STORIES FROM

Stories From Suburban Road is a unique collection of short stories that are based on the author's own childhood and adolescence. In each of these stories the writer is consciously using images, events and prople from his own life as a stepping off point for the imagination.

T.A.G. Hungerford's ability to establish an equilibrium between memory and imagination, together with his strong characterization and masterly use of narrative, description and dialogue have long established his reputation as a major Australian writer.

Stories From Suburban Road, forms a discontinuous narrative which vividly recreates a period of quiet certitude in semi-rural suburbia during the interwar years. Bird-nesting and school days, crabbing and swimming in the Swan River, chinese market gardens and the bush, South Perth Zoo and the old corner store are all brought to life through the eyes of a boy growing up in the nineteen twenties and thirties. The collection concludes with the outbreak of the second world war and the entry into adulthood.

T.A.G. Hungerford does more, however, than recapture the past. His exploration of such themes as growing up, family relationships, sexuality, racism and mateship, as well as urban encroachment on semi-rural communities and the resulting changes to the Australian character make *Stories From Suburban Road* a creative work of the first order.

Cover image: Summer Frolic, photographed by Fred Flood, painted in oil colour by L. Cutten, *Western Mail,* 1934, courtesy Maurice Jones.

T.A.G. Hungerford was born in Perth, Western Australia, in 1915. He grew up in the South Perth area and served in the Australian Army during World War II. Since concluding his army service in 1947, he has generally worked as a journalist living in Canberra, Hong Kong, New York and Perth. He has worked as a freelance writer since his retirement in 1967.

He began writing in his late teens. *The Ridge and the River,* the first of his four novels, was published in 1950, and his articles, poetry and short stories, have been published widely in journals, newspapers and anthologies, throughout Australia and overseas. His first collection of short stories, *Wong Chu and the Queen's Letterbox* (Fremantle Arts Centre Press) was published in 1976. *Stories From Suburban Road* was followed in 1985 by a second volume of stories, *A Knockabout With A Slouch Hat,* based on the author's wartime and immediate post-war experiences in occupied Japan and in Canberra, and in 1986 by *Red Rover All Over,* stories based on his experiences from the 1950s to the 1980s working as a journalist in various parts of the world. *Hungerford,* the short fiction of T.A.G. Hungerford (selected and introduced by Peter Cowan), appeared in 1989.

STORIES FROM
SUBURBAN ROAD

STORIES FROM
SUBURBAN ROAD
an autobiographical collection
1920 – 1939

T.A.G. HUNGERFORD

FREMANTLE ARTS CENTRE PRESS

First published October 1983 by
FREMANTLE ARTS CENTRE PRESS
193 South Terrace (PO Box 320), South Fremantle
Western Australia 6162.

Reprinted 1985, 1986, 1987, 1988, 1989, 1990, 1991, 1992, 1994, 1995, 1997.

Consulting Editor Ian Templeman.
Production Editor B R Coffey.
Designer Susan-Eve Barrow Ellvey.
Cover Designer John Douglass.

Typeset by Fremantle Arts Centre Press
and printed by Australian Print Group, Maryborough.

National Library of Australia
Cataloguing-in-publication data

Hungerford, T A G (Thomas Arthur Guy), 1915 - .
    Stories from Suburban Road

    ISBN 0 909144 71 0

    I. Title.

A823.3

*For
Edward Anzac Strapp,
dab hand with canoe
or crabbing-net,
first-class climber and
life-long good friend.*

Acknowledgements

Some of the stories in this collection have previously appeared in *Memories of Childhood* (Fremantle Arts Centre Press, 1978), and *Westerly*.

Grateful acknowledgement is made to the following for the use of some of the photographs which appear in this book. The photographs on pages 17, 37, 53, 83, 115, 139 are reproduced by courtesy of The J. S. Battye Library of Western Australian History; pages 1, 27, 69, 107, 149, 181, 201 by courtesy of the Pollock, P. Carroll, The Royal Western Australian Historical Society, T. Doyle, L. Lang, A. Richardson and Government Printers collections in The J. S. Battye Library, respectively; pages 95, 125, 167 and the cover courtesy of Western Australian Newspapers Limited.

The author gratefully acknowledges the assistance of the Literature Board of the Australia Council during 1976 when he was the recipient of a Senior Writing Fellowship.

Fremantle Arts Centre Press receives financial assistance from the Western Australian Department for the Arts.

Contents

King Bantam

I think she was quite the most beautiful thing I had ever seen. Every rich amber feather was flecked at the end with chocolatey-brown, her shining russet hood covered her neck as far as her shoulders and her proud little black tail shimmered peacock-green every time she moved.

Half-a-dozen times on the way back from Ian's place I stopped and lifted the lid of the shoe-box to stare raptly at my beautiful bantam hen.

She had one small defect. Her bright red comb and the little flaps of red skin beneath her beak, and much of her head, were completely covered with a hard, glistening helmet of stickfast-flea.

When they got on the dog, as they sometimes did, I had to pull them off one by one with the tweezers my mother kept on the mantelpiece in the kitchen for pulling out splinters. It was slow work, and you had to be careful not to leave the head in, or it might poison the dog. I felt it would take weeks to clean the hen up that way, and if they started breeding while I was doing it, I might be presented with another, never-ending, Saturday-morning job. What was needed was something to finish them off in one fell swoop, forever. I comforted myself that my mother, who knew everything, would know what to do to the fleas. In my memory at least she had never failed to come up with the solution to any of my problems.

Under the deep shade of the last street tree before reaching my home I stopped for the last time and lifted the lid of the box. For a moment before I did I pretended to myself that the hen had somehow got away, just to make even more tremendous the wonder of finding her still there when I lifted the lid, sitting so still and so dignified in the pad of dried grass I had provided for her comfort. I said gently: 'Tuck! Tuck!' and without so much as moving her head she turned one bright eye up to me and replied, just as softly: *Tuck! Tuck!* I thought I would shout aloud for joy. She had messed in the straw, but that didn't matter. When I got home I would put her in the old cage the cocky had lived in until he had died — of the Lewdies, as my father's friend, Mr Bader, had said one night when they were playing cards. I was the only one who hadn't laughed. The cocky had been my friend for most of my lifetime. He had never been much of a talker, but when he was inclined he could whistle *Does-your-mother-want-a-rabbit-guts-and-all-for-ninepence*, and do a little jig to it on his perch. His old cage would do as a home for the banty until a yard of some sort could be run up for her.

Although I wouldn't have admitted it to anyone, I had so longed for a bantam that I had even prayed for it. Every night before I jumped into bed I knelt on the mat and rattled off a ragbag of prayers I had assembled from what I had been taught at home and what I had heard others saying at the Convent school I attended. I always tacked on every *Oh Sacred Heart of Jesus I place my trust in Thee!* I could manage, gabbling as many as ten of them in ten seconds. I had been told at school that every time I said one it meant three-hundred days off my sentence to Purgatory — which was where I would be sent, I had decided, since I reasoned I was neither really wicked nor entirely good, although somehow different from the babies who had died without being baptised.

One night, having won myself a sizeable reprieve, I tacked on as an afterthought: *And please, God, let me have a bantam.* It seemed like a fairly reasonable request even though, of course, you weren't supposed to ask for things for yourself. You prayed for others, and others prayed for you. I made a permanent feature of my new prayer, and I got my reward.

Now two weeks after I began the prayer, when I went up to Ian's to play after my Saturday morning jobs, I'd been given the shoe-box with six holes punched in the lid. And the bantam hen inside.

I put the end of one finger gently on the glittering, pointed little red feathers under her chin, and stroked them. She sat still as a stone. Only her eyes seemed to move, flickering with a sort of blue film as my finger moved. She made a soft gurgling sound of contentment in her throat and shuffled about in the grass. I stared at her entranced, but already with the ghost of a worry rattling its chains at the back of my mind.

You could never really quite know how my mother was going to take things, especially animals. She had been fond of the cocky, and she had really cried the morning she took off the old overcoat that covered his cage at night, and found him lying on his back on the floor among all the old seeds and cocky-dirt. She liked the dog and the cat, but not the magpie: she only let me keep it because when I brought it home it had had no feathers, practically, and she hadn't expected it to live. All the same, she had given me a good woollen sock of my father's for the little bird to snuggle in until it got some feathers, and she showed me how to chew up bread and milk and dribble it into the little magpie's beak.

She roared blue murder when I brought home the possum from

3

a bird's-nesting expedition — twenty feet up a dead tree out the other side of Fremantle Road, very wild country, I had pulled my arm out of what had looked like a parrot's nest deep in the bough with the baby possum clinging to it, teeth-and-claws.

I had expected her to have a fit when it got into the belly of the sofa in the living-room and scratched out all the sawdust, but in no time at all she had simmered down and was cutting up carrots for it.

Then I brought home my first pigeon, a lovely Blue Bar I got in a trade at school for two golf balls I'd found on the South Perth links. I settled it down in half-a-kerosene-tin on the inside wall of the stable before I told my mother about it, and all she did in the end was to make a rule that I was never to bring home a cock bird — which of course had been my intention from the word go. Pigeons were not only very good to have, just to have them, they were also good for swapping. When inevitably I brought home a cock bird she made a rule that all the eggs must be broken. She forgot about it after a while, as I had known she would, and now there were forty or more Blue Bars picking up a living, somehow, around the yard and the stable.

It was touch and go every time I brought home a new animal, and there was only one way to find out what my mother would do about the bantam. I closed the lid of the shoe-box, made a last rapt inspection through one of the holes, and padded off in the direction of home.

It was nearly lunchtime when I walked tentatively into the kitchen by the back door. My sisters were doing their music theory and my mother, even before she had dished up the lunch of bubble-and-squeak, was preparing stuffed flaps for tea. *Six lamb flaps, please, Mr Rogers!* I would say at least once a week at the butcher's. *And Mum says make sure it's lamb!* Eighteen-pence for the six, plus a few coppers for the vegetables I fetched from the Chinamen's gardens, and we had enough for the whole meal with some left over for school lunches next day.

'Where's Mickey?'

'He's gone down to the Zoo.' My mother pushed back her chair and wiped her hands on her apron. She had just finished the last of the flaps, which lay in neat little bundles in the baking dish beside her. 'He's helping with the ponies.'

I was consumed with envy. My brother was a school friend of the sons of Colonel Le Soeuf, who ran the Zoo. Saturday afternoons there were penny rides on the beautiful little Shetland ponies for which the Zoo was famous, and often my brother was allowed to lead. Even, sometimes, to feed the monkeys and to clean out the cages and aviaries. It was just something else he had, like his cricket bat and his football boots and his model yacht, and going away to Kalgoorlie at Christmas with the Young Australia League. And being older.

'He's not coming home for dinner', my mother said. 'What have you got in that box?'

I held up the box and grinned at her confidingly. This was the moment. 'A banty', I said. 'Ian gave it to me.'

'Oh? He did, did he?' My mother held out her hand, palm upward, and I placed the box on it. When she lifted the lid she took one quick look and pulled her head back sharply. 'Good Lord! It's covered with stickfast fleas!' She held out the box, still opened. 'Look! Did you know?'

'Yes, Mum', I said, miserably.

'No wonder he gave it to you. The nerve.' You can take it right back to Mr Ian, with my compliments!'

'Oh, no, Mum! *Please!*'

For once, unexpectedly, I was joined in a plea by my sisters. Ordinarily they would have stopped at nothing to thwart me. 'Oh, no, Mum!' they chorused in my wake, craning over her shoulder to look at the bantam. 'She's beautiful!'

'I thought you'd be able to fix the fleas up, Mum', I said, cunningly.

'Did you, now! Well.' My mother looked closely at the bantam and said 'Tuck, tuck!' When it said *Tuck, tuck!* back to her she smiled. 'I don't suppose another mouth'll break us.' Over her shoulder she said: 'Peg, bring the dripping bowl out of the cooler. Lal, get the kerosene bottle. It's under the sink.' She turned to me, 'Get me a little tin of some sort. Skedaddle!'

When everything was assembled she put a dob of dripping in the tin, poured a few drops of kerosene on it, and mixed it around with her finger. Then she took the hen from the box, set it gently on her lap, and smeared its head with the mixture. 'There you are, banty,' she said, when she had finished, 'that'll do 'til the doctor sees you.' It was what she said to me whenever she pulled a splinter out of my finger, or gave me castor oil or put a Bates's Salve plaster on a boil. She returned the hen to the box and handed it back to me. 'You can't keep her in that box, you know. What're you going to do?'

'I thought I'd put her in Cocky's old cage,' I said, 'until I can

5

. . . sort of make her a bantam yard.'

'Oh, yes,' my mother said, 'a bantam yard. I see.' She seemed to be laughing behind her words. 'Well, clean the cage out properly. We don't want her dying of what poor Cocky had.'

'The Lewdies', I supplied, and when my mother looked at me sharply: 'You remember, what Mr Bader said that night.'

'Whatever it was', my mother said. She seemed to be laughing again. 'Put some nice clean sand in the bottom and some dried grass, and a clean tin with water. What are you going to feed her on?'

'I thought she could have some of Ginger's chaff', I said, hopefully.

'*Ginger's chaff!*' my mother snorted. 'What in the name of God do they teach you at school these days?' She leant over to the dresser for the black leather handbag which always lay there, easy to the reach, and took out a sixpence. 'Your picture money for next Saturday night, don't forget,' she said, as she handed it to me. 'Duck over to Mr Faddy's and get sixpennyworth of wheat. And don't drag your feet. Two shakes of a dead lamb's tail and I'll be dishing up!'

That night after I'd gabbled my customary litany, I crept back out into the livingroom. The wonder of my prayer and the way it had been answered had become too much for me to keep it to myself. I had to share it. My mother was sitting in the living room, doing what she called fiddling the books. They were spread out in front of her at the big polished jarrah table.

'Mum.'

'What is it?' She didn't raise her head. 'You're supposed to be in bed, Tommy-dodd. Up early tomorrow.'

'I've got a secret.'

She glanced up quickly. 'Have you, now. What is it?'

'I asked . . .' I stared at my toes. It was going to be harder than I had thought. 'I asked God to give me the banty. A long time ago. And he *did!*'

'Glory be to Holy Saint Denis!' my mother said, 'so we've got a blessed saint in the family!' She put a hand under my chin and raised my face to her own. 'Tell you what. You get down on your hunkers and ask him to let us win the Charities. Or we'll soon be in Queer Street.' She kissed the top of my head. 'You should be asleep by now, not worrying about God. Off you go.'

Once more between my sheets I lay thinking with some alarm of what she had said. The Charities I knew about, a sort of big raffle with a lot of money for first prize. We were always talking about winning it. But — Queer Street? I worried at it, trying to remember some street in South Perth called *Queer*.

And did it mean we were going to sell the shop? And shift? I couldn't imagine living anywhere else. The river and the polo grounds and the bush. And the Chinamen's gardens and the Zoo. And school, and all my friends. Perhaps Mickey would know. He was older. I raised myself on an elbow and peered across the room at the other bed. There was no movement in it. Mickey was soundly asleep.

I lay back against my pillow and tugged the covers about my neck. It was not in my nature to worry for long about anything, and soon I began to mull my way along other avenues toward sleep. On the very edge of it I remembered the Charities! I'd been going to pray for us to win it. Never mind. Tomorrow night would do as well. The shape of prayer in my consciousness changed gradually to the shape of the bantam, and my whole mind became a reflection of the little brown hen in her cage up in Ginger's stable. *Whatever happens*, I exulted, *whatever happens, I've got the banty!*

The day after her arrival the bantam hen was let out of the cocky's old cage, showing no sign of stickfast flea at all. She was perfectly at home from the first moment of freedom, and immediately all thought of building any sort of yard for her was forgotten. When she was not scratching and clucking about the stable she would sit ruffling in the black sand outside the kitchen, where from time to time my mother, working inside, would chat affably to her through the wire door.

On the morning of the second Saturday after she joined the family my brother beckoned me into the chaff-shed where he was preparing the breakfast feed for old Ginger and Biddy, the cow. 'Look behind the tea-chest,' he said, mysteriously, 'see what you'll find.'

The tea-chest, full of folded chaff bags, stood six inches from the wall of the shed, and I peered behind it. I didn't know what to expect because I was never sure what Mickey was up to. My heart leapt into my throat. In a little hollow in the sand and chaff of the shed floor there were four eggs, exquisite, golden brown, delicately rounded at one end and as delicately pointed at the other; not nearly as big as a chook's but twice as big as a pigeon's. There could be only one answer.

'The banty's?'

My brother nodded absently. He was looking at the eggs in a calculating sort of way. 'If you painted a ring of spots around the fat end,' he said, 'two sorts of brown, light and dark, you could swap them off as chicken-hawk's.'

'Don't you! They're mine, Mickey. When'll there be chickens?'

'Don't be dopey. You've got to have a rooster.' My brother, turned fourteen, stared past me at the open door of the shed. 'You've got a father, haven't you? Well.' He picked up the kerosene tin he had been filling with chaff and bran, and put a dipper of pollard in it.

'Look up now, I've got to feed Biddy.'

I stood staring at the four eggs. A rooster. Of course. It was the pigeons all over again. A bantam rooster. I knew where there were plenty of them, but it would take some planning to get my hands on one.

The back fence of the South Perth Zoo, a mile or so from our home, abutted a quiet, well-bred street of substantial private houses in what we called 'the other end' — the posh part of the suburb.

I was hampered and annoyed by the presence of my sisters, Peggie and Alice. They had insisted on accompanying me when — inadvisedly in their presence, after lunch — I had asked my mother's permission to go to the Zoo. I had protested vigorously, particularly in view of my plan, but as always the last word had stayed with my mother. She could see no reason, she said, why just for once I couldn't bear to have the company of my sisters. And that was that.

'You go on down to the gate', I told them, as we walked along the quiet street. 'I'm going to climb the fence.' I turned to Peggie, my older sister, who held the money our mother had given us — three threepences to get into the Zoo and three pennies to spend. 'You give me my fourpence, Peggie.'

'We're going to climb the fence too,' she said, as she handed it over, 'you can give us a bunk.'

'You can't! You're a *girl!*'

'Don't be stupid. I can climb better than you. I beat you up the lilac tree.'

'That's different.' I didn't like to be reminded of the defeat. 'This is a *fence*, and *high*. And people'll *see* you.'

'Pooh', she said. She glanced up and down the street. 'There's nobody. Anyway, they don't know us down this end.' She started across the road. 'Come on, Lal.'

I glanced up and down the street, as my sister had done. It was still, as if everyone south of the river had been sleeping off a heavy lunch. The hot afternoon air was heavy with the throbbing of doves and the scent of the gumtrees shading the road. There was nobody, as Peggie had said.

I crossed the road and stood with my sisters at the base of the Zoo fence. It was six feet high with a single strand of barbed wire along the top. I felt uneasy, although not because of the climb. I had done it often enough before, and by myself I would have been up and over like a rat; I could see no point in parting with a hard-to-come-by thrippence when you could get in for nothing. It was the girls. You never knew what they would do. What if they got stuck on the wire?

'Oh, *Gawd!*' I stooped and locked my arms about Peggie's knees. As she drew herself up, her sandshoes giving her some purchase on the rough wood of the pickets, I straightened my knees and heaved. When I had raised her as far as I could I slipped my grasp down to her calves and repeated the lifting manoeuvre. That put her hands on a level with the top of the pickets, and from there she could raise herself and drop over to the other side. I looked up to see how she was going. Directly above my head I could see her white bloomers, held by elastic just above the knees. If she had not been my sister I would have chanted the ritual: *I see a poppy-show all made of calico!* And if I had not been her brother she would have returned me, pertly, the ritual: *All clean and well paid for!* As it was I merely grunted: 'Hurry up, Peggie! And mind the wire!'

Before she had negotiated her way down the other side of the fence I had bunked Alice to the top. I was already on the ground, inside the Zoo, when she dropped beside me. It was a spot where I had climbed the fence on other occasions, but I stood and looked about me cautiously. We were separated from the formal area of the Zoo by a surviving narrow belt of natural bush. I knew from past experience the free-roving peacocks nested there: even as we watched, breathless, one of the great birds minced primly past us, its coroneted head bobbing backward and forward in time to its fastidious strut, the folded fan of its splendid tail swaying heavily an inch or so from the ground behind it. The nearest animal yards — some camel paddocks, the elephant's stockade and the lions' enclosure — were quite some distance down a sandy slope, but you never knew when some nosey keeper might take it into his head to have a look around. The first thing, I assured myself, was to shake off my sisters.

'I'm going somewhere. You two go somewhere else.'

'We can't', Peggie said. 'We've all got to go home together. Mum said.'

'Just tell Mum we got separated, or something. I'm not hanging around all the time with you.'

'I'll tell Mum you ran off and left us', Alice threatened. She was always the first to resort to tattling.

I took off down the slope. I knew I had her blocked. 'You do, and *I'll* tell Mum *you* climbed the fence!' You had to fight fire with fire.

I detoured to visit the big tree where the peacocks roosted after dark, and picked up a fistful of orange-coloured wing feathers, and one or two long, lovely tail feathers, which the birds had dropped overnight. The nearby elephant's stockade was empty, its occupant most likely down by the main gate giving rides to earn its keep. In the lions' enclosure the biggest lion was crouched on the cement floor worrying a huge hunk of purple meat stuck with gobs of bright yellow fat. I knew horses were killed to feed the lions. Once I had heard the sound of a rifle shot from the yard behind the pens, and sometimes there was bloody water running in the gutter under the gate. I hurried past, revolted by the stench of death and lions' dirt which clouded the whole place.

I knew exactly where I was going. I could have got there in a few minutes except that for my purpose there were still far too many people wandering the gravel paths among the enclosures.

I stood for perhaps fifteen minutes watching the crowds of tennis players on the grass courts, the girls all in white pleated skirts and most of the men in cream silk shirts and long cream pants: the few who wore shorts got whistled at and had fun poked at them by the onlookers.

In front of the bandstand at the edge of the tennis courts I spent another fifteen minutes listening to the music of the RSL band, and watching four children who sat in the front row of wooden benches sucking lemons. All children I knew believed that it would make the bandsmen blow spit into their trumpets and I stared hopefully at the uniformed men on the stage, waiting for it to happen. I had tried it myself, and although I had never seen it work, I kept an open mind on it.

At the kiosk I spent a penny on four of the lolly-balls that

10

changed colour as you sucked them. I watched the main storehouse for the animals' food until I saw a keeper wheel out a barrow of carrots and lettuces, and disappear among the yards: then I ducked in and filled my pockets hastily with the monkeys' shrivelled little windfall apples. They always tasted better than any other fruit I'd ever eaten. When I came out again there were no adults about — only a few children looking at the monkeys. I jumped the guard fence around the cages and, under their scandalised gaze, helped myself to whatever peanuts had bounced back off the bars.

I visited the snake-house just to drop one of my monkey-apples onto the head of the crocodile, I knew he would be lying asleep in his sunken pool. He blinked and yawned and went back to sleep. Better entertainment promised at the python's pit, where a stupid white hen, obviously unaware of its danger, strutted and pecked at the sand not six feet from those dreadful rainbow coils. My nose pressed against the glass, I stood entranced for ten minutes, hardly daring even to suck my lolly-ball. Momentarily I expected the snake to lunge forward, as they did in the books I read, and engulf its prey. It did nothing of the kind. It lay on the sand, its horrible spade head motionless only inches above that shimmering hawser of flesh, its yellow stone eyes glaring malevolently at nothing. Finally I gave up and walked out into the avenue. It was getting late, and I decided it was time for me to do what I had to do.

'Now or never!' I muttered grimly to myself. It was the sort of thing said by the masterful schoolboys in the comics I read every week: I wasn't allowed to have them at home, but I borrowed them at school.

I stood with my chin on the middle wire of the fence around the buffaloes' yard, considering the situation. Grey and bald, like huge baby mice in a mest, the animals crowded in the farthest corner of the yard: only one, seeming asleep, stood beside the feedboxes alongside the shed under a spreading peppercorn tree. To get to the shed I would have to pass perilously close to it, but . . . I had watched the keeper walking among the animals, and they had never taken the slightest notice of him. Still, as I prepared to climb between the wires, I was not going to deny myself the pleasure of a spine-tingling thrill of terror over something I was absolutely certain would not happen.

The door of the feedshed was open, which was practically necessary to the success of my plan. As I had anticipated, crowds of bantams were wandering in and out of it, scratching under the feed boxes and even between the legs of the dreaming buffalo. *The most beautiful bantams in the world!* I thought, covetously — bossy hens like my own banty, whole flea-packs of cottonreel chickens darting around, unbelievable roosters dripping with gold and amber and ivory. During so many visits to the Zoo I had mourned the seeming impossibility of my ever acquiring such a rooster — but I was to achieve my ambition so simply and so swiftly I would hardly have time to think about the risk attached to the kidnap.

To put off the moment of decision as long as I could I took out my lolly-ball and examined it. I'd reached the purple. I put it back, and with a last glance up and down the avenue, I stowed my fistful of peacock feathers on the ground at the base of the fence. Then I eased myself between the wires into the yard.

As I pelted across it the buffalo in the corner took absolutely no notice of me — if they even saw me at all, dreamily chewing their cuds under the burden of their wide, murderous horns, they gave no indication of it. The one by the feed-boxes watched me, but made no movement. Only the bantams, when I was half-way toward the shed, took off in panic, flying like pigeons. Those nearest the shed darted inside, as I had hoped they would. I hurled myself after them and saw in an instant that a knot of them had crowded into a corner behind a leaning bag of chaff.

Almost automatically my hands fastened around a splendid rooster of black and gold lacquer, with an ivory cowl and arching tail of iridescent green. *Oh*, I thought, staring at it in the dusty gloom. *You must be the king of them all!*

It struggled for a moment and then lay quite still in my grasp, its heart pounding against my palms. Straining it against my chest with one hand, I whipped a piece of string out of my pocket and tied its legs together. Then I unbuttoned my jacket and shirt, shoved the rooster in against my skin, and buttoned up.

My heart was pounding as hard as the rooster's when I turned to squat at the doorway. The buffalo in the corner, and the single one by the feed-boxes, were still there and, it seemed, still completely uninterested in me. The avenue was still empty of people, and — more importantly — of keepers. Within seconds I was through the fence again, and had picked up my feathers. Within minutes, delightfully goose-pimpled to think of the dangers I had faced and overcome, and congratulating myself heartily on having got away with it completely, I was well on my way to the back fence of the Zoo.

I had a shock coming to me. As I was padding along beside the high paling fence of one of the camel-yards, with the back fence in sight, a gate opened about thirty feet ahead of me. A keeper wheeled an empty barrow out. He closed the gate behind him, and began to walk toward me. Oh, gawd! *Bugger-bugger-bugger!* For a moment I thought desperately of turning around and walking away along the way I'd come, but realised that would only arouse the keeper's suspicions. I kept plodding forward, my premonition of impending disaster heightened by a sudden wriggling against my ribs. Luckily my jacket was a hand-me-down from Mickey, still too big for me, and the movement wouldn't be too easy to detect. Nevertheless I kept my hand in my pocket and pressed my arm against the rooster to keep it as quiet as possible.

As I drew alongside the barrow the keeper said: 'A bit late for you to be leaving the Zoo, sonny!'

'I'm just going home.'

'You're taking a funny way to the gate, then!'

'I wanted to see if I could find some more of these.' With my free hand I raised my fistful of feathers, and the rooster squirmed more imperatively against my side. I froze. 'I was going by the peacock tree.'

'The peacock tree?'

'That big gumtree up by the elephant's yard. The peacocks go up it at night, I reckon. You always find some feathers there.'

'Let me see those, sonny!' The keeper held out his hand for the feathers. 'Did you know boys have been catching peacocks and pulling the feathers out of their tails?' He had been examining the ends of the feathers closely as he spoke, but suddenly he looked up into my face. 'You don't do that, do you?'

'Oh, *no!*' I was really shocked, and I think it might have shown in my voice. 'I only *pick* them *up*, like at the peacock tree!'

'All right then.' The keeper handed back my feathers. 'Off you go — no, wait a minute!' My arm against the wriggling rooster, I froze again. 'When you go out the gate you can do something for me. You know Miss Le Soeuf? Good. Then tell her Keeper Hope said one of the camels in the top yard looks a bit down on it. She better tell the Colonel. Remember that?'

'One-of-the-camels-in-the-top-yard-looks-a-bit-down-on-it-and she'd-better-tell-the-Colonel!' I gabbled. I could hardly contain my longing to be outside the Zoo fence and on my way home safely, with my rooster. It would be dreadful to get so far and then be tripped up by some little thing. 'I'll tell Miss Le Soeuf, Mr

13

Hope!'

'Good lad. Here's something for your trouble.'

The keeper took a thrippenny bit out of his pocket and handed it to me. Half of next Saturday night's picture money already, and here it was, only Sunday! But what could you do with one hand full of feathers and the other jammed in your pocket to keep the rooster from jumping around?

'Thank you, Mr Hope — but I couldn't take it.' I tried to make it sound as if I didn't care very much for money at all. 'Mum and Dad don't let us.'

'Well, then — you're a good boy to do as you're told', the keeper said. 'Off you go.'

I hadn't gone ten yards from the Zoo gates before I'd opened my jacket and my shirt to let the rooster look out. He seemed quite comfortable, although very watchful. The warmth of him nestled against my side made the long walk home seem shorter. Also I was buoyed up by a feeling of virtue at having refused the keeper's thrippence: by the time I reached our own back gate I'd almost convinced myself that only obedience to my parents' wishes had stopped me from pocketing it.

As I turned into our backyard the river at the bottom of the road was already getting dark, and chips of yellow were beginning to wink here and there along the flat grey shape of the city on the other side. Light spilled from our back door, and I knew that my mother would be at the stove inside, cooking something for our tea. I could hear one of my sisters doing her practice at the piano: Peg, because Alice could only play one piece, over and over, and it wasn't the one I could hear. I knew Alice would be in their bedroom devouring one of the comics for which she traded part of her lunch, or her lunch money, at school. My father would be sitting in his chair reading the *Sunday Times*, and Mickey would be sprawled on the floor varnishing his model yacht again, or fiddling with his egg collection, or making a shanghai: he was always doing something by himself. It was nice to stand outside for a moment and think that none of them knew what I had done, or that I was going to give them the surprise of their lives.

At the same time there were problems, and I had to do some planning. I would be in for it, for sure, for being late, and perhaps also for having gone off and left Peg and Alice at the Zoo — although I hoped my own threat to them might have blocked their usual treachery. And there was the matter of the cow's grass and the morning's-wood, but I reckoned Mickey could have cut the cow's grass and brought in the wood. In any case it wouldn't hurt fat Biddy to make-do on her chaff-and-bran, for once — and Mickey would have fixed that too, by now. Boil it all down and there was really only the rooster to explain, and straight away I thought of a good way to do it. I would just tell them the plain truth. It was brilliant!

I saw him in one of the yards, and I just climbed over the fence and caught him, Mum, I would say. I tried it out aloud, but softly, for effect. It sounded good. The rooster, disturbed by my voice, shifted against my side. It cocked its head and looked up at me, questioningly. *Nobody saw me, and the Zoo's got simply thousands of them, Dad,* I would say, and they would look at the new bantam and be overcome by its beauty. As I had been. And for good measure bring in my brother, who seemed never to be able to do anything wrong. *Mickey said we had to have a rooster for the banty to get chickens, Mum!* I considered it, and it sounded wonderful. Even watertight.

They'd hardly send me back with the rooster tonight, I thought. And I couldn't see my father harnessing up old Ginger and driving right down to the Zoo himself. And by tomorrow night they'd have forgotten they'd ever been without the rooster. He'd have settled in, and become one of the family like the banty. *And even if I get a hiding for being late home, and not getting the wood in, and not cutting Biddy's grass, and for stealing, it'll be worth it!*

I pulled the rooster from inside my shirt, gently, so as not to make him squawk and spoil the surprise. I held him up only inches from my nose, and stared at him rapturously. He stared at me as if he knew me already. His comb was like coral and his eyes were like painted glass, and the fading light flowed like coloured water over his glorious plumage.

'Oh, you're the *king!*' I whispered to him, and he blinked at me. 'That's what I'm going to call you. *King!*'

I tucked him securely under my arm, unlatched the gate, closed it behind me, and trotted across the yard toward our back door.

15

The Battle
Of Barney's Hill

When I was about eight years old I was in a battle between St Joseph's Convent and the South Perth State School, on Barney's Hill.

I was going to the convent, which was on the top of Barney's Hill, overlooking the river and Perth. On the river side it dropped very suddenly to Suburban Road and the Chinamen's gardens — there was a marvellous slide of yellow sand to pelt down on the way home from school, and it led you right to a big fig tree that hung over the Chinamen's fence. On the other side, the hill sloped through the bush to where the state school was, down in the hollow.

Nobody seemed to know who Barney was, although my father used to say he'd bet it was some big fat priest who'd bought the land for the Catholic Church in the first place. '*And* for a song, too!' he'd say, at the drop of a hat. 'Trust the bloody micks to grab the best bit of land around the city!'

Just the same, he can't have been as savage about it as he pretended. He never said anything about my two sisters going to the convent, although we were Protestants. My mother wanted them to learn the piano, and everyone said there was nobody like the nuns for teaching music. And even if he had objected, my mother had a way of having her way.

Then, when I was nearly six, and ready to start school, she said why not let me go to the convent with the girls. It was a two-mile walk there and back, and she reckoned they could look after me, particularly since some of it was through the bush. I didn't like the arrangement, but of course nobody asked my opinion.

'Nobody had to look after Mickey!' I roared, when I was told about it.

Mickey, my older brother, had been going to the state school for four years already. I said to my mother that the state school was no closer to home than the convent, and that he had to walk just as far on practically the same roads, and nothing had ever happened to *him*. All my mother said was: *Dry up! You're going to the convent!* so that I had learned to recite the Stations of the Cross long before I ever got my hands on a cricket bat. The nuns were good music teachers, but there was no cricket team at the convent.

I'd been looking forward to joining Mickey at the state school, and I harped on it so much that in the end they promised me that when I'd got big enough to look after myself, in a couple of years, maybe, I'd be allowed to leave the convent. But when the second

18

lot of Christmas holidays had come and gone, and it hadn't happened, I gave up hope.

Mickey told me there was going to be a battle nearly a week before it happened. We were in the shed mixing chaff-and-bran in a kerosene tin for Biddy and Ginger. 'We're going to have a battle, Monday,' he said, 'the Staties against the Catholics.'

'Where?' I asked. I thought it would be like the Landing at Gallipoli, where our Uncle Tom had been wounded a few weeks before I was born. It was the only battle I knew anything about.

'Up the convent', Mickey said. 'We're coming up at lunch-hour.'

'Why? What's the battle for?'

Mickey stirred the chaff-and-bran for a while — all I had to do was to pour the water out of a dipper, when he told me to. I could see he was thinking hard.

'I don't know. Something', he said, eventually. 'You just be careful, Monday!'

On the following Sunday evening we were all in the kitchen waiting for our tea. I was lying on the floor with Barney reading a book called *Nomads of the North*, about a baby bear and a pup that fell out of a canoe in a river up near the North Pole and got lost in the bush. My mother was busy at the stove. One of my sisters was practising the piano in the dining-room, and the other was sitting by the dresser, out of the way, reading a comic carefully folded inside a book called *Anne of Green Gables* — I'd read it, and it was very soppy. Mickey was sitting at the table with my father, making a shanghai, and although I liked reading I would rather have been helping them.

Now and then I looked at them out of the corner of my eye — I didn't want them to know I was interested in what they were doing. I suppose I was jealous of Mickey because my father took much more notice of him than he did of me, and talked to him as if he was almost grown up. But then . . . my brother was older than me, and very good at sports, and was captain of the cricket team and the football team at the state school. He was also very beautiful, and everyone kept telling my mother and father he was a very manly little boy, which nobody ever said about me. I should have expected that any notice I got from my father could be only what was left over from the notice he took of Mickey, but somehow it didn't work.

Apart from that, I'd helped Mickey cut the rubber strips for his ging. I expected to be asked to help him make the rest of it.

Earlier that afternoon I'd been sitting in the chaff-shed with Barney watching one of the bantam hens with a new lot of chicks. She would scratch at the loose chaff and cluck to them, and they'd come running and peck at whatever she'd discovered. They'd been hatched only the day before, and I was wondering how they came to be so active so soon when it took human children so long — just lying there being stuffed at one end and being cleaned up at the other, as I'd heard a friend of my mother say, once.

While I was thinking about this, Mickey came in with an old bike tyre and a fruit case. He said: 'Help me cut the rubbers for my ging, Tommy.' He said it the way he always spoke — as if nobody would ever not do what he asked them to. He laid the tyre on the fruit case and cut a ten-inch section out of it with his pocket-knife — something else that sent me wild with jealousy of him. He slit the tube up one side and laid it out flat on the fruit case. 'Hold that end down,' he said, 'real hard, now.' Then he took his school ruler out of the front of his shirt and laid it on the rubber and cut two half-inch strips, beautiful and straight.

I felt pretty important to be helping him. I said: 'Where'd you get the tyre?' Neither of us had a bike. Whenever we asked for one my mother would just say we couldn't afford it — and then added 'Yet'. It sort of kept you hoping — but as it turned out the first bike I ever owned I bought for myself, five shillings down and two-and-six a week out of my first pay.

'Swapped for it at school,' Mickey said, 'I gave Ian Kiver two peewit's eggs and a golf-ball for it.'

'Is it for the battle?' I said. I hadn't stopped thinking about it since he'd told me, and besides, all the week the big boys at school had had us collecting gumnuts and banksia cobs for ammunition. I couldn't have forgotten it if I'd wanted to.

'Shut up!' Mickey said. He leaned to the door and looked out. 'Don't talk about the battle!'

'Well — is it?' I persisted.

He looked at me sideways. 'You'll see', he said.

I'd expected to be brought in on making the rest of his shanghai. I wasn't, and it rankled. I lay on the kitchen floor simmering and pretending to read, turning over in my mind that I'd say, as if I'd just thought of it: 'You making that ging for the battle, Mickey?' I didn't, of course. Partly because I loved him too much to get him into trouble, but mostly because he would probably have corked my arm for it when he got me by myself. He might even never have asked me to help him again.

I was still gobbling the last of my lunchtime sandwiches — mutton, on Mondays — when I crouched down behind the fallen tree trunk just inside the fence of the convent schoolhouse. We were all waiting there for the first of the Staties to come out of the bush on the other side of the road. I reckoned that Mickey would be with them, probably even leading them, since he seemed to lead everything else. I wondered if we'd see each other, and what we'd say to each other when we got home after school. After all, there can't have been many families in South Perth who had a brother on each side of the battle.

I'd given up all hope of joining Mickey at the state school, and in a way I didn't mind any more. It was very interesting at the convent, with the nuns and everything, and every Monday morning the Dean would come into the classrooms with his big red face and roar at the Catholics who hadn't gone to Mass the day before. His face was red because he drank a lot of whiskey — we used to find the bottles outside his garage at the bottom of the playground and take them to Sister Gertrude, and she told us he'd got Trench Feet during the war, and the whiskey was his medicine to take away the pain.

Besides the Mass there was Communion and Confession and Benediction. The Catholic kids used to get together and talk about it, and even if they were your friends they made you feel as if you were just a Proddie, and got left out of it.

At the convent, May was the Month of the Virgin, as Sister Mary of the Sacred Heart called it. There was a big statue of Our Lady on one side of the altar, as big as a real lady, with a gold crown on it and a lovely blue cloak over her white dress, right down to the ground, with gold shoes poking out from under it. All May the nuns kept vases of flowers around it, and lighted candles in among the flowers. It was beautiful. Every day after school the Catholics used to kneel around it and say a Rosary. I died to be with them. It was all so different from what it looked like during the day. I used to hang around the door watching, and listening to the Rosary. It was like the sound of the bees in our honeysuckle on a warm, still day. But my sisters would come and drag me off, and say they'd tell Mum if I didn't come straight away. I would have liked to be an altar-boy, too. The altar was at the far, dark end of the biggest classroom, which was really the church, and I could hardly keep my eyes on my sums and things for watching the boys practising for Sunday. They swung little silver buckets with scented charcoal in them, and hit a shiny brass gong with a little padded waddy, and knelt on red velvet cushions and said things in Latin, and put things here and shifted them there. And when it was all over they snuffed out the candles with a marvellous little brass witch's hat on the end of a long brass rod. I couldn't hope to be an altar-boy — you had to be a Catholic — but sometimes in our lunch-hour, when the nuns and the boarders were all down at the convent having their bread-and-dripping, and everyone else was out in the playground, I would tip-toe into the Sacristy behind the altar and touch the brass gong and hit it with the little waddy, and say *Tantum Ergo Sacramentum*, which I'd memorised from one of the Latin hymns we had to sing. I'd stroke the velvet cushions and the red-and-white dresses the altar-boys wore, and the priest's beautiful white lace aprons and things. I used to put my face into them and sniff them, and the smell of the incense they swung around in their little silver buckets. Somehow it reminded me of the Chinamen's shacks, down by the river.

I finished the last of my sandwiches, wolfed my slice of cake, wiped the back of my hand across my mouth and cleaned my teeth with my tongue. Then I counted my ammunition again.

By my right foot I had a small heap of hard, dried gumnuts and banksia cobs I'd gathered in the bush behind the schoolhouse. The big boys were crouching here and there along the log, and behind the ornamental palms leading down to the front gate. They all had piles of flat, sharp-edged oyster shells we'd dug out of the footpath on the other side of the school fence — the sort you skimmed out over the shallows from the riverbank down by the jetty. One Saturday morning when there was no wind I'd skipped one eleven times. Nobody had ever done more skips, but the trouble was there was nobody there to see it. I waded out to get the shell and took it home and put it on the mantelpiece for a keepsake. My mother made me throw it out, just as one day when I was at school she burned my collection of peacocks' feathers because every one of them had the Devil's Eye at the very end, and it brought bad luck.

In a way I really didn't expect the battle to happen at all. I reckoned the nuns must have seen the heaps of ammunition behind the log, and they were pretty good at finding out what you were up to — even before you did it, sometimes. Once, three of us got up Mr Edwards's fig tree in Swan Street, on our way home from school — it couldn't really be called stealing because the boughs just hung down over the footpath and once you got onto the fence you were practically in the tree. The very next day Sister Gertrude told us she'd *seen* us, up Mr Edwards's fig tree. She'd been standing on the balcony at the Convent, and that was more than a mile away, on the *other* side of Barney's Hill. So you couldn't be too careful.

I reckoned that if any of the nuns copped us it would be Sister Mary of the Sacred Heart. She was the oldest and crabbiest of the nuns who taught us. She was crippled with rheumatism, Sister Gertrude said, and that made her crabby. But I knew she just hated children. If I·made my slate pencil squeak she used to pull my hair, and it seemed that every time I looked up from my work she'd be staring at me like the python at the zoo looking at the chicken they put into his cage for food. And she was the first one who ever made me think I mightn't go to heaven anyway.

When the Catholics had Catechism in the last half-hour before lunchtime, the Proddies were supposed to do sums and things, but I used to listen. I reckoned I knew it as well as they did. *Who made the World? God made the World. Who is God? God is the creator of Heaven and Earth and of all things.* One day Sakey said to them that the Catholic Church was like a big tree that cast a shade, and all who were in the shade were saved and all who weren't were damned. And when she said it some of the Catholics looked sideways at us Proddies as if to say: And serves you right, too!

I knew quite well, from listening to them every day, just what it meant not to be saved. Millions and millions of years — *forever!* — being fried like a mutton chop in the fires of Hell. The very best you could hope for was to wander around wishing you had been better in a place called Limbo, where you got sent if you did something wicked without really meaning to do it, but did it just the same. And babies went there if they died before they were christened. I reckoned it wasn't fair, but when I told my father he said I'd find out soon enough that nothing was fair.

I looked down the pathway to the Convent, to make certain that old Sakie wasn't hobbling up it to catch me with my ammo. I couldn't see any nuns at all coming toward the school, swinging their beads, so I began wondering again how the battle had come about. I knew the big boys at the state school and the convent

23

had arranged it. But nobody had said anything about *why*, and looking back I couldn't think of any reason for fighting.

Of course, all of us used to chiack the Staties on the way home from school. We'd yell: *Convent children ring the bell, while the Staties go to hell!* from our side of the road, and from their side the Staties would yell: *Convent dogs jump like frogs, in and out the wa-a-a-ter!* But we did that all the time: it was just something you did on the way home from school, like playing follow-my-leader or drizzying alleys in the gutters. And in any case the road separated you, and you never started a fight unless there were more of you than there were of them. It was all a mystery.

I was thinking about this when three of our boys raced out of the bush between the convent and the state school. They pelted across the road, and I reckon the soles of their feet didn't hardly touch the gravel. They skimmed over the fence like plovers and crouched behind the log. A few minutes before, the big boys had sent them down the hill to see whether the Staties had started to come up it, and I could just hear what they were saying. They reckoned they'd seen mobs of Staties in the bush down by the state school, all heading up toward the convent. They sounded very full of themselves, like Tom Mix when he rode in to the fort and warned the settlers that the Indians were coming, but one of them kept looking back nervously at the bush on the other side of the road. He reckoned he'd seen a lot of what looked like metal, shining in the sunlight between the trees, and he said could the Staties be wearing *armour*, like the knights in history? Then one of them reckoned some of the Staties might have got hold of real swords, and when he said that I wondered to myself: *Or guns?* Even the big boys' oyster shells didn't seem as dangerous as they had a moment ago.

Then a lot of the others began to shout and laugh, and I stood up high enough to look over the top of the log. About a dozen of the Staties had come creeping out of the bush on the other side of the road, and every one of them had a little wooden sword and a shield made from the cut-out top of a kerosene-tin. We all started to sing out whatever rude things we could think of, rolling around and punching each other on the arm.

Then I thought of Mickey. I looked along the line of Staties but he wasn't there. Someone began to sing out something else we yelled at the Staties on the way home: *Statie dogs sitting on logs, picking maggots out of frogs!* and all of a sudden everyone behind the tree began to bombard the Staties with gumnuts and banksia cobs and oyster shells.

A lot of them pelted back into the bush, but some of them held their shields over their heads and picked up our own ammo and sent it back across the road. Another lot of them came out of the bush, but I could see right away that Mickey wasn't with them. I thought: surely he can't have *funked* it! I could hardly make myself think of such a terrible thing happening.

Just then one of the Staties dropped his shield and sword and clapped his hand to his forehead, and began to bawl — as my father would have said, *like the bloody bull of Bashan*. The blood just gushed from where he'd been hit with one of our oyster shells. It was dreadful to look at, but you couldn't stop yourself. The rest of the Staties all ran back into the bush, and then everything began to happen at once.

The big boys had made the girls stay out of the way, in the lunch sheds around the back of the school, but all of a sudden they came pelting around to the front, squealing and screaming, and ran up the steps into the church part of the school. And then the bell began to go *bong! bong! bong!*

It scared me more than the blood, or anything. The bell hung on a wooden tower between the schoolhouse and the top of Barney's Hill. They never rang it excepting for Mass on Sundays, and I knew that none of the convent kids would have thought of touching the rope, even, let alone of tugging it. We'd been told that if you did it was some sort of mortal sin, the kind that if you died with it on your soul you went straight to hell. No Purgatory, no Limbo. Straight down. I wouldn't have touched that bell for all the tea in China, as my mother said.

Suddenly everything was very quiet. While I'd been thinking about the bell everyone else had just sort of melted away from behind the log, in all directions. After the noise of the battle it seemed quieter than I'd ever heard before. I looked down the track toward the convent, where the nuns had disappeared half-an-hour before on the way to their lunch. If they'd been able to see me up Mr Edwards's fig tree from so far away, as Sister Gertrude said they had, I bet they'd have heard the bell from practically under their noses.

It was funny, because as I was thinking about the nuns, just about every nun I'd ever seen at the convent, and some I'd never even set eyes on before, came running up the path. I couldn't believe it. The Sisters never ran. I had never seen any of them — *nobody* had ever seen any of them — going faster than a dawdle.

25

In a way, I'd never thought they *could* run, but here they were practically cantering, all fluttering black-and-white like a mob of maggies swooping on you as you climbed up toward their nests.

I didn't think they'd seen me, so I swung around and galloped off around the blind end of the school-house, heading for the bush up on Barney's Hill. I passed some of the boys who were playing fly in the deep sand as if they'd been there all day.

I thought the battle was over, but it wasn't. For me, anyway, the most important part of it was still to come.

As I rounded the corner of the schoolhouse I almost ran into Mickey. So much had happened, so suddenly, that I'd forgotten about not seeing him among the Staties, and then — bang! There he was, right in front of me.

I suppose I must have been pretty excited with the blood and the noise and the nuns galloping up the path like camels, but I thought I'd never seen anything more beautiful or wonderful than my brother standing there by himself, not another Statie in sight, still carrying on the battle when everyone else had run away from it. He had his shanghai out as far as he could, so that the two rubber strips I'd helped him to cut from the old bicycle tyre couldn't be stretched any further. Against his ear, between the first finger and thumb of his other hand, he held the little leather pouch with a glass alley out of a soda-water bottle — we dug for them at Weaver and Lock's cool-drink factory on Saturday mornings, for marbles mostly, but sometimes you shot them out of your ging.

'Mickey!' I whispered. I knew now all right why he hadn't come out of the bush with the other Staties. 'You ring the bell?'

He nodded, and let go of the pouch of his shanghai. The rubber strips went *splat!* and almost at the same moment there was a most awful noise of broken glass. I turned and looked at the schoolhouse wall. *Four windows gone!* What with the bell, and that, no wonder the girls had run squealing!

'Don't you tell!' Mickey threatened.

I wanted to shout out to him there and then that they could twist my arm for a year and I wouldn't say a word, but I didn't get the chance. He was already through the wires of the fence and pelting down the road toward his own school.

The battle was really over.

Old Ally Breen
Went To See The Queen

The day I found out about Ally Breen — and other things too, I suppose — Ernie came down to our place earlier than usual. He arrived not long after breakfast, really. My mother used to keep the porridge pot for him and put a dollop of Biddy's cream and plenty of sugar into it, and he used to sit on our back step and clean it up. My mother reckoned he did a better job on it than our dog, Barney. He was my particular mate at school, in the same class as me and only a few months younger, but he was small and skinny, and my father said he didn't get enough to eat — or perhaps got the wrong things to eat, that were the cheapest to buy. His father was out of work, like a lot of the boys' fathers at school, and they got the sustenance from the Government.

If he'd come a bit earlier that morning he might have thought there was a war on. My sister Peg had told my father she wouldn't eat her porridge. We had it every morning of the week, except that on Sundays we had eggs-and-bacon afterward, but the only one of us who liked it was my brother Mickey. He used to make a business about eating it, rubbing his belly and saying: 'Bonzer!' and I think he used to do it just to make me and my sisters feel bad about not eating ours.

Every morning when my mother dished it up she said: 'Now, don't let's have a whining-match. Ernie eats it and enjoys it, so I don't know why you lot can't.' She said if he came a while longer he'd fill out his brother's old pants very nicely. When I got Mickey's old pants passed down to me my mother used to take them in at the waist so that they'd fit me where they touched me, as she used to say, but Ernie's mother didn't have a machine. You could have put a small watermelon in between his belly-button and the fly of his old hand-me-downs.

That Sunday morning Peggy just said she wasn't going to eat her porridge. She said Barney could have it, and could she please have her bacon-and-eggs straight away. My father said: 'No, you cannot, my lady. And we're all going to sit here, all of us, until you eat your porridge.'

My mother said: 'There's starving children in Russia would be glad of that porridge — without milk and cream and sugar!' She always said it, and I always wanted to say: But how are we going to get it to the starving children in Russia? I wasn't game — I would have had to walk the length of the back yard to pick up my head.

It was awful. To be sitting at the breakfast table so late, and not even talking, made the whole house seem different, and strange.

My other sister Lal and I bogged through our porridge, but only to get the bacon-and-eggs afterward. Mickey began to grizzle about having to stay inside when he wanted to go somewhere with Billy Clydesdale, the Mayor's son. Peggy sat at her end of the table staring at her plate, and the porridge on it got hard and cold like a solid grey pancake. My father sat at his end reading the *Sunday Times*, and looking up occasionally to see how things were going.

Peggy waited until he had his head down, looking at something, then slid her hand under her porridge and threw it at him, the whole length of the table. It slid over the edge of the paper and hit him where his necktie would have been if it hadn't been a Sunday. We were all frozen to our chairs with the shock of it — even Mickey, who never seemed to take much notice of what went on among the rest of us. My father got such a look on his face I thought he'd go outside and split a stick off the side of a fruit-case and take tea with Peg, as he called it. He didn't, though. He just said to my mother: 'Min, bring me a tea-towel, please', and when she handed it to him, wiped the front of his shirt quite calmly with one hand while he held the slab of porridge with the other. When he'd finished he handed the messy teacloth back to my mother with the porridge and said: 'Put that back on her plate, Min', and picked up the paper again.

He seemed to be reading, but when my mother picked up the cream jug to put some more on Peggy's plate he said: 'No — no cream. She'll eat it as it is.' He didn't even take the paper away from his face.

As my mother put the cream jug down she said to Peg: 'What I should do is tell Ally Breen to come and take you away in his bag.'

I got the scary feeling I always got, still, when she said that. It wasn't as if I still believed, like when I was little, that Ally Breen really would come and get me, but it still made me feel creepy. It made me think of some horrible old bloke with a bag over his shoulder watching me from out of the bushes, or through the window of some deserted house where he was waiting for me to go by.

He was a raggedy old man who walked all around the suburb with a sugar-bag over his shoulder. You never quite knew when he would just sort of bob up out of a vacant block or around a corner with his bag. When I was little he'd only have to show up, away down the street, and we'd take off yelling out: *Old Ally Breen! Went to see the Queen!* Of course he'd never been to see the Queen, but we had all sorts of little rhymes like that for yelling out.

Whenever we went past Billy Bew's vegetable garden down by the river we'd sing out: *Old Billy Bew! Fell in a pot of stew!* And when someone said something we didn't like we'd say: *Sticks and stones may break my bones but names will never hurt me. When I'm dead and in my grave you'll think of the names you've called me!* You could make people cry, saying that to them.

Ally Breen had been threatened at us for as long as I could remember, but when my mother brought him out for Peg that morning I had no idea it would be the last time it would ever have any effect on me at all.

I think we might still have been sitting there, waiting for Peg to finish her porridge, except that Ernie arrived and knocked at the back door. When my mother went out to give him the pot it seemed to set Peg off. She began to eat and bawl at the same time, and if it hadn't been so serious I think Lal and I might have burst out laughing. She polished off her porridge in no time at all and the moment she finished my father had her cuddled into his lap. He told us we could buzz off.

I went and sat on the steps with Ernie and Barney while Ernie cleaned out the pot, and I showed him some eggs I'd found down the river, the day before. I waxed eggs with Ernie for keeps, but it was all right to go out with another boy and wax with him just for the day if your own waxer was doing something else.

We had swum across the channel to Hierrison Island and went on up to the Causeway to look for mud-swallows' eggs under the bridge. They laid pretty little white ones with circles of tiny red-and-brown spots around the blunt end. I had some already, but if we got more they would be good for swapping. It was fun going after them anyway, crawling along the tops of the high beams just below the roadway with the deep water under you and the trams growling along a couple of feet over your head. My mother would have had a fit if she'd known.

Hierrison Island was where the Causeway crossed that part of the river, from the carbarn in Perth to where the Albany Road and Fremantle Road met on the South Perth side. For years we'd called it Harrison Island because a boy at school told us it was called after his grandfather, who had been an early settler. When he was skiting about it down at our place one day my mother said: 'Oh? Did he help to build the Town Hall too?' and my father said: 'Now, Min!'

He told us afterward the Town Hall had been built by convicts, and while the boss wasn't looking they'd shaped some of the windows like the broad arrows they wore on their clothes, just so you'd know it had been built by convicts. Next time I went into town I remembered to have a good look at the Town Hall and the little windows in the tower *were* shaped like broad arrows. So my father hadn't been pulling our legs, as I'd thought.

Hierrison Island wasn't an island at all, but acres and acres of reeds and open pools and creeks with millions of birds. The Government had begun to fill it in with muck from the river, because they said it bred mosquitoes and all sorts of diseases. My father said there was no disease like politicians and they should cover *them* with muck from the river. Rain had washed most of it straight back, so that the clean oyster shells were left behind in great heaps and hollows, and when you were in the middle of them you couldn't see anything but shining white shells, and the blue sky coming down to the ground all around you.

We were doing Africa at school then, with the Sahara Desert like a big brass tray on the map, and our teacher told us it was dangerous to travel in the Sahara because there was no water excepting a few places the Arabs knew, and they wouldn't tell anyone. We used to play we were there, and stagger around on the shells pretending we were dying of thirst.

You could almost walk out to the shell bank without going over your middle, but right at the end you had to swim about the width of our backyard across the very deep water where they'd dredged out the muck. If you could swim you could swim in any depth of water, but my mother didn't seem to think so. She'd always say, when I asked her if I could go for a swim: 'Well, don't swim in the deep water.' I could never explain it to her.

I'd only just stepped out on the shell-bank when I almost trod on two dotterel's eggs. I didn't want to go waxes in them with the other boy so I kept on walking for a few paces, thinking I'd come back later on and pick them up. Then I remembered how hard it was to see them against the shell and the seaweed, and I reckoned it would be better to have one than none at all, even though a pair was what you always wanted. So I just stopped and said: 'I think I saw a couple of eggs on the ground back there', and went back. I was lucky to spot them again. I gave one of them to the other boy, but when we were swimming back across the deep water he put it in his mouth to carry it and broke it in half, too badly to patch it up — so I finished up with the only one, after all.

I kept this egg until last, after the swallows', and Ernie was very impressed. When I'd told him how I'd found it, and how the other boy had broken his, and when I'd acted out how he looked with his mouth full of broken egg swimming across the deep part, and when we'd finished laughing about it, and Ernie'd scoffed his porridge and given the pot to Barney, he helped me with a couple of jobs I had to do.

There was always something, such as shovelling the fresh pats out of the cow-shed onto the manure-heap, and cutting up another stack of paper squares from the *West Australian* for the dunny, and anything else my mother could think of at the time. When we'd finished we just stood outside the chaff-shed looking at each other and wondering what was the best thing to do.

Sunday morning when you'd finished your jobs was a wonderful time. It was like standing at the front door of a big shop with everything in the world in it, and not knowing what to buy because there was so much. We could go down to the Chinamen's for goldfish, or catch mice in the chaff-shed, or go fishing, or go down to the Zoo or out to the bush for eggs. We could dangle our legs in old Billy Bew's well to catch leeches — a boy at school reckoned chemists bought them from you to make medicine, but every chemist we'd tried so far had hunted us out of his shop. We could rearrange our egg collection, or look at the *Chums* annual my Uncle sent us from England every Christmas, or climb the lilac tree over the stable and play Tarzan. Or we could walk along the tram track in Angelo Street and pick up used tickets — everyone said there was an office in the carbarn in Perth where the tramways would buy them back from you to use again. There were so many things to do in one day, and I thought of them one by one, but in the end Ernie just said: 'Captain's?' and I knew it was exactly what I'd had in mind all along.

Everyone around our way knew the Captain. He was older than anyone I ever knew. He must have been very big and tall at one time, but he'd grown bent and skinny, with a long yellowy beard right down to his middle. His real name was Captain Courthope, but whenever we met him on the footpath we'd just say: 'Hello, Captain!' and he'd raise a hand up to his old felt hat as if he was saluting. I don't think anyone ever heard him say a word. The Government had built him a small wooden house close to the shops because he was really too old to walk far, but before he moved into it he had lived in a very big, old white house about half-way between our place and the Causeway.

My father said that it was where they kept the convicts in the old days, and that Captain Courthope had been in charge of them. I don't think it was another of his stories, because between the house and Suburban Road there was a line of half-a-dozen or so little rooms with bars on the windows and on the little holes in the doors, and my father said they were the cells the convicts were kept in when they weren't building roads and the Town Hall.

After the Captain left we used to go up there often to play. It was a good place. There was an overgrown garden with enormous climbing roses the doves built in, and pink oleander bushes that made you feel sick if you sat under them for too long. We used to climb in through the windows, and inside the house the rooms were very big and high and empty and dusty, and if you shouted in one of them it seemed to sound all over the house, as if there was someone else in another part of it shouting back at you.

On one side of the house there was a horse-paddock with a tree trunk in it where my father said they used to hang the convicts. I didn't believe him, of course, but then found out he was telling the truth; and whenever I looked at it, especially if we happened to be driving past it in the cart after dark, my hair would stand on end to think of the men who had swung by the neck on the branches that had been cut down so long ago. There wasn't much feed in the paddock, and my brother told me once that the horses would get sanded and blow up. I didn't believe much that he said but it was something else to interest you — and just in case, I always watched for a while to see if one might.

When Ernie and I reached the Captain's that morning Barney rushed at the door of one of the little cells and barked at it. Ernie said: 'Cat, I bet!' and I went and pushed Barney aside with my foot and opened the door.

I don't think I'd ever had a bigger fright. There was a man sitting on a kerosene case looking straight back at me. He had on an overcoat, although it was summer. I bet he hadn't done his hair that morning, nor cleaned his teeth. He had a long, thick moustache like my father's, but I reckon he hadn't shaved the rest of his face for days and days. There was a heap of chaffbags and a dirty old grey blanket on the stone floor in one corner, and a sugar-bag was hanging by a piece of string from one of the bars in the window. In another corner there was a small fire between six bricks built up like a capital 'U'. Two bars had been taken out of the window in the door and laid across them, with two black billies on the bars — one full of steaming water, the other with a stew that didn't seem too bad. I could smell methylated spirits too, then I saw a bottle on the floor beside the man; although I couldn't see any little spirit-stove like the one my mother used sometimes to make a quick cup of tea. Ernie had pushed in behind me and was staring at the stew, but the man and I stared at each other. The sugar-bag was hanging from the window right behind his head and I felt my hair stand on end. Without thinking of what I was saying, I blurted out: 'You're Ally Breen!' I don't think I would have said it if my mother hadn't mentioned the name that very morning.

He looked at me in a funny sort of way and said: 'That's right, sonny. What can I do for you?'

It was my second big surprise for the morning. His voice was nice and friendly, and not at all like someone who would put kids in a sugar-bag and take them away. He sounded just like Mr Faddy, the grocer, when he put your things on the counter and said: *That's rice, tea and Golden Syrup, now. Something else?*

I said: 'We came up here to the Captain's to look around', but while I was saying it I thought: *Just wait 'til I get home and tell Peg and Lal I've been talking to Ally Breen!*

He said: 'Well, now. Would you and your mate like a cup of tea? I've just made one. And I might be able to dig up a biscuit.'

Ernie pushed past me and said: 'Too right, Mister!'

Ally Breen bent forward and looked between his legs into the box he was sitting on and took out a tin of condensed milk with two holes in the top, and two empty tins with the lids folded over into little handles. He blew into one of the holes in the full tin and milk came out of it into the teacup tins. Then he filled them to the brim from the billy: it had tea in it, not water as I had thought.

He said: 'Hand me down that sugar-bag, now', and when I unhooked it from the bar I could see it had a square board in the bottom to keep the sides out and make space inside the bag. I handed it to him and he took out a little glass jam-jar and a teaspoon and a half-emptied packet of Monte Carlo cream biscuits with the top bent over to keep the rest fresh. He gave us one each and bit one in two and gave half to Barney. He gave us our tea and I thought: *Wait 'til I tell them at home Ally Breen gave us a cup of tea and a biscuit!*

He put a teaspoon of sugar into each of our milk-tin cups and stirred it. Then he leaned over and picked up a glass jam-jar I hadn't seen standing on the floor by his box. It was full of pearly-coloured water that looked as if it had a bit of milk in it. He took a mouthful and swallowed it, pulling a face, and I said: 'You going to have some tea?'

He said: 'Not yet. Got to take my medicine.'

'What've you got wrong with you?' Ernie asked. He was always interested in anyone who was sick.

'Sort of the collywobbles', Ally Breen said. He rubbed his stomach and held up the jar of pearly water. 'This fixes them up, though.'

While we were drinking our tea and eating our biscuits we told him about our egg collection and school and everything, and when we'd finished we put the tins back on the box and thanked him. He said: 'I might be here still when you come up again. Come and have a yarn with me.'

As I was going out the door I said: 'You don't really put kids in your sugar-bag and take them away, do you?'

He looked at the water in his jam-jar for a while before he said anything. Then he said: 'Of course not. Whoever told you that, sonny?'

I couldn't very well tell him my mother had, and make her out a story-teller. I just said: 'Oh — someone.'

He turned around on his box and pointed to the sugar-bag, which I'd put back on its piece of string at the window. 'Couldn't get many little kids in that, could I, now?' he said. Looking at me as if he wanted me to say: *Of course not!*

We'd hardly left the Captain's when Ernie let out a yell and took off. Barney took off after him, barking blue murder. I'd been thinking about what I'd just found out, that my mother had been telling us a lie all that time, and wondering why. I'd asked Ernie if his mother had told him about Ally Breen taking him away in the bag. He reckoned she had, that all the mothers around our way did it. I asked him why he thought they did, and he said: 'S'pose it makes it easier for them.' He didn't seem to see much wrong with it. I decided not to say anything about meeting Ally Breen when I got home. If I did my mother would know I'd found out she'd been telling me a lie all along while she'd been saying it was wrong for me to tell them to her.

I pelted off after Ernie and Barney. Ernie was probably right about them having to tell stories sometimes, and I didn't really hold it against them. Still, everything was changed. I knew that next time my mother said anything about Ally Breen and his sugar-bag I'd see him sitting on his box in the cell with his glass of medicine in his hand, pointing at his bag and saying to me he couldn't get many kids in it, could he? And looking at me as if he wanted me to say: *Of course not!* before I disappeared through the door.

The Lucky Spinner

For a long time before the gas came to South Perth I got really tired of hearing my mother say: 'When we get the gas, so-and-so.'

My two sisters used to spend hours looking at coloured pictures of gas stoves the gas people sent out, trying to decide which they liked best, and which were the nicest pots in another set of coloured pictures that had come with the ones about the gas stove.

One night after tea when I was lying on the lino in front of the old wood stove in the kitchen, unwinding the elastic from a golf ball I'd found on the links and listening to them talking about gas stoves and pots, my father said: 'Hey, Min — who's going to pay for all this new stuff?'

My mother just said, in the way I already recognised as a cover for something else: 'Oh — we'll get them on TP.'

Everyone was quiet for a while. Even I knew what TP was. Time Payment, when you bought something you couldn't really afford. Everyone looked down on it, although everyone seemed to be doing it. Only a week or so before, when my mother and her friend Mrs Moodie had been playing cribbage after tea, my mother had said: 'Boans delivered a new bed and mattress to Mrs Wilson's this week', and Mrs Moodie had laughed and said: 'I bet the TP man'll be around *next* week!' And now my mother was suggesting that we should use TP to pay for the new gas stove.

'Like hell, we will!' my father said, and my mother said: 'Well, Arthur, you'll be lighting the kitchen fire in the morning from now on.'

Of course we got the gas stove, and on TP, too. After the first shock I didn't mind so much. It didn't have 'TP' painted on the side, as I'd expected, and in any case Mrs Moodie got one too, in the same way. Also I'd expected that it would relieve me of my daily job of getting the wood in for the kitchen stove, but it didn't work out that way.

A couple of weeks after we took delivery of the gas stove, we were all sitting in the kitchen one wet Saturday afternoon — all except my brother Mickey, that is, who was always out somewhere else apart from mealtimes and bedtime. Suddenly my mother put down her mending and said: 'Blow this for a joke. I'm going to have a fire in the old stove. The house's like a morgue!'

The house was cold, certainly. The old kitchen stove had always seemed to warm it up right through, but the gas stove didn't make any difference at all more than two feet away from the oven door.

It was good for cooking on, and very easy in the morning just to turn on the tap and put a match against the round jet and watch the blue flames shoot out. But my mother was complaining already that she couldn't bake cakes on it. When she wanted to test the heat of the wood oven she'd just put her hand in and wait a minute, her head on one side: my father always said she looked like a duck squinting down a pickle-bottle. She'd say: *Ooh! Too hot!* or *No — not just yet!* and her cakes had always come out perfect. But it didn't seem to work with the gas oven. Only the previous Saturday afternoon she'd been going to make a Swiss roll with jam for Sunday afternoon tea in case anyone came in. She tipped the stuff onto a piece of brown paper and put it on the tray in the gas oven, but instead of rising high and fluffy as it used to in the wood stove it spread out thin and hard all over the paper. She had been wild as a willy-willy. She just threw the cake onto the table and said: 'Give that to the bantams!' and stormed out of the kitchen.

My sisters and I were playing Strip-Jack-Naked at the other end of the table, and we weren't about to waste the cake on the bantams. We'd picked the lot carefully apart from the paper and eaten it, but the moment we finished my mother came back into the kitchen and said: 'Where's that sod? I might as well use it up in a trifle.' Then, of course, there was a ding-dong row — but one thing about my mother was that she never held a grudge: before your bottom had stopped tingling, she'd forgotten all about it.

While I was setting the fire in the wood stove I remembered what she'd said about a morgue, and I asked her: 'Mum, what's a morgue? You know — you said the house was like one?'

My mother had picked up her mending again, and was looking closely at one of my father's socks. She said: 'Well — a sort of room where they keep the dead people until they send them to the cemetery.'

My sisters complained, as they always did, together: 'Oh, *Mum!*' but I was too shocked to do anything. It was the thought of a room full of dead people. It could be a room of *our own house!* In the kitchen, where we were sitting at that very moment. *My own room*, full of dead people. It terrified me. I hadn't yet come to terms with the idea of dying. I didn't really believe I ever would, at least not for hundreds of years.

My mother looked up from her mending. 'Now, Tommy-dodd', she said. It was a pet name she had for me. 'Finish lighting the fire, quick-sticks!' I didn't move, and she looked at me very hard. 'Tell you what. You get a good fire going and I'll make a batch of scones in the old oven, just like we used to. How about that?'

39

It turned out to be the thin edge of the wedge in reinstating the kitchen fire. At first it had been just for the weekend baking. Then it was during the week when it was particularly cold in the kitchen. Then, practically without knowing what was happening to me, I was saddled once more with the daily job of bringing in the wood. This meant that pretty soon we'd have to harness up old Ginger one Sunday morning and go out into the bush for a load of banksia. And that was how it came about that I met the Lucky Spinner.

The drive up to Fremantle Road was one I knew quite well. I travelled it quite often when I was allowed to drive the cart on small deliveries to customers who lived in River Street. The real expedition began when we got to Fremantle Road — quite often when we got to it we had to wait for a motorcar, sometimes even two or three, to rattle by before we could cross. On the other side, the bush side, the cart bowled along on a smooth white shell track which would through the bush for perhaps half-a-mile before it petered out into a sandy cart run between the trees. Every time we turned into it my father grumbled about the way the timber was being thinned out close to Fremantle Road, and he had taken to opening up his own tracks to where the banksias were still thick enough to get a good load from just about where you pulled up. You had to be careful driving through them sometimes, although old Ginger seemed to be able to judge for himself just when the cart would go between two trees.

Mickey always sat on the seat with my father and talked about what he would do when he got to be captain of the school football team or the school cricket team. I sat on the floor of the cart with Barney snuggled between my knees, both of us quite comfortable on the chaff-bags it was my job to fill with chips and banksia cobs and dry blackboy for starting the kitchen fire.

In a tomato case in one corner of the cart there was a billy with some tea and a bottle of milk, and a small bag of fruit and a big parcel of sandwiches for our lunch. Barney got the crusts. There was a canvas waterbag swinging under the seat and, alongside it, Ginger's nose-bag of chaff-and-bran. In the other corner there were the axes and wedges, the shovel and the file and the oilstone, all wrapped in separate bags for safety.

Before we'd left home my father had spent an hour or so filing a sharp edge onto the axes and smoothing them down with the stone. He always let me spit on it. When he'd finished and had run his thumb across the edge, he winked at me and said: *That's*

40

before you bought your shovel! It was what he always said when he was pleased with what he'd done, or when he put something across you.

We pulled up at last in a patch of banksia so thick you couldn't see far before everything merged into a brown blur of trunks and a green blur of leaves. When the rattle of the cart stopped the bush was terribly quiet — and yet not so quiet when you became aware of the noises the different birds made, and the sound of the wind in the trees all around you. We sat for a while listening to it, and Ginger had a piddle as hard as any of our taps at home. He must have wanted to all the way out. My father jumped down to the ground.

'Shake a leg!' he said. 'Give me Barney, boy.'

I handed the dog down to him, and he cuddled it for a moment before he set it down, rubbing his Sunday bristles against the top of its head. *'There's* an ugly man's dog!' he said, as he dropped Barney to the ground. 'Now . . . the axes. Careful! All right, now the tucker-box. Throw out the shovel and the wedges. Now Ginger's nose-bag — don't spill the chaff! That's it! We'll make a bushie of you yet. Light the fire for the billy and then begin getting your chips together. Look — there's a nice blackboy!'

When I'd lit the billy fire I set off with my bags, and Barney danced along with me. Already he'd piddled on several of the trees — so that he'd know the place if he ever came out again, my father said. Mickey had started banging away at the biggest banksia he could see, and I couldn't stop myself from feeling jealous. I wasn't allowed to touch the sharp bush axes in case, as my mother said, I cut off one of my own legs.

All the same, I wasn't certain that Mickey didn't really like chopping down the trees and splitting them into lengths for the kitchen stove. He certainly didn't like any other sort of work.

He loved to eat the bardies my father cooked every time we went out for wood — the big, white fat grubs you found in every banksia when it was split, with hard brown heads the size of a pea. It was funny — they lay there in little holes just big enough to fit them, but there was no passage from the outside of the tree. Even my father didn't know how they got there. He would heat the blade of the shovel over the tea fire and drop a handful of bardies onto it and stir them around with a stick until, he said, they were done. He used to say until they were 'cooked enough to eat raw'. He would hold the head between two fingers and bite the body off. He said he had seen the blacks doing it when he was up in the

41

Murchison driving camels, and he reckoned they tasted like bacon-fat. I loved the fat off bacon but I couldn't make myself eat a bardie. It might have been different if I hadn't seen them wriggling around on the hot shovel first. Mickey would eat as many as Dad would cook for him, and Dad called him a 'proper little warrigal'. It put me in a fury of jealousy because he'd told us that a warrigal was a real dinkum first-rate black, and Mickie put on airs about it: just as he did about being allowed to use the bush axes.

By lunchtime I'd filled three of my four bags with chips, and Mickey and my father had half-filled the cart with wood. The blade of the shovel was ready on the billy fire, and my father had a couple of handfuls of bardies in his hat. He spat on the shovel a few times, and when the spit fizzled he tipped the bardies out onto it to cook. I really didn't want to look at the poor things, wriggling and writhing, but I couldn't help myself. I used to wonder if they were screaming with agony in their little, thin bardie voices.

'Stir them up, Mick', my father said.

He punched a dint in the crown of his felt hat and filled it with water from the bag for Barney, and as I watched Barney lapping I wondered how he could bear to cook the bardies alive when the first thing he thought of was to give Barney his drink — even before he took his own mug of tea from the billy.

He called it his *dish av tay* in his Irish voice, which he put on when he was in a good mood, or when he was going to make a joke. He said things like: *Thread on the tail of me coat an' Oi'll dance on the rim av yer hat!* which I'd been hearing since I could remember hearing anything, without ever wondering what it might mean. One day I said to him: 'What do you *mean*, Dad? *Dance* on the rim of your *hat?*' and he told me that in Ireland when a man wanted a fight he walked around with his coat trailing on the ground behind him, and when he met another man he said it: and if the second man wanted a fight too he trod on the first man's coat and then the first man knocked *his* hat off and stamped on the brim, and they began to fight. But my father didn't say: 'And then they began to fight'. He said: *And thin, begorra, it wus wigs on the green!*

It was very peaceful and quiet, sitting on the soft sheoak needles while we munched our sandwiches and swilled sweet tea out of our mugs. The cool wind just touched us and all about there were the smells of the bush and the newly-cut banksia logs, and only a few feet away old Ginger nuzzled at his own nose-bag, throwing his head up now and then with a rattle of his harness — to mix up the chaff and bran in the bag, my father said.

There was a rainbird somewhere quite near, singing its sort of sad song even though it didn't even look like rain — like the single notes of a piano going up and up and up until you could hardly stand it. Wattle-birds were crawling and yelling in the banksias all around: they always seemed to build in banksias and during the morning I'd found a mob of nests — old ones, though, as the wattlers wouldn't be laying their pretty little pink eggs for a few months yet.

'I think it's cruel to cook the bardies like that', I said, suddenly. I hadn't known I was going to say it, and I had to swallow what I was eating really before I was ready to. 'Alive'.

My father jerked his head back on his shoulders, and raised his eye-brows and popped his eyes, as if he was surprised. He was very good-looking, with thick dark hair and pale blue eyes and a moustache, and a very square jaw with a dimple in the middle of it.

'Indade?' he said. He had put on his Irish voice again, which was a sure sign he was going to have a joke with me. 'Wirra, thin. It's himself that's afther tellin' us the whys and the wherefores av ut!'

Mickey laughed, of course. I felt a bit silly, but I said: 'I still think it is.'

'You like mutton, don't you?' Mickey said. He winked at my father and I saw it.

'Course I do.'

'Well, then . . . somebody's got to kill it, don't they?' Mickey grinned at my father, and I hated him for about the tenth time that day. 'Or d'you think the poor old sheep just died by itself? Of whooping cough, or pneumonia, or something?'

I couldn't think of anything to say, because after all I *did* like mutton — especially boiled with capers, like my mother did it — and somebody *did* have to kill the sheep. And it would probably hurt, although of course not as much as being cooked alive on a hot shovel. I thought about saying so but didn't — I never won arguments with Mickey, anyway. I decided just to go on hating him. For the time being.

When we'd finished our lunch and had packed the things away in the tomato case, it didn't take me long to fill my last chaffbag with the biggest chips from around where my father and Mickey had been chopping. I lugged it over to the cart and propped it up against one of the wheels, and said: 'I'm going looking for orchids, Dad.'

My father winked at Mickey and said: 'Then keep your eyes peeled for Deaf Adders!'

He didn't have to tell *me* about snakes. We all knew the bush was alive with them, although as a matter of fact none of us had ever really *seen* one. Still I always thought about them whenever I poked my arm into the hollow of a tree looking for eggs — parrots and king-fishers and swallows and a lot of other birds all used such hollows for nesting in. Some of the boys I went out in the bush with reckoned that snakes ate eggs, and that they climbed trees to get at the nests, and found the holes made comfortable homes and stayed there. I'd never seen a snake up a tree, and really I didn't think one *could* climb, what with its slippery belly and everything.

I put it to my father, and all he said was: 'Climb! Of course they can, the cows! Climb, run, swim — anything!' And then he told me about the Deaf Adder he'd seen in Queensland, when he'd been a jackaroo on his Australian uncle's station there. Just after he'd come out from Ireland. He said they were the most poisonous snakes in the world, and the only reason why they hadn't killed off everyone in Queensland was because as well as being very poisonous they were also very deaf and very slow. He said that if you killed a Deaf Adder and opened up its head you'd see these words written on its brain: *If I could hear as well as see, no mortal man would pass by me!*

I was very interested in this, but at the same time you could never be quite certain it wasn't another of his stories — for instance, like the fairies he said lived in Ireland. Not silly little butterfly sorts of things with wings and wands but tiny brown people about the size of footballs who lived in underground villages in holes and hollows. He said you could easily mistake them for bundles of leaves and big clods of dirt and things like that.

When I asked my father if he'd ever really *seen* them, he put on his Irish voice and said: 'Well, now. Oi'm not *entoirely* sartin, yer Riverince. But Oi *think* Oi did, bedad!' Just as when I asked him if he'd ever really seen the words on a Deaf Adder's brain, he admitted that really he hadn't. But he'd seen plenty of people who *had* — mostly stockmen and drovers walking away from pubs, he said. On the whole, I decided, you didn't have to worry much about Deaf Adders because in any case they were in Queensland — but you still had to be careful about snakes in our own bush.

As I walked away from the clearing I called Barney to go with me, but he was lying under the cart, and wouldn't budge. Mickey called out: 'Don't you be too long! We'll be finished soon, and if you're not back we'll go without you!'

'I bet you wouldn't!' I yelled back at him — but that was just what happened. Although it wasn't so bad, because it was the reason why I came to meet the Lucky Spinner.

I dawdled around in the bush looking for birds' nests in the trees and orchids under them. I saw a big racehorse goanna standing at the opening of its burrow, and in the fork of a dead tree I saw a mopoke sitting on its nest with its head sticking up deadly still and silvery grey as if it was just another bit of dead wood. On another tree there was a track of claw-marks leading from the ground straight up to a hollow that had all the bark worn off at the edge. I knew it was a possum's nest, all right, but I didn't have time to go up after it: and in any case we already had one possum at home, camping in the inside of the sofa in the livingroom. It was a bit early in the season for orchids, but I found a nice patch of green cockatoos under a gum sapling, so I picked them and added them to the bunch of potatoes and spiders and blue-enamels and cowslips I'd already found.

After a while I came to a well-used cart-track and decided to follow along it to see where it went. Then I came to a most dreadful stink, and a hum of noise like a lot of people at a football match, and then a fence. I stopped dead in my tracks. The fence enclosed a huge paddock broken up into a lot of very small paddocks, and in each of them there was a small wooden shed. The whole place was alive with pigs of all sizes that squealed and grunted and squeaked until you could hardly hear yourself think. And the smell was terrible — so thick you felt you could almost scrape it off the air with a stick.

Without trying to, without even setting out to, I'd found the Piggery. Almost every time we went out the bush we said to each other: *Let's go as far as the Piggery!* but we always got sidetracked into some swamp after waterbirds' eggs, or something like that, and I'd never before got anywhere near it. It was where all the Perth butchers kept the pigs for pork in their shops, Mickey said. He'd been there, of course.

I was absolutely fascinated. I stood by the fence watching a huge mother-pig with eleven — eleven! — little pigs running around her like big white maggots. As I watched, she lay down in the stinking mud and all the little ones dived onto her, fighting and squealing to get to the two lines of tits down each side of her belly, like pointed white turnips. I picked up a piece of wood and threw it at her. She jumped up, scattering her little pigs all over the place, and stood glaring about her, very savage. I threw another stick at her. It hit her on the snout and she let out a squeal and charged at the fence where I was standing. It was wonderful. Mickey had told me once that pigs ate babies when they could get them, but I knew she couldn't get through the fence to me.

I wandered along the fence throwing sticks at the pigs until suddenly I thought about getting back to the cart. I had no idea at all how long I'd been away, and Mickey.had said they'd be leaving pretty soon.

I listened nervously for the *clop! clop!* of their axes, but the bush was very quiet — even more quiet, it seemed, than when I'd set out. I hurried back along the track, passed the possum tree, passed the mopoke, passed where I'd found the green cockatoo orchids, and at last came to the clearing where they'd been cutting wood. The cart had gone. I could still smell the cut wood, and there was a heap of fresh manure where Ginger had been standing between the shafts of the cart. I could see where they'd emptied the waterbag onto the fire my father had used to cook the bardies. But the cart had gone. They'd meant what they'd said about going without me. They'd really gone home and left me.

For a moment I couldn't believe it had happened. I called out as loudly as I could: *'Dad! Mickey!'* and then: 'Barney-Barney-Barney-Barney-*Barney!'* When I stopped to listen there was no sound at all in the bush about me — I think I'd frightened everything into silence. I felt the hair on the back of my neck creep. Even the trees might be watching me, and the possum in his dark hole listening to me, the racehorse goanna standing by his hole flickering his snake-tongue in-and-out at the sound of my voice.

I wasn't frightened of being lost. I'd spent enough time wandering around in the bush to know pretty well where I was, and I knew that all I had to do was to walk toward the sun and I'd come to Fremantle Road. Still, I opened my mouth and let out a bellow. I was wild because they should have played such a mean trick on me. I couldn't stand to think that my father would do it, and it made me cry. Then I got wilder to think that they might have laughed together about me as the cart jolted away with the load of wood piled high on it, without even looking back to see if

I might be running after them. They hadn't even left Barney to walk home with me.

After a while I stopped bellowing. There wasn't anyone to hear me, anyway. I looked around me to get my bearings, and turned toward the sun: and I bet anything I was no more than half-an-hour getting to Fremantle Road.

I stood on the edge of the road looking down it to where it disappeared toward South Perth. I knew for certain it was Fremantle Road, and that if I turned right on it I couldn't help coming to where River Street crossed it, only about a mile or so from home. Even so, it was scary. I'd never been so far out toward Canning Bridge before — except once, years earlier when I'd been little, and my father had been a carrier, and we'd all gone right down to Fremantle on one of his big lorries to pick up a family of Pommies and their furniture who'd just come out from Home.

The bush on either side of the road where I stood was thick and dark, and there was only one house that I could see, away back in the direction of South Perth. I must have been *miles out!* Still . . . if I wasn't going to be home too late for tea — or be trudging around by myself after dark, which was something I didn't even like to *think* about — I'd need to get going.

I'd only been walking for about five minutes, listening to my bare feet go *slap! slap!* in the mud of the verge, and looking ahead to where the road and the sky seemed to meet, when I heard a motor-car chugging and rattling up behind me: you could hear one coming for miles because the road was all potholes in the red gravel. I stopped and looked over my shoulder. It was a most beautiful car. It was all bright red with yellow spokes and rims to the wheels and very brightly-polished brass headlamps. I stepped off the road into the sand and turned right around to watch it go by, but when it got up to me it stopped. There were two men in the front seat and a lady and another man in the back. The man on my side of the front seat leaned out.

'What're you doing right out here by yourself, sonny?'

He had a pleasant voice, just a bit what my mother would have called la-di-dah.

'Are you lost?' the other man said.

'Not really,' I told him, 'I just got left behind?'

The man behind the driving-wheel — the one on my side — said: 'Left behind? How, left behind?'

'Dad and Mickey and me were out getting wood, with Ginger in the cart.' All of a sudden I thought I was going to bawl, just to remember how mean they'd been. But I didn't. I held up my orchids so he could see them. 'When I'd finished picking up the chips I went looking for orchids. And I found the Piggery. And when I got back they'd gone without me. They didn't even leave me Barney to come home with. He's our dog.'

'Golly,' the first man said, 'that's no good, is it? Where d'you live?'

'South Perth.' I pointed the way I was going. 'I go down River Street.'

'Well, you'd better hop in, eh? And when we come to River Street, you tell us.' The man turned half-way around to the people in the back. 'Make room, Belle?'

'Why, of course!' the lady said, and the man beside her opened the door of the car on my side.

When I got in I sat between them staring at my bunch of flowers. I'd never been so close to such beautiful people — except, of course, at the pictures. Like Marion Davies and Billie Love and the Gish Sisters: and Ramon Navarro, even if he was a Dago.

The lady had on a tiny little green hat that fitted tightly on her head so that her shiny gold hair only poked out here-and-there, like on her forehead and by her ears. She was wearing a beautiful piece of grey fur around her shoulders, like a whole animal with ears and little brown glass eyes and the inside of its mouth painted crimson like a pillar-box. Her green dress hardly seemed to reach her knees, and when I looked quickly at them out of the corner of my eye I could see her pink silk stockings. She had a lot of lovely scent on — as my mother would have said, she must have had a bath in it. Her cheeks were very pink and white, and you could tell the red on her lips was lipstick, but it just made her look more beautiful.

The man on the other side of me smelled of beer and tobacco, but nice and clean as if he'd only just drunk the beer and only just put out the cigarette. Not like some of the men who came into our shop, stinking as if they'd been smoking and drinking in the same clothes for years, without ever taking them off. And his suit wasn't made of blue serge, like my father's and every man's that I knew. It was very thick, rough stuff the colour of Barney, almost, a sort of honey colour with a bit of green in it somehow, and he had a dark brown hankie in his top pocket to go with it and his tie. The men in the front seat seemed to be very well dressed too, and they all smelled of some soap nicer than Solyptol.

I supposed they must all be real toffs, and all of a sudden I felt dreadfully ashamed of my muddy bare feet on the little mat on the floor of the car. And for the first time in my life I really *knew* my pants were a hand-me-down from Mickey, and patched and dirty.

'These are my old pants', I said, and I touched them as if they didn't matter. It was a story, because they were my only pair apart from my very best for going to town and to the pictures, Saturdays. 'I only wear them out the bush.'

'Of course!' The lady smiled at me, and I fell in love with her right then. 'Nobody wears their best clothes out getting wood, do they?'

'What does your Dad do,' the man behind the wheel asked, 'besides getting wood?'

'Oh — the wood's only for our own fire', I told him. 'We've got a shop — although Mum says she's going to give it up when her ship comes in. What do you do, Mister?'

'Well, now.' He smiled across me at the lady, and then turned back to his driving. 'I guess I'm what's called a Lucky Spinner.'

'You hope so!' the man sitting beside me said. He laughed, and turned to me. 'We're all Lucky Spinners. We're going to the game.'

'The footy?' I said. In Perth in the winter there was only one game, and sometimes they played it on Sundays.

'No — another game', the lady said. She put an arm around my shoulders and pressed me against her side. I felt I should pull away, but I couldn't make myself do it. Besides, it might have been rude. 'You know,' she said, 'I've got a notion you might be a bit of a Lucky Spinner, yourself.' She pressed my shoulder. 'You are lucky, aren't you?'

I thought for a moment. It was hard to think, pressed against her like that, with my head full of the smell of her clothes and her scent. 'I don't really know,' I said, after a while, 'we've never won the Charities.'

'Oh, that's nothing, the old Charities!' The lady picked up her handbag from the seat alongside her. It was made of shiny black leather like her high-heeled shoes, and where a clasp was on my mother's bag there was a big lump of green stone the same colour as her dress. 'Will you do something for me?'

'You bet!' I said, straight away. I reckon I'd have jumped off the top of the T&G if she'd asked me to. 'What?'

'Hey!' she said, and she laughed again. 'When a lady asks a gentleman to do something for her, he never asks her what. Remember?' She opened her bag and took out a lot of notes rolled up in a tight bundle. I couldn't help staring. I reckoned there must be a hundred pounds, at least. She held it out to me. 'I want you to touch it for me. I reckon you're a Lucky Spinner, and maybe you'll make me lucky, too.' She smiled at me. 'You're good-looking enough to, anyway!'

'Oh, crikey, Belle!' the man behind the wheel said, laughing. 'Any age, nine to ninety!'

'Go on,' she said to him: and then, to me: 'Will you?'

'Course.' I stretched out my hand and touched the money, and she took a note off the top of the roll and handed it to me. It was one of the red ones, for ten shillings. Right under it was a blue one, which I knew was for five pounds. Five *pounds!* And lots more under that.

'Oh, no thank you', I said. I couldn't quite keep it out of my voice how sorry I was that I couldn't take it. *Ten shillings!* 'Dad doesn't like people to give us money.'

'I'm not *giving* it to you', the lady said. She folded the note tightly and put it into my palm, and closed my fingers on it. I just couldn't stop her doing it. Her hands were soft and white and her fingernails were shining pink, like a celluloid Kewpie doll.

The man who was driving had begun to slow down. 'River Street, just ahead of us', he said, over his shoulder. He pulled in toward the side of the road. I looked ahead, between him and the other man in the front seat. It was the River Street sign, all right. In a moment I'd have to get out. I held up my flowers for the lady to see.

'Would you like to have my orchids?'

'I'd love them!' she said. 'But . . . where I'm going tonight I couldn't look after them. They'd just die.' She smiled at me. 'Tell you what? I'll just take two or three of them, and wear them.'

She leaned across me and slipped three of the stems of green cockatoo orchids out of my bunch. She held them to her cheek for a moment, and then put them down the front of her dress. 'There! *That'll* bring me luck!'

I stared at them, the little green parrot's-beaks all up the stalks. They stood so stiff and hard against the white skin of her neck. I knew that if I lived to be a hundred I'd never forget how she looked.

The car pulled up and the man next to me reached out and opened the door.

'There you are, Spinner,' he said. 'Time to hand over the kip.'

The lady squeezed my shoulder and said: 'Off you go — and

don't dawdle. It's getting late, and your Mum might be worrying about you.'

I scrambled out, taking care not to muddy the man's trousers. I stood by the side of the road and said: 'Goodbye. Thank you for giving me a ride in your motorcar.'

I began to walk away down River Street, but as soon as they pulled out into the road I turned to watch them go. I wondered what the man had meant about handing over the kip. For an awful moment I'd thought he might have meant the ten shilling note the lady had given me. I thought: *I'll ask Dad when I get home.* I'd be there in a jiffy. No — I'd dawdle. Mickey could feed Biddy and Ginger, and get the wood in. And serve them right for buzzing off and leaving me, the way they had.

I stood on the roadside staring at the back of the car until I could hardly see it. The lady was sitting in it with my green cockatoo orchids down the front of her green dress. I wondered if they would really bring her luck in the game they were going to play.

After a while the grey canvas hood disappeared over the edge of the slope leading down to the Causeway. I began to walk home down River Street.

The Day
Of The Wonderful Eggs

When I put my foot out from under the covers and onto the floor, I found Barney had got back inside somehow. Not that there was much of a surprise in that, because he was always doing it. When the cat was put out and the house was locked up for the night he would sneak back in again. My mother reckoned he was some sort of magic dog who could come in through the keyhole, and although I didn't really believe that, it was some sort of magic to find him there in the morning, and to put my foot down onto his warm back rather than onto the cold lino, and then let him jump up onto the bed and lick the side of my face while I sat there remembering the night.

It had been a dreadful one. After the storm we'd had it seemed funny to be able to look out on such a lovely morning. It was all so still, and blue and gold. The bantams' tree, the one they roosted in, drooped across the window with millions of rain drops like little glass beads, so that when I half-closed my eyes and looked at it, it was like being on the inside of an iceberg, looking out. I got up and walked to the window, and Barney dragged at my pyjamas.

'You tear my coat and Mum'll give you what for!' I threatened him, but he took no notice.

After such an awful night as we'd had I couldn't believe everything could look so ordinary. Nothing had been washed away. No boats had floated up from the river and been left high-and-dry in our yard: they never had, but you couldn't tell. When you lay there and listened to the rain pouring down in the dark, you could *see* the river getting fuller and fuller and then beginning to creep up Rover Street, and if it kept on raining, what was supposed to stop it?

However much rain we'd had it hadn't worried the bantams, who'd been out *in* it. They were all scratching away around the manure heap outside the stable. There were twenty-six of them now, and although I often had bantams' eggs for breakfast, there were two hens sitting in the chaff-shed with seventeen between them. Of course my mother shouted, from time to time: 'No more bantams! I *insist!* Break the eggs!' but she always forgot — or was too busy, or didn't mean it.

Once my father killed four of them and she cooked them for Sunday dinner, but although we liked chook my sisters and I cried all through it, and would only eat the vegetables. Mickey was the only one who ate any bantam.

During the night there'd been terrible thunder and lightning as well as the rain. The lightning was so bright, green and yellow, you'd think it would set fire to the curtains, and the thunder followed right behind it. My father said that was a sign that we were right in the middle of the storm. It's funny how they tell you different things at different times: I could remember him telling us when we were still little that the thunder was only Mr Roberts rolling his new rainwater tank down his driveway from the road, where the carrier had left it, and that lightning was just the angels lighting their cigarettes. They tell you one thing, and then another and then another, and in the end I suppose you find out for yourself what it really is. When it crashed right over the house it seemed as if the whole world had split in halves, and you could hear it rolling away over South Perth and Victoria Park and the hills, and then Kalgoorlie and the rest of Australia. I was scared of it because it seemed to be mixed up somehow with Eternity that the nuns were always on about at school. *For ever and ever and ever!* they warned us, again and again, whether you were a happy saint in Heaven if you were good, or whether you were being roasted in Hell if you weren't. I could never really decide which I thought would be the worst.

Nobody else in the house had seemed to be worried about the rain. In the night I could just make out Mickey's shape on the other side of the room, humped up under his covers. I wondered if I should wake him and the others so we could all crawl up onto the roof before the black water flowed into the house and filled up the rooms like buckets. I had a terrible picture of all of us pinned against the ceiling like drowned frogs.

Once when I was little I *had* wakened everyone. I'd crept across the freezing lino and shaken Mickey by the shoulder and told him the water must be up to the windowsill. They chiacked me for weeks, and my father kept calling me Noah and asking me how the Ark was coming along. They even told my friends, so that it got about at school and for weeks afterward I had fights nearly every day on the way home.

After a while I reckoned I should just climb up onto the roof myself and leave Mickey to be drowned: but I couldn't stand the thought of my brother being dead. In the end I decided to stay where I was and say as many *Oh Sacred Heart of Jesus* as I could, but I'd hardly started when I went back to sleep anyway.

Mickey was up and gone long before I woke up — he was always going somewhere or doing something, especially on Saturdays. The rain had stopped and the flood, if it had happened at all, had drained back to the river. Perhaps the Chinamen's gardens would be covered as they had been for a while in the very wet winter a couple of years before. From the roadway down to the ferry you could see rows and rows of cabbages shining like weak street lights under the brown water, and the Roads Board had put up little bridges of planks so that people going into town could get to the jetty. The water was only knee-deep but some people, mostly ladies, stumbled off into it, and men had to take off their boots and roll up their trousers to go in and help them. We had a wonderful time until the water went down, and maybe it was a bit much to expect that it might happen again.

Even if it didn't, things were still pretty good. I'd got through the night without letting anyone know I was scared stiff, and I *knew* all of a sudden I'd never be frightened of the rain again. I had Barney and the bantams. And my pigeons — even as I thought of them they all swooshed up from the roof of the church next door and wheeled away into the sky. It almost seemed to stop my heart just to see them do it. And then, in about twelve hours, I'd be off to see Milton Sills in *The Sea Hawk*. It seemed as if I'd been waiting half my lifetime for it to come to South Perth.

I gave Barney a cuddle for a moment and then got up and pulled off my pyjamas and jumped into my shirt and pants — I'd perfected a way of doing it all in one movement, almost without stopping. Before I had to go back to school on Monday morning, anything might happen.

My usual Saturday morning jobs didn't take me very long. When breakfast and cleaning up were done my mother picked up her black purse off the dresser and put it on the kitchen table in front of her. She did it every Saturday morning at the same time, and I loved it. It was her way of doing things, and I thought that as long as she kept on doing it we'd all be together, and nothing would change. She took out a two-shilling piece. Then she fossicked around until she found a half-crown, and planked it down on the table in front of me.

'That's for a roast of beef, and tell Mr Rogers a nice big one. Then it'll do.'

She didn't have to tell me what it would do — hot lunch for Sunday, cold for tea Sunday night, with salads; sandwiches for Monday's school lunches, and in a curry for tea, Monday night. She looked at the two-shilling piece for a moment and then said what she'd decided. 'Two pounds of stewing chops for tonight's tea. Two lamb's fries and — let's see.' She poked around with one finger in her purse, rattling the coins, and scraped out a thripenny bit and three pennies onto the table alongside the two-shilling piece and the half-crown. 'Two pounds of mince. Remember that? and if Mr Rogers's got a lamb's kidney, tell him to throw that in, too.'

'What're we having for dinner today?' Just to think about the roast beef and the lamb's fries made my mouth water, even though we'd just finished breakfast.

'Bread-and-pullet', my mother said. She always said something like that — *duck-under-the-table* or *saveloys-and-wheat*. She pushed the money along the table toward me, counting it as she went.

'Two-and-six, four-and-six, four-and-nine, five-shillings. Golly Fritz! *Five shillings* for the weekend meat!'

'Better tucker bills than doctor's bills!' I said, and grinned at her. It was something else she said, every Saturday morning when she counted out the money for the meat and vegetables. I'd been waiting for a chance to get in before her.

'Less of your old-fashioned chat', she said. 'Off you go, now — oh, and tell Mr Rogers to throw in a few soup bones. They'll do for Barney, afterward.'

Lamb's fry! I thought, as I ran along the footpath to the butcher's. My mother cooked it with onions and bacon and boiled rice, and it was gorgeous.

My next message was to the Chinamen's for vegetables, with Barney dancing along behind me. My mother had wrapped one-and-eightpence in a piece of paper — I hated her doing it because I wasn't a baby, but she insisted. Sixpence for a nice big caulie and thrippence for a bunch of beetroot for Sunday night's tea: *Drink up the juice*, my mother always told me. *It makes blood!* Eightpence for two pounds of beans and thrippence for a bunch of soup vegetables, and make sure he put in some sprigs of thyme and parsley with the carrot, the parsnip, the onion and the couple of sticks of celery. I never had to fetch potatoes because they were sold in our shop. My mother reckoned they were free, but my father said he didn't know about that.

When I got back from the Chinamen's and dumped the vegetables on the sink in the kitchen I thought I was through, but my mother came out of the diningroom with a bundle of papers in her hand. I really felt my heart drop down into my heels.

'Now, there's something else you can do for me.' She licked a finger and flicked it through the top sheets, reading out the names of a few people who lived around our way as she went. 'You can take these accounts and go and see . . .'

'Oh, *no*, Mum!' I'd been hoping it wouldn't happen, for once, but I knew it would as soon as I saw the papers in her hands.

'Oh, *yes*, Mum!' She handed me the accounts she'd picked out. 'And here's a couple more while you're at it — that's supposing you want to go to the pictures tonight?' She looked at me hard, with her eyebrows up.

I nodded.

'I beg your pardon?'

'Yes, please, Mum.'

'That's better. Now . . . shift your shanks. When you've done that you can go and play — providing I can't think of anything else for you to do.'

I took the accounts from her and trudged off toward the back door. I wondered sometimes if she really loved me, or just kept me for a slave, or something. I was really wild, and I suppose she could see it.

'And lift your bottom lip, young man!' she called out after me. 'Or I'll hang the kettle on it!'

Of all my jobs it was the one I hated most, even though it only came around every so often. It was what my father called going round the traplines, and it was to see if I could collect something off customers who'd run up big accounts at our shop. The houses were so poor and the people were so hopeless and ashamed and sorry about it all. *Tell your father I'm sorry*, they said, *but I'm only able to give him* . . . or *Tell your father I'm sorry but Mr Wilson's only worked two days this week* . . . or *Tell your father I'm sorry but I've had the baby to the doctor this week* . . .

I got swamped up to pussy's bow with their troubles, and I hated asking them as much as they hated it. Sometimes I began worrying on Monday that I might have to do the traplines on Saturday, and every time I set out with the accounts I swore that when I grew up and got married I'd never, never, *never* be poor.

But as it turned out I was walking on air when I got home. I'd got such a lot of money. I felt prouder with every tinkle as I dropped it on the kitchen table coin by coin, counting it up for my mother.

'Four-and-sixpence!' I said — and then, because I felt so good: 'Next week I'll take *ten* accounts, and perhaps I'll bring home a *pound!*'

'Bless your eyes and whiskers', my mother said. She put her arm around my shoulder. 'Where are you off to, now?'

'I reckoned I'd go up to Ernie's.'

'Then you'd better have a piece. You won't get anything up there.'

I knew what my mother meant. Ernie's father was out of work, and he had to go into town every week and get the sustenance. It was something the government handed out to the unemployed. I'd been in their kitchen once with Ernie when his father came home and emptied it out onto the table, a big hunk of corned beef and some potatoes and carrots and other vegies, and a few groceries. As he dropped the sugar-bag onto the bare wood floor he said to Ernie's mother: *I don't know what I went to the bloody war for.* I'd wondered about it, afterward. The war had been over for years, and it couldn't have had anything to do with the sustenance.

I was only half-way across our backyard when Ernie came through the gate. He stopped in front of me and stared at my piece of bread-and-jam.

'Where you going?' I asked, through a mouthful.

'Come to see you.' Ernie's eyes stayed right on my bread-and-jam. 'Thought we might go down the river, or something.'

We were almost the same age, to the month, but I was taller and fatter than Ernie. I suppose that is why I usually took the lead in our games and expeditions. We both wore hand-me-downs from our brothers, but mine still weren't all that bad. My mother had a machine, and she took them in here and there, and when they had to be patched she always tried to do it with the same sort of stuff, or something very like it. Ernie's were always frayed and worn out even before he got them, and they were patched with any old stuff. He had on a grey flannel shimmy much too big for him, with short sleeves and no collar. His pants were held up with an old pair of men's braces and his lower half disappeared into them without touching the sides. Another thing was every time he got a knock or a scratch it turned into a yellow fester — his knees and the backs of his hands were covered with them. My mother called them school-sores because only school children got them. She said they came from some germ in the sand of the schoolyard. I'd heard my father say, once: *School sores be damned, Min! It's scurvy!* He'd been studying to be a doctor before he left Ireland, and he knew a lot about fixing up people and animals, especially horses. *Those poor damn kids aren't getting enough tucker,* he went on. *Our kids don't get sores!* We did, but not as many as Ernie.

I turned and went to the back door. Ever since I'd heard my father say that I was always worried that Ernie might be hungry. 'Ernie's come down, Mum. Can he have a piece, please?' I put my lips close to the wire. 'A big one!'

She handed it out to me a moment later, and I loved her more than ever. It was even thicker than my own, and it was simply covered with butter and jam.

We'd almost given up trying to catch the goldfish in the Chinamen's ponds. Our plan had been to take them around in a bucket to sell to the neighbours as pets, but the only one we'd ever caught had died before we got it home. I was thinking of asking my father for a piece of the muslin off one of the hams he sold in the shop, and then put it around my crabbing net and catch them that way, but I really hadn't thought it out yet.

We looked for crabs on the piles of Douglas's jetty, but there weren't any: it was where old Mr Douglas's grandfather had tied up the little boat he'd sailed over to town for supplies in the early days. Then we walked along the bank of the river to Billy Bew's garden, and dammed the stream running out of his springs. When a lot of water had collected we broke the dam and pretended it was Mundaring Weir collapsing, and climbed up a paperbark to save ourselves. While we were there I found a greeneye's nest with four of their pretty little greeny-blue eggs in it, but I didn't touch it — they were so common you could get a hatful whenever you wanted them.

When we got to Manning's paddock we stood on the safe side of the fence for a while waiting for Manning's bull to jump onto one of the cows and make a calf. Nothing happened, so we got through the wires and paddled along the shoreline to the point. We kept an eye on the bull, just the same, in case he came our way.

Before you got to the point there was a reef of flat sandstone rock that edged out into the deep water. It was covered with birdshit from the hundreds of pelicans and gulls and shags that roosted there all the time during the summer — sometimes wild ducks and even black swans. Once I'd found a dirty white egg there, but when I showed it to my mother she just said one of the birds had dropped it in a careless moment. I would have liked to be able to say it was a pelican's or a swan's, but it was much too small. When I put in my box I labelled it SHAG because it was about the right size, and I knew a shag laid a dirty white egg. I didn't care much for it, really, because you had to get the egg out of the nest yourself for it to be any good.

Some of the most beautiful eggs I had were not my favourites. The fishermen who worked on the river used to go up to a place called the Moore River, a very lonely place nobody else ever went to, about fifty miles up the coast from Perth. I was listening when one of them called Huby Woods was telling my father how mobs of seabirds nested right on the beach there, and you were able to walk around among them and pick up a bucketful of eggs in a couple of minutes. I told him I collected eggs, and one time when they came back he brought me a whole box of seabirds' eggs. I think they were the most beautiful eggs I'd ever seen, all brown and green and red and purple streaks and splotches like coloured seaweed. My father said the birds made them that way because they used seaweed in their nests, and if the eggs and the nests all looked just like seaweed it made the eggs very hard to find.

I used to take the Moore River eggs out now and then and look at them and handle them, and try to imagine that I'd walked around among those swarms of seabirds on the lonely beach with the sea breaking only a few yards away, and the fishermen's camp just up in the sandhills. But it wouldn't work.

Yet I loved looking at my maggies' eggs — the pale blue ones or the pale green ones with reddish spots in a ring at the fat end, or the chocolate maggies' with chocolatey-brown squiggles instead of spots. I used to love remembering how I'd got every one of them, and when I picked one up out of its little nest of cotton-wool I could really see the tree the nest had been in, and where it was in the bush, and how hard the climb had been, and the way the maggie had attacked me with its beak and wings, right up there at the top of the tree, to make me go away. You really had to get your own eggs, and the harder it was the more fun you had showing them off and skiting about them, or even just looking at them by yourself.

We didn't often go past the fence on the other side of Manning's paddock, unless we were with big boys. The swamp was very thick, and down toward the river there was a forest of bulrushes, tall and tangled, that completely hid the open water from sight. It looked mysterious, and we thought it was dangerous. And the vegetable gardens on the top side of the swamp belonged to Chinamen we didn't know: not 'our' Chinamen, who came into our shop, and gave us specked fruit for helping them. They didn't meet us all the time on the footpath and smile and say: *Welly ni' day, eh?*

We used to spy on these strange Chinamen from the rushes while they were working in their garden. They wore exactly the same blue jackets and trousers and the same wide hats of plaited straw. Their faces were just as brown and sort of *slanted*, and they had just the same sort of big, white teeth. But you just didn't *know* them.

That day, the day of the wonderful eggs, we climbed through the fence on the other side of Manning's and walked a fair way into the swamp. Then we heard the strange Chinamen talking on the other side of the ditch at the bottom of their garden, and we hid in the rushes and spied on them. After a while I began to wonder what they would do if they found out we were watching them. They might do *anything*. The skin began to crinkle on the back of my neck, and I started to crawl away, backward, from the bottom of the garden. Ernie didn't waste any time following me, and we didn't stop until we'd put the whole width of the swamp behind us, and had reached the edge of the bulrushes.

We'd hardly come to a halt on the tiny beach when I caught a glimpse of a bird. I'd never seen anything like it before, even in a picture-book. One moment it was walking across the mud, jerkily, as if it was on stilts. The next, just like the flicker of something in the corner of your eye, it disappeared into the bulrushes. For a moment I thought I must have imagined it, not just because it had disappeared so suddenly, but because it was so strange-looking. It had long red legs and a brilliant blue front and dark-brown wings, almost black. Its beak was very short and brilliant red, and between its beak and its forehead there was a funny sort of red shield. No wonder I thought I was having a fit.

'Did you see that bird?' I whispered, to Ernie.

'Nuh.' Ernie shook his head. He never said a word more than he had to.

'I did. I think.'

I sloshed over to where the bird had been and there were its tracks, all right. They were much bigger than a chook's — so big you might have thought a peacock had made them. For a moment I thought it might have *been* a peacock, but then I knew it couldn't have. You couldn't have *missed* seeing a peacock. Ernie had run after me, and we stood looking at the mysterious prints. They pointed straight into the thickest part of the bulrushes. I started to follow them.

'Come on!'

'Nuh,' Ernie said again, 'snakes.'

'Snakes? In the *water?*'

'Water-snakes.'

'Gawd!' I wondered if Ernie had just made it up as an excuse for not going into the swamp. I wasn't all that keen on it myself, and even less when I thought about water-snakes. But I kept thinking of the strange bird, blue, red and black, so unlike anything I'd ever seen before. 'All right,' I said, 'you stay here. There might be a nest.'

'We still waxing?' Ernie said. He sounded a bit anxious.

'Oh, well . . .' I thought it over. By rights you had to be together when the eggs were found, if you wanted to share. Still. 'All right,' I said, after a while, 'waxes.'

I parted the bulrushes and pushed in among them. I was on a narrow, winding stretch of open water, only a few feet wide, between the banks of green. I was a bit scared of being there by myself, but at the same time I was glad there was nobody else to share what might be a marvellous discovery. I had no doubt I'd find the strange bird's nest — big birds have big nests, and they're easy to spot; not like a chickaree's, about the size and shape of a gumleaf, with a long tail of dried grass, and always built in a gum to make it even harder.

When I'd gone around a couple of bends, and the rushes had sort of closed in behind me, I could hardly believe I wasn't in the African jungles I'd read about in my Tarzan books, so still and hot and quiet. I could see nothing but the reeds and the sky above them. Nothing of South Perth at all, and on the other side of the river only our three tall buildings — the T&G, the Town Hall tower and St Mary's Cathedral. The only sound I could hear was one of the trams clanking across the causeway to Vic Park or South Perth. It was creepy, and seemed to be a million miles away.

I found the nest all right. I really didn't know what to expect, but I knew what it was the moment I saw it. It was like a raffia shopping basket hanging on the reeds, well above the water, and twined to four or five strong rushes to keep it up. It was really very well hidden, and I might even have missed it if one of the big birds hadn't flopped away from it just as I got abreast of it; but even so I wouldn't have missed out. There were dozens of them all around me, and the moment you see one nest in a colony you see them all.

I'd just reached out and had begun to pull the nest toward me, stalks and all, when something right behind me let out a loud *honk-honk* that scared me out of my skin. It could only have been the bird that owned the nest, I knew, but it was scary being there by myself in the middle of the swamp, and hearing that noise. And it gave me an uncomfortable feeling to know that the bird was hiding there in the rushes, watching me rob it. It was something I'd never felt before when I'd been out nesting.

I forgot all about that when I saw the eggs. Three, five, *eight* of them packed among the dried kack and feathers and bits of reeds in the bottom of the basket. They were big eggs, almost as big as a chook's, and they were dark greeny-yellow with a ring of red and purple blotches around the fat end — which is where the spots almost always are. My father told me it was because the bird turns the eggs over and over while they're hatching, and the ring of spots gives it something to go by. I said how did the chooks get on because their eggs don't *have* any spots, and he said he'd think about it.

I picked one of the eggs out of the basket-nest and just stared at it for a while. Then I put it up to my nose to smell the wonderful wetness-and-feathers of it. Then I held it to my cheek to feel the warm smoothness of it, like silk. Then I put it back into the nest and turned my back on it.

I used to play a game with myself when I found a special nest or orchid or something like that. I used to pretend I hadn't found it, or I'd forgotten where it was, so that when I looked again it was like finding it again, for the first time.

I stared at the tall bulrushes with their sky-rocket heads of tightly packed fluff that broke away and sailed on the air like snow, and at the drooping brown fronds of the sedge; and at the deep-green tops of the paperbarks, standing up like giant broccoli where we'd come into the swamp.

I was so excited about the new eggs that it all seemed to be something completely new, as though I really was on the banks of some unknown river a million miles from Perth. I was standing so still that a tiny green reed-warbler landed on the stalk of a rush not ten feet away from me and began to sing its heart out. I could see, more clearly than I had ever before, the way its claws clutched the rush, and its little twig legs, and the beating in its throat as it sang. A little further off a black moorhen bobbed along the way they do, in little jerks and starts, and for a moment a whole mob of fork-tailed swallows seemed to blink all around me in the air, after a cloud of midgies. The moorhen steered itself into the rushes in a bit of a hurry, and in a moment I saw why — two water-rats were swimming toward me, side by side. They made little arrows on the surface of the water just like the ferries, and a tiny wake just like the boat's where their tails joined their bodies. As I watched them they suddenly changed their course toward the rushes and disappeared, as the moorhen had, and a moment later I heard what had disturbed *them:* the slush-slush-slush sound of someone walking into the swamp. A moment later Ernie was standing alongside me, looking into the nest. I suppose he'd got more scared of waiting there by himself than he was of meeting up with a water-snake.

'Gawd!' He looked around where we were standing, and saw the rest of the nests. 'Gawd — *cart*loads! For swapping!'

'Well . . .' I wasn't so sure about taking cartloads. My mother was dead set against collecting eggs, but when I'd asked her if I could start she couldn't say much because Mickey already had one of the best collections around our way. What she did say was: 'How would *you* like to come home and find all your eggs gone, if *you* were a mother-bird?'

'You don't take *all* the eggs,' I explained — and at the time I suppose I really believed what I was saying. 'You *always* leave *some*, so the mother-bird won't desert the nest.'

'Yes — so she'll lay more and you can come back and steal *them!*' my mother said. 'The mother bird can *count* her eggs. She'd know *some* were gone!'

I said I didn't think birds *could* count, and she said then how did I think the mother-bird knew when to stop laying? I was going to mention that more often than not we took the bantams' eggs before they'd had a chance to get cool, and it didn't seem to worry the bantams any. In the long run I thought better of it. After a while you got to know when it was best to stop.

I went ahead with my plans anyway. I knew my mother would forget she had forbidden me to, as she always did. As a matter of fact, when I reckoned later on she'd had time to forget, I showed her the eggs I'd already collected, she was just as interested in them as I was. She said how pretty they were, and asked me where I'd found this one and that one.

I reckoned I could let my head go on the new eggs. There were plenty of nests to choose from, and if you could judge from the one I'd already looked into, plenty of eggs in every nest. I reckoned I wouldn't have much trouble going easy on the mother-birds' feelings.

'One out of each nest', I said to Ernie. I thought about it for a while and then said: 'We can come back later on for more. When they've laid them.'

I hefted the beautiful egg in my hand, wondering about its weight. If an egg was youngketty it seemed heavier, and more solid, with the chicken inside it. I held it against my ear for a moment, to see if I could hear anything inside it — sometimes you could. Ernie was watching me anxiously. Then I held it up against the light — with some eggs, particularly the light-coloured ones, you could tell from the colour of the shell if there was a youngun inside. When an egg was youngketty it was very hard to blow it properly. The hole you blew the yolk and the white out of had to be as small as possible, and the bigger it was the less the egg was worth to you, or as a swap. Sometimes you blew the whole end out of an egg, and that euchred it, of course. I'd never been able to make myself put a youngketty egg on an antheap and let the ants eat the chicken out, like some of the others did.

'Can't tell', I had to say, in the end. 'Shell's too dark.' I put the egg carefully in the front of my shirt. 'Come on — one from each nest.'

As we waded around taking the eggs and putting them inside our shirts the big blue-fronted birds seemed to follow us, honking at us and now and then showing themselves among the rustling bulrushes. Before we left I took careful note of the spot — not for the big nests, because once you knew where they were you'd always be able to find them, but for the reed-warbler. I knew from other times in other swamps they always sang loudest close to where their nests were.

In the last half-hour before tea, after I'd got the morning's-wood in and fed the cow, and had done a last-minute run down to the Chinamen's for white onions, I brought out my egg boxes and sat down at the kitchen table with them. Peg and Alice were crocheting around their doyleys, which my mother was teaching them how to do. My father was at the other end of the table oiling the beautiful cricket bat he'd given Mickey for getting into the school team: I loved the clean smell of the linseed oil, and I was wild with envy — but this time at least *I* had something that might make the great Mickey sit up and take notice.

As I'd walked into the kitchen I'd noticed a bowl of liver on the dresser, cut into strips and dipped in flour. It looked as if we were going to have lamb's fry for tea, instead of the stew my mother had mentioned that morning when I was going to the butcher's. I glanced at the stove, and there was the big, heavy pot she cooked the rice in. That settled it. *Lamb's fry!*

I took out two of the new eggs and laid them carefully on the oilcloth. A moment later my father looked up in my direction — maybe he'd been wondering why I'd been so still for so long. He stared at the eggs for a while and then got up and walked to my end of the table.

'Where'd you get those, boy?'

He picked up one of the eggs and stood staring at it for a long time, in the palm of his hand. Watching him, I had the feeling he was really looking through it, or past it, at something else entirely.

'Bald coots', he said, and looked up at me. 'It's a bald coot's egg. Used to see mobs of 'em up and down Cooper's Creek, long time ago.' Again I had the funny feeling he wasn't really in our kitchen, talking to me. He seemed to be talking to someone not even in the room, maybe someone who'd been a friend of his in the days he told us about, sometimes; when he'd been a drover in the middle of Australia. He sighed, and put the egg back on the oilcloth.

'And the Diamantina.' He spoke the way he always did when he was telling us about his other life — as though he was reminding himself of something he'd forgotten for a while.

'In the reed-beds', he went on, in the same dreamy way. 'Mobs of 'em. Bald coots.'

I looked at him suspiciously. *Bald coots!* He was, well, such a terrible story-teller — I didn't like to think of my own father as a liar. Yet . . . I remembered how the birds' heads had looked sort-of bald, behind that funny red shield that covered their foreheads. And shiny. Perhaps, for once, my father wasn't pulling my leg.

'It was a big bird, with a blue front, Dad', I said.

'That's right.'

'And it had a funny red shield in front of its forehead.'

'That's right.'

'And it *was* sort-of bald.'

Mickey walked into the kitchen. He didn't even bother to look at his cricket bat.

'Gee!' He reached out to take one of the eggs, but I moved the box back from him. 'Where'd you get *those*, Tommy?'

'Up Cooper's Creek.' You never told anyone where, unless you'd agreed on a bargain beforehand. I smiled at my father, and he smiled back at me. I felt as if I'd absolutely burst with skite.

I'd had a wonderful day. I hadn't told anyone about being

scared the night before, and I knew now I'd never be scared of the rain again. I'd collected more from the accounts than I'd ever brought home before. I'd seen the strange, beautiful bird — *just by chance, too!* — and found the nests and got the eggs. And for once I had Mickey where I wanted him.

And now, best of all, there was lamb's fry for tea, and Milton Sills in *The Sea Hawk* afterward.

It *had* been a wonderful day.

I knew I'd remember it when I got old. I'd still walk down to the river with Barney and look at the Chinamen's gardens, and walk along the shore to the great bulrush swamp and watch the blue-and-black birds. The bald-coots.

I knew that no matter how old I got I'd stand in my own kitchen with Ernie and remember it — just as my father stood in ours and remembered Cooper's Creek and the Diamantina, and the bald coots *he'd* seen *there*.

And I'd always remember it as the day of the wonderful eggs.

Coodie Crab Co.

I found out about the crabs one morning during the Christmas holidays when I was pottering around down by the river on my own.

It was a real scorcher, absolutely calm, the water clear as glass and blue as the sky, and hundreds of snow white pelicans wheeling around in big circles above the river, so far up they looked like confetti flung at a wedding.

Out in the middle of the river where the sandbanks were, there was a great mob of shags and divers rounding up a school of mullet. While they swam and dived in a circle to stop the fish from getting away, mobs of gulls flew around above them screaming their heads off and waiting for the scraps, as they always did. The ferryboats were chugging along between the tall wooden posts that marked the channels between Perth and South Perth, one to Mends Street and one — ours — to Coode Street. The river wasn't very deep, really, so that when you were riding on the ferry you could easily make out the shelly banks on either side where the channel had been dredged. Blue manna crabs crawled all over them, and sometimes you'd see huge stingrays basking on them, half-buried in the mud like wet chaffbags and just gently lifting and dropping their wings. One of the fishermen told me once that a stingray could cut a man's leg right off with a swish of its tail, and could kill you dead as a doornail with the big sting under its bottom, like an ivory dagger. He called them stingarees.

The old *Zephyr* was out early, steaming down river with some picnic party or other, and then over to Rottnest, I guess. As I watched her she came to the Narrows, and I began to wonder about the bridge everyone said they would build there, one day, to link Mill Point with Mount's Bay Road. If ever they *did* build it they'd be able to send the trams across it to South Perth, instead of all the way round by the Causeway at the other end of the city. The air was so clear I could see them quite plainly, clanking across among the horses-and-carts and the bicycles and the occasional motorcar. The *Zephyr* went out of sight behind the Old Mill, and I decided to get on with my kylieing.

I'd started off from Coode Street jetty by myself, to see if I could get enough mullet for my dinner. Ernie would have been with me excepting that he had to go to the dentist. He had a lot of dreadful decays, and he'd been grizzling with toothache on-and-off for weeks. His teacher sent a note home to his mother and said he had to get them out, and they'd waited for the holidays. Ernie reckoned he'd be glad when he turned twenty and got false teeth,

70

like everyone else.

The young mullet schooled in hundreds in the shallow warm water close to the shore, and it was pretty easy to kill them with a kylie. My mother always promised me she'd cook what I caught for my dinner, but when she saw what I brought home, all mangled and messy with their guts where they'd been hit by the kylie, she always said: 'Get that mess out of my kitchen! Give them to the cat!'

Once I tried to cook them for myself in an old frying-pan I'd cadged from her. I made a little fireplace with two house-bricks behind the stable, but it wasn't as easy as she made it look. They stuck to the bottom of the pan and all I got out of it in the end was a sort of fish mince that tasted more of burn than it did of fish.

I'd worked my way along the foreshore for a couple of hundred yards, throwing my kylies well ahead of me to where I thought the fish would be. I'd half-filled my bag — my mother had made it for me out of a two-pound flour bag — when I came up to some of the fishermen pulling their nets in the shallow bay down below Billy Bew's garden.

Several fishermen lived around-about our place, and I knew all of them. They came into our shop for their cigarettes and tobacco and things, and I went to school with their children. They made a good living from the mullet they caught in the river, and sometimes they went right up the coast to a place called Moore River, where they could fish in the sea as well as the fresh water.

As I got close to them one of them yelled at me, pretending to be wild: 'Gawd Almighty, it's bad enough we've got to fight off the flaming pelicans and shags to get a few fish without you killing thousands of them with your kylies!'

He was the one who'd told me about the stingarees and for a long time it frightened the stuffing out of me every time I went crabbing. He was a big fat man who never wore boots even when he came into the shop, and he always had his trousers rolled half-way up his legs. He used to throw his head back and look at you with his eyes closed, half-smiling at the same time, so that I could never really tell if he was pretending or not.

'I don't take many, Huby', I said. I held up my bag.

The three men all laughed, and one of them said: 'Crikey Moses, Tommy! You won't get very fat on that lot. Not even your *cat!*'

Huby, the one I knew best, said: 'You lend us a hand taking the fish out of the net and I'll give you enough for your tea. How about that?'

I put my bag and my kylies in the bow of their boat and went to work. The net was out in a wide circle of corks around the boat. While two of the men pulled it in, I helped the third twist the mullets' gills out of the net and threw the fish into the bottom of the boat — before I even started there was already a beautiful silver heap of them flipping kicking there. As the net was freed of fish it was coiled neatly on the back seat of the boat. Every now-and-then we'd pull in a cobbler, with one white ivory sting sticking up behind its head and two hidden, one behind each side flipper. When that happened the man working with me picked up a heavy wooden waddy and stunned it before he very carefully took it out of the net. Then he dropped it into a wooden box and covered it with a wet bag. Cobbler was very nice but it was dangerous to handle: and you had to skin it with a pair of pliers before you could cook it.

We got a few crabs which we put into a bucket by themselves. The men swore about them because they tangled up the net, and if you weren't careful getting them out they tore the mesh. Something struck me while I was taking out a browny-green female crab, which I'd have to throw back anyway — you never kept them because they laid the eggs for next summer's crabs. I realised that you just didn't *get* crabs in the shallow water during the daytime. In the evening, after tea, was the time for crabbing. Then my brother — and sometimes my sisters, but just to pull the bag — went down to the river and caught dozens before it got too dark to see them against the white bottom: although on nights when there was no moon every crab moved in a little cloud of greeny-white fire that made them easy to catch.

If you wanted to catch crabs during the daytime you had to do it with drop-nets off the end of the jetty, or from a boat anchored out in the deep or tied up to one of the channel-posts. I got to thinking about this and I said to the man I was working with: 'Where are the crabs coming from? I didn't know you could catch them as shallow as this in the daytime?'

'You don't know much, do you?' he said. 'In the daytime they burrow themselves into the sand on the bottom. Just their eyes sticking out. When you get used to it you can see them easy as wink.'

'Where?' I pointed out to the bobbing line of corks holding up the net. 'There?'

'There. And maybe a bit further out. You know on the bottom, how there's patches of weed and patches of clean sand? Well, there. Where the sand meets the weed, mostly. That's where they seem to like to get.'

'I reckon I might have a go, after', I said.

When I walked into the kitchen my mother was standing at the table with a lot of pins in her mouth, cutting around some paper patterns she had pinned to a piece of blue stuff. She was always making things for the girls, and often when I was doing my homework at one end of the table, Peg or Lal would be standing up on it at the other end for her to trim a hem, or something.

When she saw me she looked up in surprise — as she reminded me often enough she never expected me home before it was time to get the wood in or to feed the cow. She said that in the long run nothing but an empty belly would ever get me home one split second before I was supposed to be there.

She took the pins out of her mouth. 'What brings you home, Tommy-dodd? It's a long time to dinner.'

I didn't say anything. I walked over to the sink cupboard and took out her mixing bowl. Then I opened my fish into it. I stood looking at them, feeling very proud. They were so beautiful, their shining little black eyes and the dark blue-black scales on their heads, the wet silver of their bodies, their filmy fins and tails that had sort of rainbows in them. And they'd taste so good, too. And I'd *worked* for them, for tea for the whole family.

'Mullet!' I said.

'So I see', my mother said. 'Where did you get them?'

'Kylied them.' I looked sideways at her, making a joke.

'Your story.' My mother picked one up and examined it. 'Where's the marks?'

'No — Huby gave them to me.' I grinned at her. 'Two for you and two for Dad and one each for Mickey and Peg and Lal and me. *Eight!* I helped him and Henry and another man pull in their net. Can I have a piece?'

'Well . . . seeing you've got us our tea, I can't very well say no, can I?'

My mother rinsed her hands at the sink and dried them on her apron. Then she got the bread out of the bread-bin.

I put my crabbing-net and my crabbing-bag into my tin canoe and put the lot on my head. As I walked down to the jetty I steadied the canoe with one hand and used the other to eat my piece with.

I wanted to finish it before I got down to the jetty. I could see there was a mob of the other boys there, fishing, and I didn't want to have to share it — my mother had *smothered* it with lemon-and-melon jam from a tin she got specially out of the shop.

There wasn't much to do during the Christmas holidays, unless you went away somewhere, like on a YAL tour, or to somebody's farm. You could go down to the Zoo, or to Como for a swim, or to the Museum in town if it rained, or out the bush on the other side of Fremantle Road after birds' nests. There was always a mob fishing from the jetty, although nobody ever caught much — just trumpeters and gobblies and blowies, and sometimes the pretty little yellow-tail with their golden scales and blue spots. The gobblies were no use for anything — not even the cat would eat them, but you kept on catching them to see how many you could get. You rubbed the blowies on the wooden planks of the jetty until they swelled up and then you stamped on them: if you did it right they went off with a bang like a penny cracker, but the man who drove the ferry went mad about the guts all over the boards for the people to walk on.

Sometimes you fried the trumpeters over a little fire in the rushes, but a new kid who'd lived in Perth reckoned they ate the muck from the sewerage works at Burswood Island, up by the Causeway. He called them shit-fish, and reckoned nobody should ever eat them.

I'd decided not to let anyone in on my secret until I'd tried it out. I waded out, towing my canoe behind me on a piece of string, until the water was up past my middle and the patches of weed were all about me like the maps of countries drawn on the hard yellow sand of the bottom. I'd soon know whether the fisherman had been pulling my leg. I half-expected he had been.

It took a bit of time before I could really make out the shape of a crab where it had half-buried itself in the sand, with its eyes poking up like the heads of matches. I had a few hit-and-miss shots at them before I worked out how to go about it. When I'd found a crab I'd just tap the sand in front of it with the edge of my net. It would jujp up in a little cloud of sand and before it could take off I'd have it in my net and dumped into the canoe.

I think it was the best canoe I'd ever had. I'd made it myself out of a sheet of flat galvanised iron my father got for me from a builder who came into our shop. It was sharp at one end but square at the other, to give it better balance. I'd blocked the holes with bitumen I'd scraped off the roadside down at Mends Street, where they were doing some repairs to the tarred road. I always used it when I went crabbing by myself. It was hard to handle a net and a bag at the same time, but with the canoe you just banged the net on the side and the crab fell out — and the iron was too slippery for it to climb up and get over the side into the water again.

There were lots of crabs buried in the sand. I lost some but I got a heap more, and before long I must have had nearly three dozen scratching around in the bottom of the canoe. I reckoned it was time to go and spring my surprise on the mob at the jetty.

I dragged my canoe through the shallows to the edge of the deep water around the jetty, pushed it off and swam behind it to tie it up to the piles: you had to be careful because they were covered with barnacles, sharp as razors.

When I climbed up the slippery steps onto the jetty there was quite a crowd gathered there, at the edge, looking down at my canoe-ful of crabs. One of the grown-ups just off the ferry was a real toff with a stiff black moustache halfway across his face, like a fence between his bushy black eyebrows and the little black tuft of beard on his chin. I think he was a Dago of some sort. He had a black bowler hat and a high white collar, stiff as a board, and a black tie with little red swords on it. He pointed at my canoe with the end of his walking-stick, and smiled at me. He had beautiful white teeth.

'How many have you got, young feller? Eh?' His voice was just like he looked, real nobby.

'Thirty-three, I think, mister.'

'D'you want to sell them?'

I was a bit surprised. Nobody around our way ever *sold* crabs — there were so many in the river that you just went and caught them. Excepting that we often gave a few dozen to the Chinamen just to get rid of them, and for letting us take the short cut through their garden to get to the river. I didn't have any idea of how much a crab would be worth, but if I got a penny each for them, I'd get — I added them up by mental arithmetic, twice twelve is twenty-four and maybe nine or ten more — *two-and-ten!* With the fish I'd got from Huby it would make a very nice morning's work, jut pottering around. On the other hand, I thought, the bloke looked like a toff. He might even pay more — you couldn't imagine him sloshing around in the mud in his bowler hat catching his own crabs.

'I suppose', I said, when I'd thought it out. 'How much would you pay, mister?'

'What would you say to — ah — threepence each?'

'Crikey!' *Three times two-and-ten!* I could hardly speak for the way my heart was thumping. 'That'd be bonzer, mister.'

'You'd have to deliver them for me, of course.'

'That'd be all right', I said. I knew just about every street for miles around our way, and if it was very far I could borrow a bike and wheel the crabs there in a bag. 'Where to?'

'D'you know the Weld Club?' The man raised his walking stick and pointed out across the water to Perth. 'In town? In Barrack Street?'

I nodded. I knew the Weld Club, all right. You passed it as you walked up from the ferry, when you went to town. It was a posh place with a tower on it, and a lovely garden and a tennis court at the side. Sometimes when the blinds were up you could see old men sitting around inside reading the paper and smoking in big leather chairs. My father said he'd like to get in there sometime with a whip, and stir up the useless old bulls that ate up all the good grass.

'Get them there this-afternoon?' the toff said. He reached inside his coat and took out a little flat leather case. 'I'll be back at the club at about half-past-three.' He took a little white card out of his case and wrote something on it with a gold fountain pen. 'There. Give that to the man who opens the door, and he'll pay you.' He put his hand in his trousers pocket and rattled the money there. 'Thirty-three, you said; that'll be eight-and-threepence for the crabs — and twopence for the ferry-ride over and back.'

'Thanks, mister.' I noticed he didn't say *thrippence* and *tuppence*, the way we did.

'And I'll add a shilling for delivering — nine-and-fivepence all told.' He smiled at me. 'I always say the labourer is worthy of his hire.'

I didn't know what he was talking about. I felt as if I was dreaming it all, and in a minute I'd wake up with Barney licking my face. *I'll have to duck up to the Chinamen's and borrow a couple of sugar-bags,* I thought. *That'll get the crabs over in the ferry and up in the tram to the Weld Club.*

'Thanks, mister,' I said, 'that's bonzer. I'll have them there before you get back.'

As the toff walked away down the jetty I turned the card over. On the back it had: *Charlie. Pls give the boy 9/5 for the crabs and put in coolroom. Back abt 3.30.* I couldn't read the man's name —

it was like the squiggles you see on the dunny walls at school, and the printed name on the front was just some shop or something in town.

Everyone was crowding around me and saying things like *Gee!* and *Crikey!* and *Gawd! Nearly ten bob!* I offered one of them thrippence, when I got paid, to watch my crabs while I went up to the Chinamen's for the bags.

My plan got busted before I got started on loading the crabs into them. The next ferry came in and I asked the driver if I could take the crabs across in the bags, but he wouldn't let me. He was the snotty one who was always growling about us diving off the jetty into the ferry's wash.

'Not on your bloody life!' he said. 'Old Ohlson'd have my guts for garters if I did! And get those dead blowies off the jetty. The mess you damn kids make!'

I had another look at the writing on the card, and I reckon the figures '9/5' stood out as if they'd been written in gold. I thought about it for a moment, and decided what I'd do. I pulled my canoe around to the steps and promised another kid thrippence, when I got paid, to steady it for me while I put the crabs in – one bag at each end to balance it. Then I got in myself, very carefully, and settled myself in the middle, between them. Then I paddled away from the jetty.

'Gawd!' someone yelled out after me. 'You gone barmy, or something? Paddling to *Perth!*'

I don't think it was all that much to shout about. We used to run canoe-races out to the second and third channel posts, and it was nothing. I reckoned to paddle to Perth would be just like doing maybe five or six races out to the third post. I looked around me. The water was as smooth and shiny as our dining-room lino, and when I looked over the side of my canoe it was so clear I could see the bottom as plainly as if I was looking at it through a pane of glass.

It would have been different if it had been like the floods last winter when the waves had been as high as the sea, and the current in the middle of the river was like the rapids in Canada, and the water was dark-brown with mud: some of the best paddocks in the State going down the river, my father said, just because some silly cows had chopped down all the trees. Already people had begun to talk about it as if it had been 1066 or something like that, out of history. Even one of my teachers said: 'Remember the 1926 floods. You'll never see anything like them again!' and made us write a composition about them. On the second day of the storm the jetty broke up and some of us tied four of the planks together and poled them out as far as we were game to, until the current began to turn our raft around in circles. The snotty ferry-driver told my father he'd seen me out in the middle of the river, and I reckon I didn't sit down for weeks afterward: and I hadn't even been anywhere near the middle of the river.

There was no current now, though, and not even a wave. I reckoned all I had to do was to keep on paddling and not worry about how far it was, and sometime I must get to the other side. And if my canoe did sink, all right: I'd lose it and the nine-and-five-pence, but all I had to do was to swim to the nearest channel-post and hang onto it until one of the ferries picked me up — and I guess I'd get another hiding. But I wasn't afraid. We'd all played around the river since we could walk, almost, and nobody but our parents worried about it.

It took me a bit more than an hour to get to Perth. I could judge how long by the ferry — it took fifteen minutes to cross and it made nearly five trips while I made my one. I was tired, though. By the time I was getting near the Barrack Street jetties my shoulders were aching a bit and my right leg had pins-and-needles, so that when I pulled in alongside the slips of the nearest rowing shed I could hardly get out of my canoe.

I soon stamped the blood back into my leg, and then I took the bags of crabs out and laid them on the wet boards. While I was pulling my canoe up beside them two men, a fat one and a thin one, walked out of the clubhouse with a two-man scull on their heads, like a crocodile with four long legs. I waited for them to see me.

'Do you mind if I leave my canoe here, mister?' I said. 'I've got to go up to the Weld Club.'

The fat one, who was in the lead, looked a bit surprised.

'Oh? You're a member there, are you?'

'I've got to take these crabs to a bloke up there.' I touched one of the bags with my foot. 'He bought them off me.'

'Where did you come from?' the thin man said, as they stooped and laid the scull on the slips.

I pointed across the river to the Coode Street Jetty. It looked about the size of a match-box, and South Perth looked just as hot and sleepy as Perth did from there.

'From *Coodie?*' The fat man pointed at my canoe. 'In *that?*'

'Jesus Christ!' the thin man said, without even bowing his head.

It would have got him a clip on the ear from any of the nuns up at the convent, where I went to school: even from old Sister Mary of the Sacred Heart, who was over ninety they reckoned.

'The Weld Club?' the fat man said. He pointed at my bags of crabs. 'They're pretty heavy. How're you going to get them up there?'

'On the . . .' I said, and stopped dead. I'd forgotten. I wouldn't have any money until I got to the Club. I couldn't go on the tram at all. 'Oh', I said, as though I'd worked it all out. I didn't want them to know I didn't have a penny. 'I reckon I can carry them.'

'Go on!' The fat man winked at his friend. 'We can't have the manager of the Coodie Crab Co. hoofing it around town, can we!' He turned to me. 'Come on into the club with me, and I'll advance you a penny for the tram.'

'Gee!' I said. 'Thanks, mister!'

'Just 'til you make your first million!' he said.

I was back at the rowing club within half-an-hour, with my money, but the two men were way out in the river by that time. I took a penny and laid it on the boards where I reckoned they'd drag their scull out of the water.

I'd had no trouble delivering the crabs. When I dragged the two bags up to the front door of the Weld Club I'd half-expected to be hunted: it was so shining clean and so sweet-smelling with floor polish and Brasso and Flytox, and the coloured tiles of the floor were so clean and glossy, and the glass swinging doors like diamonds.

The man who answered the doorbell just took my card and read what was on it. He told me to wait on the steps and not to dirty the tiles, and called another man in a striped apron to take the crabs. Then he pulled a handful of coins out of his trousers pocket and counted out the nine-and-fivepence into my hand.

'There you are.' He spoke as if he couldn't stand me. 'There *are* thirty-three crabs, I suppose?'

'There's thirty-*five*.' I felt like telling him to count them. 'There's two more than I thought. Tell the bloke he can have them for a present.'

As I put the money into my pocket I thought of the bulls. I'd probably never have another chance like this to find out.

'Where do you keep the old bulls? The ones that eat all the good grass?'

He looked at me as if I was a bad fish under his nose. 'Off you go, and don't be cheeky', he said, and closed the door.

The trip back to Coode Street was harder than paddling over. I reckon I was already a bit tired, and the Fremantle Doctor had come in. It did, every afternoon, blowing up the river to cool the city down. It wasn't as hot paddling as it had been before, but on the other hand the water was choppy enough to make paddling harder. I tried to stop every so often to bail out with the jam tin I always carried with me.

Sometimes, as I got closer to South Perth side, it seemed as if Coodie jetty was moving away from me all the time — but suddenly I was at the third channel-post again, and then the second, and then the first, and then I was walking up River Street towards home.

I had my head in the sharp end of my canoe, and the rest of it hung down my back like an Indian head-dress of tin feathers — the way we always carried our canoes when they were empty. The money in my pants pocket weighted them down on that side, and rubbed against my leg as if to remind me it was there: as if I'd needed any reminding.

The boys I'd promised thrippences to had been waiting for me at the end of the jetty, and I'd paid them. So that with that and the tuppence I'd spent on tramfares I was taking home eight-shillings-and-ninepence — and I'd even be home in plenty of time to get the wood in and go the messages and feed Biddy and Ginger.

As I walked through our back gate poor old Barney pounced on me. He'd probably been waiting there for me all afternoon. I tipped my canoe onto the ground and gave him a cuddle, and he danced ahead of me right across our backyard and into the kitchen.

My mother was standing by the table beating up a bowl of batter with a fork for the mullet I'd brought home that morning — they were stacked on a plate on the dresser, like blue pancakes. I could hear one of my sisters practising her scales in the living-room. I walked to the table and plonked my money down on the oilcloth.

'He*llo!*' my mother said. She put down her bowl. 'Where did you land that lot?'

'Crabs', I said. 'The Coodie Crab Co!'

'Glory be!' my mother said. 'Who did you sell them to?'

'A bloke', I said. 'A real toff. He offered me thrippence for each of them if I took them in to that place, the Weld Club. You know? In town?' I suppose I was too full of myself to see how dangerous it was getting. 'I took them over in my canoe.'

'You *what?*' My mother sat down suddenly and leaned her head in her hands, hiding her eyes. I stared at her. I wondered what had happened to her. After a moment or two she took her hands away and stared back at me.

'You paddled right over to *Perth*, in your *canoe*, with *two bags of crabs* in it?'

'Yes, Mum.' All of a sudden I knew what I'd said, and what I'd be in for. 'It wasn't . . .'

'Jesus *God!*' my mother said. She almost never swore, and even though I was so worried I noticed that she didn't bow her head, either. She dropped it into her hands again, and I stood staring at her.

It seemed terribly quiet in the kitchen, even with my sister still banging away at the piano on the other side of the door. Barney was sitting on the lino with a puzzled look, and I dropped my hand onto his head. Just for comfort. After what seemed like a week my mother took her hands away from her face. I'd never seen her look so upset, even the time Mickey and I stayed at Roberts's dairy to watch the calves having their throats cut, and got all covered in blood.

'Now . . . listen to me, young man,' she said, 'and listen carefully. I'm not going to tell your father about this, because if I did he'd kill you. But if you *ever go out in the deep water in your canoe again*, I'll kill you myself. And I mean it. Do you understand?'

I nodded — when she was like that you didn't dare say a word. But she'd given me something else to worry about, mentioning my father. The snotty ferry-driver was sure to tell him he'd seen me: all I could hope was that he wasn't on at the time.

'You can go *right now* and put your canoe up on the stable roof,' my mother said, 'and you can leave it there *for the rest of the holidays*. And let me warn you. It depends *entirely on how you behave for the next couple of weeks* whether or not you *ever take it down again!*' She stood up and lifted her mixing bowl off the table. 'And now get. There's Biddy and Ginger to feed, for a start. And the wood to bring in. And if I can't find half-a-dozen messages for you before dark you can paddle across to Perth in your canoe *tomorrow!* Pick up your money and *get!* Before I take to you with this bowl, *right now!*'

I got, I can tell you. And Barney got too, right behind me. He always knew what was what.

Just to be outside again, away from that look on my mother's face, made me feel better. It would be terrible to be without my canoe in the summer, but then — you could always borrow one down the jetty. And my mother would forget, as she always did. And if I never found another bottle, I had my picture money for months. *And* enough for chips at interval.

It was bad luck not being able to keep on with the Coodie Crab Co, but maybe I'd be able to sell them on the jetty, without having to paddle across the river.

I didn't feel too bad about it all as I pushed my canoe up onto the stable roof and went on over to the woodheap.

The New Kid
And The Racehorse Goanna

The clearing the racehorse goanna lived in was in the middle of the long stretch of bush between Fremantle Road and the Canning River.

We came on it one time when we were out there nesting, and we got into the habit of going back, just to see him. Maybe there had been some sort of homestead there, burned out in a blaze-up of the scrub long before we got to know about it.

A bit of a cart-track, very faint, still straggled in to it on one side and out at the other, and the open ground was littered with bent and rusted sheets of galvanised iron. I bet it hadn't been disturbed for years before we wandered into it that day.

There were mobs and mobs of green-and-scarlet kangaroo paws under the banksias — so many they seemed to float on their long green stems; and the cowslips and the little orange-and-red cats-paws and white everlastings and blue hovea were so thick on the ground it was hard not to walk on them.

It was the middle of the day, that first time we got there, in the mid-summer Christmas holidays. It was so hot, and so quiet. The hush and the gold of the Christmas trees seemed to cover the whole world, and in some way the moment I saw the racehorse goanna, standing at the entrance to his burrow, the hot day and the silence and the loneliness of the bush all seemed to be a part of him. I stared at him and he stared back at me, blinking the way they do with that blue film going over and over their eyes. I thought of the dark, damp tunnels of his hole, where he could go but I couldn't, and the hair on the back of my neck tingled and shivered the way it did sometimes when I listened to my mother and father talking about the Yilgarn, where they used to live before I was born.

I would sit behind the sofa in our living-room when they had visitors on Sunday afternoons, old friends from the Goldfields, all blue serge and lace fronts and gold all over them, big lumps of it on the men's tiepins and pretty funny-shaped nuggets fastened to the ladies shoulders on gold chains so fine you could hardly see them. My mother had a gold nugget almost the perfect shape of Australia: it was given to her by a man in a place called the Nullagine, but she sold it once when, as she said, we were on the way to Queer Street. They'd say: *The Yilgarn, Arthur! When we were in the Yilgarn, Min!* and it made my hair stand on end the way it did when I looked at the racehorse goanna.

He and the place they called the Yilgarn seemed to belong to some world I could never know about, hard and scaly and secret, older than Australia and deeper than the mines at Kalgoorlie, and hotter than any summer I'd ever known.

I don't know how long we kept on going to see the goanna — maybe all that summer, maybe only for the six-weeks Christmas holidays that raced past us and away like a fire in the grass. We must have gone pretty often, because we were always out the bush, and as we padded along single-file in the tracks of some wood-cutter's cart among the banksias and the whispy sheoaks, someone would always remember him. Someone would always say: *Let's go and see the racehorse goanna!* and we'd wheel like ducks in flight and make for his clearing.

Sometimes he'd take off the moment we appeared, in the funny way of running they have — standing up almost straight with his tail curved over his back like a boomerang. As you watched he'd melt like magic into a patch of pig's-face near his burrow — we called it that because the little dried-up seed-pods looked just like a pig's face, or so we reckoned: you had to find a name for everything so you could tell other people about it. We used to squeeze the seed-pods for the stuff in them — it was sort-of-sweet, and we used to call it raspberry-jam. My father said the blacks told the first settlers about it, and they passed it on to us.

The racehorse goanna would stop at the edge of this patch for a moment, still and stiff, and stare back at us. Then he would just disappear. Melt into the green and grey without seeming to have moved at all — there one moment and gone the next. We'd race to where he'd been and search for any hole he might have ducked into, like the magician in a pantomime. We never found one, and I think it was this way he could just suddenly become nothing that made us go back again and again, just to see him do it.

When he didn't run away into the pig's-face he'd just stand there, stiff-legged with his tongue flickering in and out, watching us from the entrance to his burrow under a heap of burned logs. The black sand was so hot that it burned through even our feet, which my mother used to say were as hard as a goat's knees; and the sun was so hot it seemed to burn in your head like bees buzzing in a hive.

Don't stand up straight! we'd whisper to each other, as we stood watching him. *He'll think you're a tree, and run up you!* So we lolled around like melted candles. Everyone at school, and everyone I played with, knew that much about racehorse goannas — that they mistake people for trees, particularly if there's a dog around, and run up them and perch on their heads, and claw their scalps and rip their ears and tear out their eyes. *Just like golf-balls!* someone reckoned. So as we backed away from him very carefully: *Watch him!* we'd warn each other. Softly, from the corners of our mouths, as if he could hear us, and could understand what we were saying about him.

The new kid was just as strange as the goanna, in his way. Maybe even stranger, because at least the goanna *belonged* in South Perth.

The new kid had arrived among us from the other side of the river, where they had sewered toilets and everything. He had shoes, black *and* brown, and suits and coloured shirts and ties and dinky little felt hats, just like the ones our fathers wore: we had brown cloth fisher-hats for summer and oil-cloth ones for winter. And his family had shifted — for no reason that we could find out, although my mother said afterwards that it was because the kid was getting into trouble with a gang where he lived in Perth. They were going into the big shops and stealing, so the kid's family decided to come to South Perth where there were no big shops.

South Perth stretched from the Causeway at one end to the Old Mill at the other, and we divided it into two parts — 'our end' and 'the other end'. Our end was all dairies and the Chinamen's gardens, and patches of bush and paddocks. There were vacant blocks with old houses on them and fig and apricot and loquat trees you could just rob when you wanted to. Everyone kept chooks and ducks in their backyards, and there were cows and horses poking their heads over the fences to be petted as you walked down to the ferry or the shops. Our mothers and fathers went to euchre parties, and we went to school bare-footed, and we left school when we turned fourteen unless we happened to get a bursary or a scholarship.

The other end was the lovely old Windsor Hotel and big old homes in rambling gardens full of pampas grasses and elephants-ears and climbing roses and pink oleanders. A lot of the families had squatter and pioneer names, and my father used to say, when some of them were mentioned: *Bloody old gin-jockey!* or *Bloody old black-birder!* but when I asked what he meant my mother would just tell me to go outside and play, or to 'stop waggling my ears'. A lot of them had motor-cars, and their fathers and mothers went to bridge parties and the Repertory, which was a theatre in town. The kids wore shoes to school, and if they happened to be boys they had some chance of going to the university, whether they had any brains or not. Some of the girls went to the university too, although my mother reckoned it was only to get in early on husbands who might be lawyers and doctors, and live down the other end.

The new kid's family seemed to have some money, so we could never understand why they came to live in our end, where nobody ever had any at all. As a matter of fact they took a house in our street, which meant that I made friends with the new kid before anyone else, and sort-of edged him into all our swimming and fishing and crabbing and making canoes, and going birds-nesting, and robbing the Chinamen, and prowling around the Zoo.

He was only a year older than me, but he seemed to be much more. My mother said it came from being brought-up in Perth. *He's been here before, that one!* she said to my father, after the first time he came to our place to play. She didn't mean he'd been to visit *us* before. It was one of her sayings, such as: *Stop that old-fashioned chat!* and *You're born but not buried, my boy*, which she brought out all the time to set me back on my bottom. If she said: *He's been here before!* to a new mother, it meant that the new baby was very intelligent and maybe forward for its age, like smiling when it was spoken to. But when she said it about the new kid I was pretty sure she didn't mean it as a compliment.

He was saucy and cocky, that was his trouble. He had shrewd blue eyes and curly fair hair like turkey-lolly. He was hard and brown and wiry, and although he wasn't very much older than any of the others who came to our place, his *body* seemed older. Or that's what my mother seemed to think. He certainly knew a lot more than we did about a lot of things. I remember one Saturday morning not long after he came to South Perth we were all sitting at the edge of the dam down the bottom of the polo-ground, sharing out some half-ripe watermelons we'd lifted from the closest Chinaman's patch, when he started to talk about girls and what you could do to them, and he certainly opened our eyes.

We still called them 'the tarts', but he called them 'brush' and 'swell kakas'. The only time I ever used one of those words in my mother's hearing I had to walk half the length of our backyard to pick up my head. *And don't you let me hear you bringing that new kid's dirty talk into* this *house, young man!* she sent after me. She knew where I'd picked it up, all right.

Maybe she didn't like the new kid because she was so leery of his mother. She was a good-looking but discontented sort of lady who 'made-up' her face too much, everyone said — far more, anyway, than the dab of rouge and face-powder my mother and her friends reckoned was enough for what they called 'any decent woman'. Also she had a silver-fox fur and fussy hats with violets on them, and she had far more clothes than anyone I'd ever known.

To be fair to my mother, however much she didn't like the new kid she didn't say he wasn't to come into our yard — or our kitchen, for that matter. She iodined and bandaged his cuts and scratches and vaselined his burns whenever he was down at our place, just as his own mother would have. He came to play with me far more often than ever I went to his place, and whenever she gave me a 'piece', with jam or dripping, which was several times a day between meals, she gave him one too. The way he wolfed them made me think that maybe he didn't get enough to eat at home, and I'm sure my mother liked to watch him gobble them. She loved to feed people and animals, and another of the things she always said was: *Better tucker bills than doctor's bills!* She made it work for all my friends as well, just as it worked for me in all their homes — except the new kid's. No-one was ever invited inside there, and nothing was ever even passed out through the kitchen door.

In no time at all he was lining up for the handout as regularly as our chooks, but there was only one time I ever heard my mother say anything about it. She was standing at our front window looking through the curtain at his mother on her way down to the ferry to go to town, in the silver-fox fur and one of the fussy hats. *Lah-di-dah!* she said, letting the curtain fall. *She puts on her back what I put in that kid's belly!* Maybe she was thinking of what we called 'Mum's bit of duck's-waddle' around the collar of her five-year-old winter coat.

On the first Saturday morning the new kid came down to our place to play we circled around each other for a while, getting each other's measure. I showed him the chooks, one of them with chickens that I could watch for hours, but he hardly looked at them. We threw stones down the well at the frogs until my mother threatened us from the back-door. I showed him my egg collection, but I had the feeling he wasn't really very interested. He kept on about the things he'd had before, and how wonderful it was to live in North Perth — as though it was all way up in the Kimberleys, or some place like that, instead of just across the river in plain old Perth. He'd say: *Oh, up in North Perth we had.* or *we did.* Or *there was,* until I found myself thinking, like my mother: 'He's been here before, the bloody skite!'

Well, I would have bet my shanghai against a green fig there was one thing they hadn't had in North Perth.

'Like to go down and see Manning's bull?' I offered.

'Oh, I dunno', the new kid said. I reckoned he wasn't going to be trapped into being too keen on anything in South Perth.

'Where is it?'

'Down by the river.'

'Oh . . . all right, then.' He looked at our back door for a moment, listening to see if my mother was around. 'A bull?' he whispered. 'Can you see him do it to the cows?'

I felt a bit silly, because I don't think I would have told even my best mate Ernie that I liked watching the bull with the cows. None of us ever let on we went down to Manning's just to see him at it. You went because the paddock finished up right at the water's edge where you took off for crabbing, or to swim across the deep channel to Hierrison Island after birds' eggs. Also there was a stretch of coarse brown shingle at the bottom end where you might find a dotterel's nest, if you were lucky. You lay out on the shingle and the seaweed with one eye on the bull and one on a dotterel. Where a bird dropped suddenly out of sight you might find a little hollow with two of their round, grey-brown-and-green eggs in it. The first time I showed one of them to my father he told me their proper name — we'd always called them sand-snipes — and he said they flew all the way from Siberia every year just to lay their eggs at the bottom of Manning's paddock in South Perth. He pulled my leg so much I didn't know whether to believe him or not, but it was still a wonderful thing to think about, and sometimes before I went to sleep I used to imagine those tiny little birds flying all that way across the ocean, and wondering how they knew which way to go.

There was certainly plenty to do down in Manning's paddock, and I suppose we really didn't go there just to watch the bull. At the same time I bet there was one thing every one of us was hoping every time we raced across the bottom of the polo ground to get there — and that was that we'd arrive just in time to see the big red bull climb up onto the back of one of the cows, and do it.

I'd never have admitted that to anyone, but the new kid was what my mother called a new kettle of fish.

One day after he'd been around for a while he came out the bush after birds eggs with us. We went to see the racehorse goanna, as we always did, but on the way we had a bit of an adventure: and I reckon if the new kid hadn't got so puffed up by his part in it, things mightn't have happened the way they did.

A big stretch on the bush side of Fremantle Road, a mile or so in, had been cleared only a little while before to plant what was called the Collier Pine Plantation, after the Premier of the State who said it had to be done. 'Just as well he stayed sober long enough to do *something* good', my father said, when he read it in the paper.

Of course the whole shebang was out of bounds to everybody, and of course when we came to the five-wire fence around it we climbed through. We wanted to see if any water-birds had begun to build in a little swamp that had gathered from the water the trees had used up before. When we were halfway back to the fence I spotted the manager riding his horse toward us — he was a man called Mr Traynor, and he came into our shop. He would have known right away what we'd been up to because we were all still sopping wet from wading around in the swamp up to our middles, but luckily he wasn't looking in our direction. We dropped like quail behind a clump of the axed trees.

'Oh, gawd!' somebody complained. 'It's old Traynor! He'll tell my Dad, and I'll get a hell of a hiding for going in the swamp!' I reckon what he said was going through all our minds.

'Don't be such a bloody sis!' the new kid said. He was still standing up, looking at the manager. 'He don't know me. I'll go and talk to him. You all stay here, and when he goes, you duck out. I'll wait for you on the other side of the wires.' He walked straight on toward the fence, so that he couldn't help meeting up with Mr Traynor and his horse. It wasn't very far from where we lay hidden among the dried branches, so we could hear everything they said. Even above the thumping of our hearts.

'Well, young fellow', Mr Traynor said. He sat on his horse, looking down sternly at the new kid. 'What d'you think you're doing here? Don't you know you're not allowed inside the fence?'

'No, sir,' the new kid said, 'I didn't know.'

He looked straight up into Mr Traynor's face like the respectful, manly little boy I was always being told I should be: but suddenly I thought of how his voice went flat and thin and mean when he was telling us about the brush and the swell kakas and all the things he'd done with them.

'I only came to South Perth a couple of weeks ago,' he went on, 'we used to live in North Perth. I don't know any of the South Perth kids yet, and it's a bit lonely. I came out here for a walk.'

'Where d'you live, sonny?' Mr Traynor asked, and his voice was

90

much kinder. I was very surprised when the new kid told him. 'And what's your name?' Again the new kid told him, truthfully.

I couldn't understand it all, and I don't think any of us did. We'd all made up names and addresses we could reel off without thinking for if ever we got caught, and I'd expected the new kid to have done it too. Yet here he was . . . and only a few days before we'd been sitting on the bank of the polo ground dam talking about what to do at different times, and he'd said, in that skiting, show-off voice of his: 'Well, what I reckon is, you never give your guts away. No matter what happens.' *Give your guts away?* It was the first time I'd ever heard that expression, and it took some careful asking around to find out what it meant without letting on I didn't know.

'Well,' Mr Traynor was saying, 'you just buzz off through that fence and don't come back. I catch you in here again I'll tan your hide. And what's more, I'll see to it that your Dad does it, too. All right?'

'Yes, sir,' the new kid said, 'thank you, sir.'

When Mr Traynor had disappeared over a sandy ridge a good way off, riding carefully to avoid trampling the tiny pines, we pelted across the few yards to the fence. We crawled through it so as not to set it twanging, and joined the new kid in the shelter of a low-hanging sheoak. As we came up to him, someone said: 'Why the bejesus did you tell him your *real* name?' I reckon it was what we all intended to ask him.

'Why not?' the new kid said, very cheeky. He was full of himself, all right. 'It don't hurt to tell the truth, *some*times. When it can't hurt you.' He turned to where Mr Traynor had vanished. 'That bloody old warb on his bloody old horse.' He placed the thumb of his right hand to his nose and waggled his fingers. It was what we called the 'Kaiser's Salute', and it was the rudest thing I knew. If ever I got caught doing it I got a good clip on the ear.

When we got to the edge of the racehorse goanna's clearing he was standing by his burrow. High on his front legs, with his tail curved over his back as if already he had made up his mind to dash off and disappear into the pig's-face. As we came to a standstill at the edge of the scrub he had his head turned toward us. It was long and fine, and beautiful in a way I'd never noticed before: like one of the wedges my father used to split logs. It was as though he'd been expecting us, or maybe he'd heard us coming, or had felt our footsteps shaking the ground long before he could see us.

We stood staring back at him as we always did, very careful, every one of us but the new kid stooped and bent so as not to look like a tree. The new kid looked from us to the goanna and back again, quite a few times. On the walk from the pine plantation we'd been trying to explain to him something of the sort-of mystery of the racehorse goanna and his clearing, which in a way I suppose we regarded as our own special secret. I don't think we'd made him understand. I don't think we even understood it ourselves.

'Well . . . what's so great about the bugger?' he said, at last. 'You come all this way to look at a silly old lizard?'

As easy as that, in a split second, he killed it for me, perhaps for all of us, what we'd felt was so wonderful about the racehorse goanna. *A silly old lizard.* I knew that never again would I have the neck-tingling feeling that he'd been standing there by his burrow since long before they'd killed that black, Yagan, up at Guildford, or put in the Kalgoorlie pipe-line, or planted the first orchards of apple and pear and fig and grape on the riverside slopes of South Perth. In the few weeks I'd known him this kid from North Perth had taken everything I'd grown up thinking was wonderful and made it look silly. Girls. And the colony of bald-coots we'd found in a riverside swamp — *Silly buggers'll all get drowned next high tide!* he'd said, and I'd known that for me no more giant snakes would ever slither around in the branches of the overhanging paperbarks. And Manning's bull, doing it to the cows: *That's what your old man does to your old woman, in their bedroom, at night!*

And now the silly old lizard.

'I'll show you how to deal with Mr Bloody Goanna!' he boasted. He picked up a length of charred timber and stepped out into the full glare of the clearing.

Don't you touch him! I wanted to shout, but all I said was: 'He'll run up you if you don't look out!'

'Run *up* me?'

'He'll think you're a tree', I explained. But even as I said it I knew I no longer believed it myself. It sounded ridiculous. 'And run up you', I finished, because I had to.

'Run up my Royal Irish *arse!*' the new kid shouted.

He turned and trudged through the heavy sand toward the racehorse goanna. It stood still, watching him. Its tongue flickered in and out, and that pale blue film came and went across its eyes. Maybe, I thought, watching it, it's been told, sometime, that this would happen — that it had to happen, and that there was no escape anyhow: because, in a funny way, that's what I thought

92

myself. It didn't move even when the new kid raised his waddy and brought it down fair in the middle of its curved, green-and-yellow back.

Before the stick fell again, I was at it with the new kid. And then the others, howling like Indians and banging away with whatever bits of wood they could grab from the ground.

I think the first blow might have paralysed the racehorse goanna. It still hadn't moved, and as our sticks rained down on it it stood perfectly still. After a while, though, its stiff front legs just folded, and it lurched to the ground. Its busy tongue lolled out like a bit of crimson string. A small trickle of blood ran between its jaws, and stopped. The flies were onto it before you could have said 'knife'.

'And *that* buggered *him!*'

The new kid looked down at the goanna. There was nothing at all in his voice. No pity. He wasn't savage, or satisfied, or anything, really. He threw his charred stick onto the goanna's back.

'Come on, I want to see a few of these damn swamps you been gas-bagging about.' He turned around and stared out of the clearing. 'Which way?'

Someone pointed, silently, and he took off between the trees. He didn't seem to care whether we followed him, or not.

Chinamen
On The Footpath

When I heard Aunt Kate mention Chinamen I was sitting on the floor of the dining-room at our place reading *Tarzan and the Jewels of Opar*, my favourite book that year. Maybe for the tenth time. I really didn't know how many times I'd gone through it — as soon as I finished it I'd turn straight back to the front and into the jungle again, and Tantor the Elephant and Horta the Boar and all the other animals Tarzan went around with. When I heard my mother singing out for me to do some job or go some message I pretended it was only some wonderful red-and-blue-and-yellow tropical bird screeching in the ruins of Opar, the way the writer said they did.

Aunt Kate's voice was a different matter.

'Seems to me every time I come over here to South Perth I see Chinamen on the footpaths . . .' she said. She had a creaky sort of voice and it sounded in my ear like sand-paper being used n another room. It broke into one of my favourite bits where Tarzan has a fight to the death with the repulsive little henchmen of La, the beautiful High Priestess of Opar. She spoiled it a bit because I couldn't understand why she had to be brought into a story of Tarzan in the jungle. She didn't swing around in the trees with him, or anything, although she did seem to be pretty keen on him.

When I heard Aunt Kate say *Chinamen* I looked up from my book. The red-blue-yellow-green light from the glass in the door leading out onto our side verandah seemed to dance in the room, and make it look strange, as if I'd never seen it before. I tried not to look too hard at Aunt Kate because my mother went off about it, even though I couldn't help doing it. She said it always made me look as if I was hearing something she couldn't, and if she hadn't been so interested in what Aunt Kate was saying to her she would have told me to get that old-fashioned look off my dial, as she always did.

'Of course, Min,' Aunt Kate went on, dry as weatherboard, 'I know it's nice getting your vegies from them. And so *cheap*. And fresh, of course. Those peas at lunch were just beautiful. But . .' she pulled the corners of her lips down and seemed to look up at her eyebrows, and I knew what to expect. It was the way she looked when she was telling my mother about things that happened in East Perth, where she lived. Everyone reckoned it was a pretty rough place.

'I don't know,' she went on, 'always seeing Chinamen on the footpaths. And they walk so *close* to you!'

Where I was sitting on the carpet, half-hidden behind a chair, I

96

could watch her jawbone going up and down as she spoke, under her brown, wrinkled skin. It moved in the sort of slow way a goanna's did, when it was eating a tomato. I found myself wondering why she should grizzle about the Chinamen.

As far as I could see there wasn't anything wrong with them. I played in their gardens and caught frogs and goldfish in their ponds — and black gilgies that turned red when we cooked them in a billy of river water, down in the rushes. Sometimes I helped them around the beds pulling onions and cutting lettuces, and carrying the little flat boxes they grew their seedlings in under panes of glass. They gave me apples and bananas, a bit specked sometimes, but I didn't mind. You could eat around the speck. Sometimes they'd give me a sixpence, and once they put a long-necked, brown-and-white duck right into my hands. *For Clismas dinner.*

'Glory be!' my mother said, when I took it home, 'I didn't know they even *thought* about Christmas!'

I knew it wasn't just for Christmas. It was for me. I liked the Chinamen, and I think they liked me. Sometimes I woke up long before morning, when it was still dark, and heard the soft sound of the horses' hooves, and the jingle of their harness, as the Chinamen's big, hooded carts creaked along past our place to the markets in town. I always felt safer and warmer in bed to hear them.

'I get the vegies from them, for Mum', I said to Aunt Kate: although I don't think I really intended to say anything at all. My head was full of Tarzan and the High Priestess, and I wasn't quite certain what she'd said. I had an idea she thought the Chinamen were dangerous, or shouldn't be there, or something — and I thought I knew why. Where she lived in East Perth, on the other side of the river, it was all houses side-by-side in tiny little yards with never a vacant block to play on. Hard black tar roads and footpaths, no trees, no paddocks, no horses, no cows: and of course, no Chinamen — so she really couldn't know what they were like. I was sorry for her, and I reckoned I should say something to show her I was on her side.

'You can get a stick of sugar-cane off them for a penny', I said. 'Purple. It's real sweet, and you can suck it for hours.'

Aunt Kate didn't move her body, but she turned her head and looked at me — again, the way a goanna does. She was a tiny little woman, all shrivelled up as if she'd been left out in the sun too long — like the trumpeters and gobblies we caught down the river, and left out on the hot boards to dry. She always wore grey and black, and her little grey-and-black bun of hair seemed to be stuck onto the back of her neck with tortoise-shell pins as big as clothes-pegs: I always wanted to pull them out and see if it would fall off.

Most of the ladies I knew wore their hair the same way. My mother and a few others fluffed it out a bit at the ears, and I thought it looked prettier.

'Sugar-cane' Aunt Kate said. She grinned at me, but I don't think she was amused. She had two rows of beautiful false teeth, and suddenly she pushed the bottom ones out with her tongue. My mother did the same thing, sometimes, just to tease me when I went to kiss her, but that was different. It made Aunt Kate look more like a goanna than ever.

'You don't eat sugar-cane with *them*, my boy!' She spoke as though it was rude to talk about eating sugar-cane, and it made me blush. For a moment I hated her.

She and Uncle Kirk weren't really what my father called blood relations — which I found out the way I found out everything, by listening to what the grownups talked about. Uncle Kirk had been my father's partner in camel teams they'd had years before, on the goldfields. Hungerford and Kirkpatrick. All my life, it seemed, I'd been hearing them talk about it, sitting around the table for old-times-gossip after Sunday lunch at our place. *We come in from Yilgarn with a load of ore an' wool* . . . Uncle Kirk would say, and they'd all nod, remembering it. And my father would say . . . *met Eustace Cashman out Lake Way, that trip:* or: *That's the time we camped two nights outside the Nullagine, bogged up to the axles.*

I knew all the names — Sandstone, Nannine, Peak Hill, Daydawn — and sometimes when they'd gone home I'd take the aluminium nose-peg down from the mantelpiece and think about the camel its nose had been stuck through, and the Never-never feel and taste of it. *When we were up the Never-never, Arthur* . . . my mother would say time and time again, and just the sound of it made me feel sad. Perhaps because I hadn't been there with her, in the Yilgarn.

'Well, I just wouldn't feel comfortable,' Aunt Kate's dry voice rustled on, 'you know . . . well, how they *feel* about *white women.*'

For some reason I couldn't understand, Uncle Kirk began to bellow laughing. He rocked himself backward and forward on his chair like some enormous walkie-doll in its blue serge Sunday suit.

'Oh, *Gawd*, Kate! Oh, Gawd, oh *Gawd!*'

My real Uncle Tom was there that Sunday. He was my mother's only brother, and he was a lot younger than she was. He grinned sideways at Aunt Kate, and said: 'Godalmighty, Kate! Aint you kiddin' yourself?'

He'd been Wounded at the Landing, and we all called him Soldier Tom. He was tall and handsome and well-built and mean. My two sisters and my brother and I all loved him, but I don't think he could stand us at all. When any of us tried to climb onto his lap he'd say: 'For God's sake, Min! Get the little sods off me! There . . . look at my blasted pants!' Or my blasted coat or my blasted hair or my blasted something else. Once he said to me: 'You want to see smoke come out of my eyes? Then come here! Put your hand on my chest and look right into my eyes!' And when I did he pressed his lighted cigarette onto my bare skin, and brought up a blister.

My father smiled at Aunt Kate and said: 'Swim out, Kate, your swag's bobbing!' It was what he always said when he thought anyone was trying to take a rise out of him.

'They wouldn't be wantin' to *kill* you, Kate!' Uncle Tom said. He winked at my father. 'Not *kill* you, I don't think!'

My mother gave her particular hard little cough and looked around at all of them. I turned my head to look at her, and as I did the coloured lights from the door seemed to float across the room like clouds. I'd known for years what the cough meant, and there were even times when I'd have missed out on hearing something if she hadn't done it. I could never understand how it was she'd never caught on that I knew. She gave me her look.

'Golly Fritz! D'you *always* have to be sitting around inside, little Mister Bigears?'

'I'm reading, Mum', I said.

'Reading-reading-reading!' She rattled it off with a sort of crossness. I couldn't understand, ever, why she did it. Mickey came home late from school all the time, and he just said he'd been playing football on the way. She didn't say *Football-football-football!* as if he'd done something wicked, or even worse, somehow queer. About all she ever said was to tell him to go and wash his hands because she was dishing-up.

'It's Tarzan of the Apes, Mum.' I held my book up for her to see. I thought she'd understand if she saw the picture on the cover, with Tarzan riding on the back of his elephant, Tantor. 'He finds this old city called Opar, and there's all these jewels . . .'

'Then take Tarzan and his jewels outside and read', she said. She seemed very impatient.

'You heard your mummy, boy!' my father said. 'Skedaddle!'

I know I blushed again, to be sent outside as if I was Barney. Uncle Kirk had stopped laughing, and was picking at his ear with the nail of his little finger. He kept it long for the purpose. Soldier Tom was rolling another cigarette, carefully moving the tobacco to the centre of the paper. His fingers were long and thin and stained brown from the nicotine, and you could see the marks of his Gallipoli wound crawling over them like a white cobweb. Aunt Kate was sitting bolt upright in her chair, and I thought of the way a praying mantis stands so still on a twig and stares at something a thousand miles behind you. Something good to eat. As I walked through the doorway I heard my mother say: 'He's always got his nose stuck in a *book!*' As if I had some terrible disease she felt she should warn them about.

When I got out into the yard I looked around to see nobody was following me. Then I ran across to the Cape Lilac tree by the stable and shinned up it. It was easy with my bare feet on the rough bark, and I reckon I used to go up it as quickly as a possum.

I'd made myself a hammock out of used chaff-bags and fixed it up on a long bough that ran along the roof only a few feet from the iron. It was my secret place. I went up there to read my Tarzan books, so that my sisters wouldn't interfere with me sitting at the same table and talking across me, or even snatching my book and running away with it whenever they got the chance. I reckon I'd read about every Tarzan book there was, and up there on the roof, with the leaves and boughs all around you, it was just like being in Africa.

I stood on the roof for a while pretending there was a native village down in our yard, and that they were after me. I'd sniff the air, like Tarzan did, for the acrid stink of Numa the Lion. Then I'd lower myself carefully into my hammock and pretend it was a litter, and my faithful blacks were going to carry me hundreds of miles across the swampy plains of the Zambesi. I had to get into it carefully: the hessian was pulling away from the bark I'd fixed it to with nails from my father's tool-box.

When I was in the hammock, but not reading, I could look up at the sky through the leaves and the clusters of tiny little Cape Lilac flowers. It looked like pieces of torn blue paper pasted on the ceiling. In one end of the stable beneath me I could hear old Ginger munching his way through his manger and stamping the flies away. Sunday was his day off. At the other end Biddy would be standing chewing her cud and staring at nothing, as she always did. On the other side of the three-strand wire fence around our yard they were holding Sunday School in the Baptist Church. The outside weatherboard had been painted yellow, once, but it'd been standing there so long, summer and winter, that it was about the colour of an old bone. The windows were little panes of red and green glass, although you could really only see the colour from the inside. They were open, and I could hear the organ very plainly, but not so plainly the people reading the Bible and singing hymns.

I went to Sunday School once, when things were pretty slow in the cool weather — someone told me that if you stuck it for a year you got a gold medal. While I was going I got invited to a magic-lantern show about a missionary in China. Someone offered him a helping of stew, so he pointed to it and said: 'Quack-quack?' but the Chinaman shook his head and said: 'Bow-wow!' We went around for weeks afterward saying *Quack-quack!* and *Bow-wow!* to each other, but apart from that I didn't like Sunday School much. I soon stopped going when it got really hot, and time for swimming.

When I said I wasn't going to go any more, and stuck to it, my mother used to say, just about every Sunday when the kids started singing: 'They're *good* little boys and girls!' Just to make me think I *wasn't* good, I suppose. But I played with them, and she didn't. I knew they weren't any better than the rest of us. They used to rob orchards and tell lies and fight and go into the bushes with girls, just like the rest of us.

The noise of the hymns and the bible classes and the organ wasn't all I could hear from the church. When my homing pigeons weren't flying around they seemed to spend most of their time on the roof, and the mess they made of it was something awful. At night they roosted in the stable, but all day they perched up there, strutting up and down and bowing to each other and messing, and *rickety-cooing* a storm. Particularly on Sundays, it seemed.

I knew there'd been some talk about it between the parson and my father. The parson said he didn't want to cause any trouble, and he wouldn't dream of insisting that a boy should get rid of his pets. At the same time he was worried that the people he was preaching to *inside* the church couldn't hear what he was saying for the row on *top* of it. And of course, there was the mess. And it was well known that the birds spread some very nasty sorts of diseases.

My father said yes-yes-yes, he'd do something about it, and

thanks for bringing it to his notice, but of course he never did a thing. When the parson had gone my mother said pigeon pie every Sunday for a month would fix a lot of troubles, particularly the weekly meat bill. I was still worrying about it. You couldn't really tell when she was joking and when she wasn't, and usually all you could do was to wait to find out.

When I'd listened to the Sunday School and the pigeons for a while, and had worried over it a bit, I opened my book where I'd turned back the corner of the page. My father would have had a fit if he'd found out, but I knew he wouldn't — he refused to read my Tarzan books and said he didn't know what I could see in such stuff. Before I began to read I looked around just to make sure things were all right. I couldn't hear my sisters down in the yard. Ginger and Biddy were munching away in the stable, and Barney had stopped whining at the bottom of the tree. I'd been afraid he'd give me away, but he'd gone off somewhere for a snooze, I reckon — probably onto a heap of chaffbags in the shed. My brother had gone somewhere and, inside the house, the grownups were still remembering the Murchison. Everything was in order, so I settled down to read.

After a while I came to the part I couldn't understand, where Tarzan gets caught by the repulsive henchmen of the High Priestess. They tie him up and leave him lying on the floor of a dungeon, and when it's dark La, the High Priestess, comes to visit him and begs him to do something. It says: *She ran her hands in mute caress over his naked flesh. She covered his forehead, his eyes, his lips with hot kisses* and it goes on like that, very soppy, for quite a while. It seems she was pretty gone on him, but then — and this was what I couldn't understand — she turns round and hands him over to the dwarfish henchmen to be sacrificed on the altar with their sacred knife. I could never make out what it was she wanted him to do and he wouldn't.

She was a bit of a mystery all round. I'd never been able to picture her to myself at all. I knew exactly what Tarzan looked like, and I drew him all the time — riding on his elephant and swinging through the trees and spearing poor old Horta the Boar. The first time I ever read *Tarzan and the Jewels of Opar*, I knew the dwarfish henchmen would look just like Tramway Suzie, the South Perth Zoo's girl chimpanzee who had just been adopted by the tramway men as their mascot. And I had no trouble with the warthog Tarzan was always teasing because it was so ugly and bad-tempered — although I used to think that maybe if he hadn't teased it so much it wouldn't have *been* so bad-tempered. I'd had warts plenty of times — my mother reckoned I got them from playing with frogs. And if a hog was really a pig, as my father said, I'd seen one of them being killed, and cleaned out and boiled in the copper behind the butcher's — although of course my father didn't know that: so a warthog must be just a kind of pig covered with warts.

I'd worked all of them out, but I still couldn't make head nor tail of La, the High Priestess. I reckoned, once, that she must be some sort of nun, a sort of lady priest. It didn't work, though. I couldn't see her getting around in the jungle in the long brown skirts and brown hoods the nuns at the convent wore, any more than I could see the nuns at the convent going around with nothing on and living in the jungle with a crowd of dwarfish henchmen.

And then, all of a sudden, as I lay there on my hammock reading about her, it was as though someone had done a picture of her on the page for me. She was exactly like the painting of a lady in my mother's bedroom, with lovely pink cheeks and long hair, standing between two marble pillars in a black dress. The stuff was so thin you could see her chest sticking through it, like two of the Chinamen's little, round, pale-gold rock-melons. And she was sort-of looking down at you, with her eyes half closed.

All right, I thought. I've got that fixed. I know what she's like. But what was she panting and crying and crawling all over Tarzan for? What was it she wanted and Tarzan didn't? What was it all *about?*

I stopped reading and lay my book down on my stomach, and looked up into the tree. Just then, as I was thinking about it, there was a break in the hymns. As clear as crystal I heard my pigeons up on the church roof, *ricketty-coo! ricketty-coo!* and I said to myself: *I'll shove it up you, shove it up you!* It was what the boys down at the jetty said, when they were watching the wild doves chasing each other up and down the branches of the trees. *Ricketty-coo! Ricketty-coo! I'll shove it up you, shove it up you!*

Shove what up you?

Manning's big red bull jumped into my mind and climbed up onto one of his cows. I remembered what the new kid had said one day when we were leaning on the top wire watching him, about your mother and father in their bedroom at night, and when I asked Ernie what he meant, Ernie said: 'Gee! Didn't you know? That's how they make the calf. That's how your mother got you from your father!' Aunt Kate walked down the grey shell footpath to the jetty, past the Chinamen's garden, scared stiff one of them would get too close to her. They stared at her through the pickets of their fence, their hard bare feet and their hard brown legs and their thin blue trousers, and in our diningroom she said it again for me: *You know how they feel about white women!* There was a thread that joined the pigeons to the bull, and the bull to Aunt Kate, and Aunt Kate to the Chinamen. I could barely see it, but I was just going to take hold of it and follow it wherever it went, when I heard my mother's voice.

'Tomm-e-e!'

I sat up so suddenly the hammock creaked and tore along the line of nails.

'Oh, *Gawd!*'

Everything fled out of my mind but my mother, standing at the back door looking around the yard, listening like a magpie, wondering where I was. If she discovered I was up on the roof I'd never be safe there again.

'Tom-m-m-e-e-e!'

I could tell she was getting impatient, the way she dragged out my name. If I didn't make a move the next thing would be Barney barking and dancing around at the bottom of the tree, and she'd really know. I stood up, and my hammock ripped some more.

'Bugger-bugger-*bugger!*' I swore to myself. 'Go to the shop! Get the morning's-wood in! What about the grass for the cow! *Bugger!*'

Once I'd stirred I could feel the cold air on my bare arms. It must be getting late, all right. Uncle Kirk and Aunt Kate and Soldier Tom would have gone by now, on their way back to their homes on the other side of the river. The Baptist Church was all quiet excepting for the last of the people crowding around the porch to talk to the parson and his wife before they all went off. They reminded me of the bees crowding around the entrance to a wild hive I'd seen once, out the bush.

I tiptoed across the roof to the side of the shed facing away from the house. I was careful to step on the clumps of dead leaves to cut out the sound of my footfalls — my sisters could climb like monkeys, and if they ever found out where I went I'd never have another moment's peace.

At the edge of the roof I stopped and looked down. Barney was there, waiting for me, whining softly. My father reckoned he could tell the time.

It'll be the Chinamen's, for starters, I told myself. *Sunday. A lettuce and some white onions, I bet.*

I stooped and grabbed the edge of the iron that jutted out from the wall of the stable, and eased myself over. For a while I hung at full stretch, pulling myself up and down to develop my muscles. Every time I got near enough to him, Barney stood on his hind legs and licked the soles of my feet, and it tickled. Then I dropped to the ground.

I reckoned I'd think about it all some other time, Tarzan and the Priestess La, and Manning's bull and the pigeons and Aunt Kate and the Chinamen. For the time being I had other things to do.

I walked around the end of the stable. 'I'm coming, Mum!' I yelled, as though I'd only just heard her.

Of Biddy And My Dad

The day our cow died it was overcast and rainy. Squally winds jumped and bumped across the river from under Mount Eliza, turning the surface of the water so grey it was almost black. They howled up River Street to our place as if all they had in mind was to shake the last of the summer leaves and berries off our Cape Lilac trees — and that might be just why poor Biddy died. The little berries were supposed to be poisonous — lots of people said they killed chooks, and nobody I knew had a chook-yard under a Cape Lilac: my father said afterward Biddy might have picked up too many berries with the grass I'd cut for her down the river that afternoon, and tipped out onto the ground under the tree.

We'd have to buy another cow, of course, because we were four kids in our family and if we didn't have one, milk would be a big item on the weekly food-bill. My mother had used Biddy's in just about every way you could think of — raw, boiled, as cream for our porridge and in custards and junkets — but there was always plenty over to sell in our shop.

Biddy was a jersey, and the people who bought her milk really liked it. I think it might have been because most of them actually *knew* her. Biddy and I used to meet them when I was taking her down to the river to graze, and they'd always stop and say: *Hello, Biddy! How's my milk coming along?* and things like that: and they'd rub the places on her forehead where her horns had been polled, which was what she liked more than anything else.

It wasn't only the milk, though. When she died I think we were sorriest because she was our friend. She'd been our cow most of my childhood, and we loved her nearly as much as we loved each other, I reckon. We'd had other cows before her, sharing the stable with old Ginger, our horse — their feedbox in one corner and his in the other, with his harness hanging on nails driven into the uprights. I hardly remember them. It's Biddy I always think of when someone says, now, *Remember that cow we had, one time?* Pale-gold and soft-eared, with a snout like black velvet and eyes — my mother reckoned — like big purple pansies.

She belonged to all of us, of course, but I had charge of her, and because of that I suppose I spent most time with her. After I got home from school we used to stand on the river bank for hours, while she grazed and I read, and both of us watched the world go by. Sometimes I'd ride her around our place like a horse until my father caught me — she didn't mind, but he did. Sometimes I'd lie beside her in the hot sand of her yard with my head against her smooth side, listening to the grass I brought her rumble and slurp through her ten stomachs — or so my brother told me; and all the time, no matter where we were or what we were doing, she'd poke out her long grey-and-pink tongue and give me such a loving lick whereever she could land one. It was half like the good-night kiss my mother used to give me, and half like the feel of the rasp my father used to smooth down old Ginger's hooves.

We should have known there was something wrong with Biddy the day before she died. When I put the bucket on the kitchen table after the evening milking my mother sniffed at it suspiciously.

'Have you been putting cabbage leaves in with Biddy's grass again?'

It was a dodge I got up to sometimes when the grass was scarce, or when I had something better to do with my time than to spend it cutting grass for Biddy down the Chinamen's garden. Although Biddy grumbled about the cabbage-leaves she still ate them; but according to my mother they gave the milk a taste.

'No Mum', I was able to claim — truthfully, for once.

'Well, we can't sell it, and that's that!' My mother wouldn't have dreamed of putting anything over Biddy's customers, but she didn't say anything about us not using it up ourselves. She knew lots of ways of fixing it up, with a shake of nutmeg or vanilla or cinnamon, and if we complained she'd just say: *Get it into you! What won't fatten 'll fill!* It was an old joke, and we'd all sing out, together: *And what does neither 'll probably kill!* — but let me tell you we ate it just the same.

The very next day — the day Biddy died — there was something else we should have noticed. My mother milked that morning — she did, sometimes, when the mood took her — and when she came back to the kitchen she complained that Biddy had been acting up.

'She swished her damn tail so much I had to tie it to the rail!'

Then Biddy had kicked the bucket over — luckily when there wasn't much in it, so it wouldn't be one of those gloomy days when you had to say to the customers: *No milk today! Biddy kicked the bucket over!*

My mother went on about it, but I wasn't very interested in what Biddy was up to. I was wolfing my porridge and thinking about the two-mile walk to school in the wind and rain. In any case Biddy had kicked the bucket over before, and she *always* twitched her tail while you were milking her. She'd stung me with it plenty of times when I'd been tugging at her tits, my forehead against her side, a million miles away from our cowshed with the buzz and ping of her milk into the bucket.

I grabbed my lunch and put it into my school bag and set off for school in my slicker and my sou'-wester. I wasn't to know I'd felt the last switch of my friend's tail and the last lick from her loving tongue, the last nudge from her soft muzzle begging me to tickle her stumps.

I got home late that afternoon, soaked to the skin from playing in every puddle on the way. When I walked into the kitchen my mother was sitting beside the stove doing nothing: it seemed strange, because for as long as I could remember she always seemed to be doing *something*. I'd expected to get roused at for being so late, and so wet — maybe even a hiding. All she did when she saw me was to cover her face with her hands.

'Biddy's dead, Tommie-dod', she said, between gasping and snuffling.

'Biddy? Dead?' I don't know what I felt just then, but I don't think I was really all that sorry. Not then. 'When did she die?'

'About lunchtime.'

'Gee!' I said. 'Is she stiff yet?'

'You nasty little beast!'

It was all my mother needed to set her going again. She wiped her eyes with the corner of her apron and got up and cut me a piece with Golden Syrup — I loved it when it soaked into the bread and went hard, like honey-comb. 'And when you've finished that, feed the chooks and get your morning's wood in — there's some dry I put in the shed. And don't dawdle over it — you'll have to help your father bury Biddy when he comes home.'

She was like that. She'd had her cry and she could turn around and talk about digging Biddy's grave, just as if she was telling me off to another of my jobs.

'Why not Mickey?' I protested. Not because it was Biddy, not yet; because I just didn't like work. 'He's older than me!'

'Mickey's gone to Scouts early, there's something on,' my mother said, 'and Peg and Alice are still at piano', she added. She always knew what I was going to say next. 'Now — skedaddle! Or I'll take a stick and warm the seat of your pants!'

Biddy was lying outside the chaff-shed, and when I'd got the wood in and everything, I went to have a good look at her. I'd never seen a dead cow before. I put my finger-tip against her soft muzzle, to see how it felt. It was rubbery and cold, and there was no sweet breath from her nostrils to warm my hand, the way it always had, with the summery smell of grass and flowers. I know it was then that I realised I'd lost my friend, and I began to cry.

I'd hardly got really going when my father drove our creaking old cart into the yard. He got out and stood with me for a moment, looking down at Biddy: he always stopped at the front of the shop to take in things he'd bought in town, and my mother must have told him.

He used to say he had no time for any bloody animal that didn't earn its keep, and he was always going off about our Barney being a lazy loafer who needed a bit of hard work to make him know what's what. Animals that didn't earn their keep didn't include Bibby, and he'd always stop to stroke her back or tickle her stumps whenever he walked by her; but all the same I think he was pretty fond of Barney, too. When we stopped for a smoke-oh out the bush, when we were getting wood, the first thing he always did was to punch a dint in his old felt hat and fill it out of the waterbag for Barney to drink.

'Never mind, boy', he said. He put his arm around my shoulder. 'We'll get another cow, one day.'

He was a funny, quiet man. He never gave his guts away, as one of the boys said once. He didn't raise his voice very often, but you could tell when he was wild. He got that sort of look that if it had been me my mother would have said: *All right! Come off the boil!* Usually he treated the four of us as if we were friends he really didn't want to be troubled with too much — yet some mornings he'd come in before I was awake and tickle me, and rub his whiskers on my face and chest.

'Look,' he said, 'Old Ginger's laughing at you!' He patted my shoulder. 'You begin on the hole, down there in the corner by the church fence. I'll take Ginger out of the cart, and then I'll come and give you a hand. Off you go.'

It was dark before we'd got the hole dug. The light from the kitchen door threw a yellow streak across the yard, and my mother brought the hurricane lamps down to where we were working. She put one at each end of the hole and stood at the middle, holding up the other. She held it high, so that the lilac leaves sticking to our clothes and our faces looked like big golden spangles in the light. It was still raining, on-and-off, and I reckon that was why my sisters said they wouldn't help us. They screeched and reckoned they weren't going to dig poor Biddy's grave, and they were crying to each other in the kitchen, where it was warm.

111

When we got down to the really damp sand, and can't have been very far from water, my father climbed out of the hole. He pulled me out after him and walked over to where Biddy lay, with her legs sticking out stiff as pickets.

'Go on up to the house, Min,' he said to my mother, 'we won't be all that long, now.'

As the kitchen door closed behind her he went into the shed and brought out his bushman's saw, and very quickly cut off Biddy's legs at the knees. I was fascinated. There was practically no blood at all, really just like sawing a banksia branch out the bush.

'Why did you do that, Dad?' I don't know why I whispered, but it seemed you shouldn't talk out loud.

'So she'll fit in the hole', my father said. 'If I hadn't her legs would have got stuck on the sides. We'd have had a time getting her in.'

He tied one end of a rope to Ginger's collar and the other around Biddy's neck, and then hupped Ginger to drag her to the edge of the hole. Ginger didn't like it at all — you'd have sworn he knew Biddy was dead, and he didn't want to put her into her grave. He showed the whites of his eyes at the edges of his winkers, and stamped and snorted and shief until my father grabbed a clothes prop and laid what he called a persuader across his rump.

When they'd got Biddy into position he shoved the end of the prop under ribs and heaved once. In she went, and he threw her legs in after her, one by one. I looked down at her. Her eyes were still open, and the light of the hurricanes shone in them so that she looked to be staring back at me, accusing me of cutting off her legs. I began to cry again.

'Come on, boy, stop that,' my father said, 'we'll fill in the hole and then go and have our tea. What've we got, do you know?'

'Stewed chops and treacle pudding.'

'My word!' my father said. 'And just the night for it, eh? Pick up your shovel.'

He slipped Ginger's collar and bridle off and smacked him with one hand to start him in the direction of the stable. The lonely stable now, I thought, watching him go. No dear old Biddy at the other end of it to keep him company, belching and chewing her cud and dropping pats while he worked his way through his manger.

I hadn't heaved more than a few shovelfuls into the hole when my father came back and picked up his shovel to help me. Straight away he threw it down again. 'You bloody little heathen!' He stepped right across the hole and knocked mine out of my hand. I was too frightened to bawl. I thought he'd gone mad. 'Throwing sand into her face like that!' he roared.

He jumped down into the hole beside Biddy and brushed his felt hat backward and forward to clear away the sand. When he'd finished he closed her eyes with his fingertips, and then looked about him in a helpless kind of way I'd never seen on him before. In the end he took off his patched working weskit and laid it across Biddy's face.

'Go on up to the house, boy.' He said it very gently. He'd stopped roaring.

The light of the hurricane at the middle of the hole shone straight down onto him. I could see drops of water sliding down his cheeks into his moustache. It must have been raining harder than I'd thought.

Oh Mr Gallagher,
Oh Mr Sheen

Every Friday night Mrs Moodie and Rudolph came down to our place to play cribbage with my mother and father.

Mrs Moodie's husband had died some years before — I think his was the first funeral I ever saw go by our place, the big glass box on wheels and the horses with black ostrich feathers on their heads. I heard my father and mother talking about it once, and my father said Mr Moodie had died of some gas he'd swallowed during the war.

Mrs Moodie was a lovely lady. She wasn't quite fat, and she had soft white skin covered with powder: it reminded me of some flower. Her hair was long and wavy and thick, and she kept it piled up on top of her head in a bun like my mother's, before she had it cut off — although my mother had worn hers on the back of her neck. We thought Mrs Moodie was keen on Rudolph.

He was an American who'd turned up in South Perth that winter to be the head trainer at the polo ground. He was very big, and good-looking in a kind of way, and much younger than my father. He had black hair and white teeth, which is why my sisters christened him Rudolph, for Rudolph Valentino.

They played crib in our living-room behind the shop. We kept open until ten o'clock every night — just to squeeze out the last little bit, as my father said — and of course every so often while they were playing the bell on the door would tinkle. When that happened my father would push back his chair and excuse himself to go and attend to the customer.

As he sat down to take up the game again my mother would look at him with her eyebrows up, and he'd say something like: *Mrs West. Half-a-dozen eggs and a stick of Bates's Salve:* or *Bert James after his Champion finecut and his papers:* or *Just some kid — wanted a bottle of American Creaming Soda.*

On the night I'm telling about, though, one time he went into the shop he stayed there much longer than he did usually, and when he came back into the living-room he just sat down without saying anything.

'Myrtle Floyd?' my mother said, after a while.

My father just nodded, staring at his cards.

'Oh . . . tea.' You could tell that he didn't want to talk about Mrs Floyd and what she'd bought. 'And bread and butter.'

'And you let her have it?'

'For God's sake, Min! They've got to eat!'

My mother stared at her cards then, and said: 'Was it your play, Mrs Moodie?'

They'd known each other since long before I was born, and they were best friends, but I never heard them call each other anything but Mrs Moodie and Mrs Hungerford. Never Fannie and Minnie, as most people I knew would have.

On the Saturday before, in the afternoon, I'd been up to the Floyds'. It was part of my weekly job of going around to the people who owed money to my father and asking them if they could pay something off the account. I hated it, I can tell you, and not just because I would rather have been over on the Reserve playing tip-cat, or sitting on our side verandah going over my egg collection, or something like that. It was because it was so hard at school on Monday mornings, when some of the boys and girls, even if they weren't my friends, must have known that I'd been up to their places on Saturday trying to get some of the money their fathers owed mine.

I'd been given a note for the Floyds, in an unsealed envelope. I took it out and read it, of course, and I got a shock. They owed us the enormous amount of fourteen pounds six shillings and ten pence. The note asked Mrs Floyd please to give me whatever she could spare, and I wasn't surprised to see it was addressed to her rather than to her husband.

Mr Floyd was almost always drunk. He was very flash and good-looking — big and weak like a boarding-house cup of tea, my father reckoned. Before he got married he used to wear gold cuff-links in the coat sleeves of his blue serge suit: I suppose he was what we used to call a lair, although he was very popular around South Perth. He played football for the suburb, and everyone said he would go a long way, but something must have gone wrong. One day they were talking about him down the jetty and one of the big boys said the two birds had got him, and it was a long time before I found out he meant the Swan and the Emu, which were two brands of Perth beer.

Mr Floyd had worked in the cool drink factory until he got the sack for being drunk. They were frightened one of the bottles might blow up, as they did, sometimes, and blind him, and they'd be in trouble. Then he worked in a factory somewhere in town, and sometimes for one of the Chinamen when they were pulling onions or picking beans or setting out the thousands of little lettuces they planted every year. But mostly he worked on the roads: the Roads Board foreman and he had played in the same football team, and he got any odd jobs that were going.

I don't think he ever earned much, and my mother reckoned

that poor Mrs Floyd didn't get much of what he *did* earn. She was a pretty lady, but terribly skinny, and she always seemed to look so sorry for herself — like Barney, when he got a hiding for fighting or barking at the cow or chasing the bantams or digging holes. I'd heard them saying she'd been got into some sort of trouble by Mr Floyd, and that her parents had hunted her. Her father was a very stuffy Pommie, a boss at the brewery: he always wore leather leggings, and a weskit and necktie, no matter how hot it was.

When I got to the Floyds' I stood on their back verandah for a while before I knocked at the door. They lived in a tumble-down old place on the hill, and I could look down over the roofs of the houses and across the Chinamen's gardens to the swamps on the edge of the river. And then across the water to town, with a tower or a spire sticking up here and there above the other buildings — most of them were only two or three storeys high.

It was Saturday, and there were lots of yachts out. I remember hoping the yachties were throwing plenty of beer bottles overboard to float in to the South Perth shore. We collected them and got a ha'penny each from Mr Faddy, the grocer, who used them for kerosene. If you found a dozen it was your picture money for Saturday night, and you could spend your pocket money on chips at interval.

When I knocked at the Floyds' door Mrs Floyd came out, and I gave her the note. She had her baby balanced on her hip, and the smell of its stale piddle would have knocked you over, as my mother would have said. She closed the door, and for a while I could hear Mr Floyd shouting at her. After a while she came out again and handed me a sixpenny bit.

'Tell your father I'm . . .' she said, and closed the door quickly. But not before I'd seen she was crying.

There was a mob of boys splashing around in the shallows up toward Douglas's jetty, throwing their kylies into the schooling mullet: I could see them quite plainly as I walked along the Floyds' verandah toward the steps. At least some of them had to be friends of mine, and I was dying to be among them to try out the new cross-kylies I'd hammered out of hoop-iron one afternoon after school during the week. The ordinary kylie was shaped like a V, but my new ones had two pieces of iron about a foot long crossed and fastened at the middle. My father had taken the pieces of iron up to the blacksmith's near the Causeway, where Ginger was shod sometimes, and he'd put the rivets in for me. I just couldn't wait to see how they worked, and to feel the water soaking me up to my middle, and the lovely smell of the river and the rushes and the mud. And no poor skinny Mrs Floyd to worry about, crying inside that busted-up house with her drunken husband and her dirty baby.

On the way down the hill I tried to work out how many sixpences there were in fourteen pounds six shillings and ten pence. That way, I'd know how long it was going to take me to collect all of the Floyds' bill at sixpence a week. With forty sixpences to the pound and fifty-two weeks to the year — those were easy — I reckoned if would take me nearly a year to collect just one pound out of them. That meant that if you added fourteen years to the ten I was already I'd be *twenty-four* before I could stop going up there every Saturday afternoon. I might even be *married!* And of course you had to add all they'd tick up in the meantime. And the six shillings and ten pence, which were too hard for mental arithmetic.

I was thinking about all this, and worrying about it, when I heard Mrs Moodie say: 'And one for his knob, Mr Hungerford!' as if she'd won the Charities. It was what you said when you turned up a jack.

I stopped worrying about the Floyds, and all the Saturday afternoons I'd have to go up to their place before they'd have paid their bill, and watched the game of cribbage going on around our own dining-room table.

Before Rudolph started coming to our place one of my sisters, Lal, used to play with my mother, and my father used to play with Mrs Moodie. I was usually doing my homework while they played, or if I'd finished that I'd be reading a book at the far end of the table: they didn't disturb me, whatever I was doing, they were so quiet.

They laughed and gossiped while the cards were being dealt and shuffled, and after almost every hand there'd be what my mother called 'a bit of a port-mortem'. Then you'd hear the soft sound of the cards being shuffled and dealt again, and someone would start off by saying something like: *A four to begin with!* and then someone else: *And eight with a pair!* and somcone else: *And seven makes fifteen-two — you peg, partner?* Every so often my father would say to my sister: 'Come on, now, Lal! No shoving the peg along with your blooming elbow!' and they'd all laugh.

It all buzzed in my ears like the sound of being in church,

everyone saying the same things and making the right answers. I used to close my eyes and listen to them, and look at them on the back of my eyelids. That way I could see them just as plainly as if my eyes had been wide open, and I'd been looking straight at their reflection in the sideboard mirror.

It all changed when Rudolph started coming Friday nights, and playing with my mother.

He didn't seem to be able to do anything without shouting. He used to bang his cards down on the table, hitting the wood with his knuckles, and he'd say things we'd heard before only in the pictures. *Holy cow!* and *Son-of-a-gun!* and *Jeepers-creepers!*.

When he took Lal's place as my mother's partner, and it became him and my mother against Mrs Moodie and my father, they never seemed to gossip and laugh any more. You would have thought they were fighting a war rather than having a friendly game of cards. There were no port-mortems after each hand, and discussions of what might have happened if someone had played a different card into the crib. When Rudolph and my mother won a game by more than one row on the board he'd bang the table and shout to my father: '*Hey*, you old son-of-a-gun! *Skunked* ya!' and he'd pretend there was a dreadful smell in the room, holding his nose and waving a hand in front of his face. Or he'd say: 'Ja know any *other* games? Skipping rope, maybe?' and things like that.

My mother and Mrs Moodie used to laugh, but I could see my father didn't think Rudolph was so funny: and neither did my sister Lal. She'd stare at him the way Barney looked at dogs he didn't like, so that you'd almost expect her to show her teeth and snarl. And when Rudolph and my mother lost by more than a row it was Lal, not my father, who'd yell: 'Skunked ya! Skunked ya! *Skunked* ya, Rudolph *Vaselino!*'

She hated him all right, but so did my other sister, Peg — they told me so, and they used to screech at me when I said I liked him. They used pretend to ride bucking horses in front of him, in a way they meant to be rude, but didn't seem to be. And when we played cowboys-and-Indians they'd yell: 'Bags I being the one who shoots Rudolph with an arrow!' and one of us would always shout: 'In the B—U—M!'

The crib game lasted until about half-past nine, when they stopped for a cup of tea and cream biscuits from one of the Mills and Ware's or Arnott's tins on the shelves in the shop. As well as that we'd have heaps of Minties and Toffee-de-Luxe from the glass jars on the counter, so I suppose it's no wonder the shop went bung, later on, like all my father's other businesses. We children had a cup of tea with the grown-ups, then we had to go to bed. We were allowed to stay up until ten on Friday nights because there was no school the next day, but there was never any whining and begging to stay up longer. My father would say: 'All right, you kids. Bed-oh!' and we'd go.

As soon as they stopped for supper Mrs Moodie would always ask me to recite. She'd smile at me and say: 'Come on, now, Tommie. Let's hear your latest piece of poetry!' They'd all look at me, and Rudolph would say what he said every time: *OK! Bring on the Harleywood Kid!* I knew *Harleywood* was his American way of saying *Hollywood* — my sisters used to make fun of him behind his back, imitating what my father used to call his *damn Yankee twang*. And I knew Hollywood was where the pictures were made, but what I could never decide was whether or not he was making fun of *me*.

I never had to be asked twice — unlike my sisters, both of whom had been learning the piano for years. When they were asked to play they'd wriggle and giggle and say: 'Oh, *no!* I'm not good enough!' Not me, though. I loved the limelight. I'd taught myself a lot of poems from books I got here and there, and of course we got plenty at school. I was given a lot of encouragement from the nun who was teaching me at the time — she put me in all the school plays, and she used to say she'd offer up a dozen candles if my name wasn't up in lights one day.

On this particular Friday night I had a surprise for them.

I'd already memorised a nice poem called 'The Relief of Lucknow', about a town in India where there was a war on, and a girl heard the bagpipes before anyone else. It begins: *Pipes of the misty moorlands*, and I really tried to make my voice like a pipe the way the nun told us: she said we mustn't only *say* a poem, we must *be* it. I'd been going to say this piece of poetry, but just at that time there was a song going around called *Oh Mr Gallagher, Oh Mr Shean*, and one afternoon down at the jetty I'd heard one of the big boys singing it. It had an easy, catchy tune, and I memorised the words as he sang them. I think he must have made them up himself because they were about a place in Perth — and almost every song we sang had been an American song in the first place.

'I won't say a piece of poetry', I said to Mrs Moodie. 'I'll sing you a song I just learned.'

'That'll be lovely,' she said, 'and if I like it I'll give you a

121

thripenny bit.'

My usual place for reciting was on the far side of the table from the sideboard, looking straight into the mirror so that I could admire my own actions and expression, as the nuns called it. It was a beautiful sideboard like a castle, shiny red jarrah with little points and knobs on it, and glittering with all the glass and the polished brass of the door-handles. It had been given to my father as part of the payment for a job he'd done when he was a carrier, and he always said he'd got his hernia from shifting it.

When nobody was about, I used to stand in front of it and look at myself. I used to wonder whether I'd still be *me*, the way I looked and felt, if I'd been born Les or Bobbie or Eddie; or if anyone would ever find a way of getting into the room in the mirror, and what it would be like in there. I didn't know then that in a few years the shop would go bung and we'd have to sell the sideboard — and the big red jarrah table we played cards on, and the chairs and the sofa the possum had lived in for years. When everyone was quiet, and looking at me, I began. *Oh Mr Gallagher*, I sang, *Oh Mr Shean!* jigging about on my feet and making movements with my hands and nodding my head, the way the nuns had shown us.

> *Oh Mr Gallagher, Oh Mr Shean!*
> *There are places here in Perth you've never seen!*
> *Down in Roe Street there are houses*
> *Where the girlies wear no trousers!*
> *Will you come with us, Mr Gallagher?*
> *Absolutely, Mr Shean!*

I could tell as soon as I'd finished I'd taken them by surprise with the song rather than a poem. Nobody did anything for a moment, and then my mother said, in a funny way: 'Glory be to Holy Saint Denis!'

Mrs Moodie put her handkerchief up to her face as though she was going to cry, which surprised me a bit. There was nothing to cry about. Rudolph hit the table with his hand.

'Hot diggety!' He roared laughing, and then wiped a hankie across his eyes. 'Ain't *you* the little expert! How d'*you* know the girlies don't wear no trousers?'

'Of course they don't,' I said, 'girls don't wear trousers. *They* wear *bloomers. Men* wear trousers!'

My father had swung his chair around to watch me when I began to sing. He turned it to the table again, and I could see only the back of his head. His neck was brown and wrinkled, and there was a lot of grey in his black hair. His ears — he'd been born in Ireland, and he always called them 'my years' — sat close in against his head: because his mother had made him tuck them under his hat, my mother told me all the time. *Not like yours, sticking out like the handles of a jerry!*

'I think you kids can go to bed', he said, quietly.

'But it's suppertime, Dad!'

'Just do as you're told', he said. 'Get off to bed.'

Rudolph stopped laughing.

'Godsakes, Arthur!' He always called my father by his Christian name, although my father never called him anything but McKean, which was his real name, not Valentino. Harry McKean. 'Godsakes, Arthur! Why d'you always have to be such an old killjoy?'

I'd been watching it all in the mirror, so I could see the expression on my father's face. He didn't larrup us very often, but when he did he looked exactly like that. I thought: *Golly! He's going to larrup Rudolph!*

Just then my sister Lal pushed her chair back from the table. She didn't say anything. She just stood there with her savage dog look, staring at Rudolph. And then at my mother.

'I know a better Gallagher and Shean song than that', she said. 'I'll sing it to you.'

I thought it was funny, her offering, because when anyone asked her to play the piano you just about had to leg-rope her. And I thought she had a cheek, too, when nobody *had* asked her: or perhaps she was after the thrippence Mrs Moodie had promised me. She didn't even know how to stand properly, the way the nuns had shown us — with your belly in and your chest out, and your hands at your sides unless you needed them for expression. She was holding onto the table for dear life, as if she would fall over once she let go, and her knees were bent forward by the edge of the chair behind them. She didn't even bow.

> *Oh Mr Gallagher, Oh Mr* McKean! *she sang.*
> *There's a hotel in town where you've been.*
> *And someone goes there too,*
> *Every Wednesday after . . .*

'*Alice!*' I had never heard my mother speak so loudly in the house before. 'Go to bed, at *once!*'

She needn't have bothered anyway, because Lal was already half-way to the door. I thought what a bad sport she was, running away like that and crying just because they didn't like her song as much as they liked mine. I reckoned Mrs Moodie's thrippence was as good as in my pocket.

I was still looking into the mirror. It's funny the way things reflected in it always seemed closer and sharper than the real things in the room. I really saw the grain in the jarrah of the table, and the shine of the little ivory pegs on the crib-board. And the colours of the cards, clearer and brighter than ever.

And the people. My mother and Mrs Moodie and Rudolph, all still as paintings of themselves, staring at their cards as if they were looking for something they'd lost. And my other sister, Peg, watching my father the way you watch a sky-rocket on bonfire night, waiting for it to go off.

And my father. Looking at my mother, his braces over his striped shirt. His necktie. His mouth a bit shrunken because he would never wear his false teeth, and the ginger moustache he grew, long and straggly, to hide it. You saw these things every day, but in the mirror, at night, they seemed different in a way I couldn't even explain to myself.

My father was the first to move, and to speak. He picked his cards up and stared at them for a moment.

'Fifteen-two, fifteen-four,' he said, 'and the rest won't score.' I thought it was strange, because they'd already finished the game, and he'd counted them before.

I stood behind him watching them all, sitting there like paintings. I thought: *This is how I'll always remember them, sitting like painted people in the room behind the mirror.*

So Long, Rudolph

All winter I used to get up before first light to help train the polo ponies with Rudolph.

We lived a mile or so from the stables, and as I ran along the footpath to get there I used to feel there was only me alive in the whole world. I had to keep telling myself the shapes I could just see moving about under the shadowy trees in old Douglas's paddock were only his cows and horses — and in any case I knew every one of them by name. I had to tell myself something I mightn't want to see *wasn't* hiding behind the black piles of empty crates outside Weaver and Lock's cool-drink factory. I liked passing the early-milking hullabaloo of Roberts's dairy, all lit up and clanking like a tram in the long, sandy paddocks between Suburban Road and the Chinamen's gardens down by the river; but I wasn't all that keen about running under the enormous peppercorn tree at the side of the old Teagardens Hotel, which hadn't had a licence to sell beer for years, and had been empty for as long as I could remember.

The stables were right behind the old hotel, in the middle of a grove of old gumtrees — marri gums, and even in the almost-dark you could see the big bunches of their white blossom. When I got there it was warm inside with the glow of the lanterns, and busy already with the rattle of bits and the snorting of horses and the men hurrying around getting some fed and some ready for their exercise.

I would hurry along between the loose-boxes, saying good morning to the men and my favourites among the horses. I was really dying for Rudolph's hand to fall onto my head, and to hear him sing out, as he did every morning: *Hi, there! You young son-of-a-gun!*

He was very big and good-looking and noisy, with a tanned face and oily black hair brushed back hard. The way he did it was called the push-back, and all the big boys around our way were doing it. He had small brown eyes — monkey's eyes, my sisters said — and a hooked nose and whiter teeth than anyone I'd ever known. Every other man I knew wore blue serge for his only suit and denim for work — with black boots for both. Rudolph had cream moleskin riding trousers like my mother's suede gloves, and cream silk shirts and coloured cravats, and beautifully polished brown leather leggings and riding-boots.

He was an American, and he said he had lived and worked in Hollywood, where the pictures were made. His right arm had a tattoo on it — a heart with HMER inside it — and when he worked

126

his muscles he could make them do a little jig. His real name was Harry McKean, so I'd worked out the HM were his initials, but one morning as we were coming back from our ride, walking the horses for the last little bit to cool them down, he told me the ER stood for Esther Ralston. I knew she was an actress, and I'd even seen her a few times Saturday nights, when I'd planked down my hard-earned sixpence at the old Gaiety. He said he'd had the tattoo done one weekend when they were in a place called Santa Barbara, because he and ER were keen on each other — *sorta sweethearts, sorta kidstuff* was the way he said it.

It was funny to think that the beautiful lady I saw up there on the screen had been Rudolph's girl. It was like a comet or the Great Wall of China, which I'd read about in the Children's Encyclopaedia: you *knew* they were there, because everyone said so, but somehow you just couldn't quite believe it.

Rudolph came to Perth to be head trainer at the polo ground near our place, although my father said he didn't know why they had to bring in a blasted Yank to do what a good Western Australian could have done as well, and probably better.

He started to come into our shop for his cigarettes and things, and because he was a stranger and a long way from his home my mother and father asked him to Sunday lunch. Then they introduced him to the people who were our special friends, and used to come to our place pretty often, and before long it was as if he'd been around forever.

I worshipped him from the very start. Maybe it was because he was the first American we'd ever had in South Perth, but I think mostly it was because he was a tip-top horseman, and he'd worked in Hollywood. He'd known cowboys like Ken Maynard and Tom Mix, and some of the others who set us screeching like Indians ourselves on Saturday nights, when they galloped across the prairie to rescue some Yankee fort, or to beat the Indians back from some blazing ring of prairie schooners.

It was because he came from Hollywood — I thought — that my two sisters nicknamed him Rudolph, which stuck. But they insisted it was because of his greasy black hair and his hooked nose and his dark Dago eyes, and said they'd hated him on sight. *Rudolph Vaselino*, they'd say, saucily to his face, but behind his back with a sort of *grown-up* hate I couldn't understand.

I said to them once I couldn't see why he let them get away with their cheek, and my elder sister said: 'For the same reason that he offered to teach you riding.'

I said: 'I still don't know what you mean, Peggie.'

'You'll find out', she said.

One evening when we were having tea they were talking about him, and my other sister, Lal, said she hoped he'd go back to America, soon. My mother told her to keep a civil tongue in her head, but my father just laughed.

'Don't worry, dear heart. He'll buzz off when he's ready. He's only dropped in here to pick up what he can and put on a bit of fat. When he's done it, we won't see which way he went!'

In that very instant I thought of the little birds we called sand-snipes, that flocked in their hundreds on the river every summer. My father told me once that they were really dotterels, from Siberia, and that they flew down to the Swan every summer just to lay their eggs and raise their chicks. Then, when it was summer again in Siberia, they flew all the way back. He said they had a bit each way, with warm weather wherever they went.

I thought maybe Rudolph was like one of them, a sort of travelling bird that just dropped down among us for a while to rest his wings and smooth his feathers, and like my father said, to put on a bit of fat before he took off again for another kind of life. In some place we just couldn't imagine, like the snipe's Siberian home.

Rudolph and I used to leave the stables in the starlit freezing darkness just before the sun came up over the Darling Ranges. It was easy and comfortable going for us and the horses on the deep-red loam washed off the gravel surface of Suburban Road by more winters than I could remember. The thud of hooves was softened by the foliage of the trees above us — gums and kurrajongs and peppercorns, lillipillis and Moreton Bay figs made that section of our ride almost like a tunnel.

On the river side of the road there were an orchard or two with a house here and there, but mainly paddocks that went right down to the Chinamen's gardens. They were covered with dandelions in the spring, so golden-thick that you had to be careful walking through them or you'd tread on a bee and get stung. As we rode past the houses I often wondered if the people sleeping inside them could hear — maybe through their skin — the soft clip-clop and jingle-jangle-jingle of Rudolph and me ghosting by on the other side of their fences.

We never changed the way we went — right down through South Perth to Mill Point, out onto the beach near the old mill, off for a gallop on the hard sand and then into the water for a splash. As we trotted back along the beach to the point the first sunlight would be trickling down the sides of Mount Eliza like water. The brewery's big horse-drawn lorries would be creaking out onto Mount's Bay Road, heading for pubs all over Perth — every one was pulled by two enormous Clydesdale horses that always took a part in processions through Perth, dressed up with shiny horse-brasses and red-white-and-blue ribbons plaited into their manes and tails. The first trams would be clanking and clanging around the bays under the side of the Mount, and every now and then a motorcar would chug along like someone with a bad cold. It was so still as we sat on the horses, giving them a breather before we started home, we could hear the soft hum of the city from across the water, like the sound of a travelling swarm of bees.

I loved every bump, every second and yard of it. I suppose I was a skite, because if anyone I knew came out early for bread or milk or a paper or something, and saw me riding with Rudolph and sang out to me, I reckoned I was made.

I usually got back from my ride in time to join the others for the tail-end of their breakfast. There'd be a slab of porridge just keeping warm between two plates on top of the stove, and a jug of our Biddy's wonderful milk to put on it. There was always cream to go with my slice of toast and jam, too, because every night my mother put the left-over milk in a basin at the back of the stove, and in the morning it was covered with lovely thick, yellow cream.

I don't know why, but my father seemed dead-set against those early morning rides of mine. Almost every time, as I sat gown at the table, he'd say to my mother: 'All this damn galloping around in the dark! And on horses he doesn't even *know!*'

'I *do*, Dad!' I said, once. 'I lead them around between chukkas, polo days!'

'Ballyhooley!' he said. 'You don't get to know a horse leading it around on a bit of blasted string! You've got to *ride* it — and ride it for a *long time!*'

He knew about horses. His father had owned a lot when he was a boy in Ireland, and then when he came out to Australia he'd worked on his uncle's station in Queensland — and then he'd ridden all over the place with cattle.

One Saturday he came up to watch the polo, and while I was cooling one of the ponies down he hopped up into the saddle — and of course while he was still there along came the owner, a big farmer from Beverley way. When he saw my father on his horse he stood staring as if murder had been committed. You know how people say your eyes pop out, well, his *did*. I thought: *Oh, gawd!* and although the man was not a yard away from us, I sort-of whispered: 'Dad! *Please get down!*' He just sat there smiling, and I'm sure it must have been just heaven for him to be sitting a horse again — I know when he and my mother had a row she used to say: *All you want to do is to get back to your damn horses and camels! You should never have got married!* After a while he said to the farmer: 'Nice little pony you've got here!' Then he patted its neck and swung his leg over its back and dropped to the ground — light as a feather even though he was old as anything — maybe even forty. The farmer just grabbed the lead off me and stamped away without saying a word, but he gave us both a look for luck. I thought I'd die of shame.

One breakfast-time when he was on about me going riding with Rudolph my mother said: 'It will do him no harm, Arthur.'

'The boy needs his full sleep, Min!' my father said. He moved his cutlery around, impatiently. 'Damn it! He's got *school* to go to!'

'He's learning to ride', my mother said. 'Properly. From someone who knows what he's talking about.'

That same morning while we were on our way back from Mill Point we'd pulled in at the Windsor Hotel, and Rudolph went inside for a while. When he came out again he told me he'd been talking business with the manager, although you could smell the beer on him from the corner. I was going to tell them about this, and how I'd sat outside and held *all* the horses, and how the people going down to the Mends Street ferry had looked at me. I'd got no further than *Rudolph and I*, through a mouthful of warm porridge, when my father blew up.

'Just finish your breakfast and get ready for school! We'll do very well to get through *one* meal without having to listen to your stories about that half-baked bloody Yankee!'

It was quite a burst for him, and he spoke in a way we knew enough to take notice of, although we didn't hear it very often.

Later on, between finishing my breakfast and leaving for school, I heard him say, in their bedroom: 'It's not just McKean, at all, Min. There *is* a danger, and the boy *does* need his sleep!'

'So you keep saying, Arthur', my mother said — and she spoke the way I would have if someone at school had tried to kid me they were cutting out homework.

'So I keep saying', my father said.

And neither of them spoke again.

One Saturday afternoon not long afterward I went up to the polo
ground looking for Rudolph.

On home-match days three or four of the boys from around our
way used to put in a couple of hours there making ourselves useful
in and out of the stables, fetching and carrying and walking the
ponies between chukkas to cool them down. It was worth
sixpence to us, and it saved us the business of collecting bottles for
chips at interval. Once a Mr Lefroy asked me to pick up a saddle-
cloth he'd dropped when he was leaving the field, and when I
handed it to him he gave me a half-crown, just as if it was a penny.
I told my father about it later that evening, and he said: 'Lefroy?
The cow could have given you five pounds! Owns stations all over
the State!'

Once, too, as I was leaving the stables to go home after a game,
Rudolph handed me a two-shilling piece.

'Here — this is just for you. Don't tell the other boys!'

I did, of course, skiting, and one of them said: 'Gawd — *I* know!
He's keen on one of your sisters!'

'Go on!' I said. 'They're only kids. Anyway, they hate him like
poison!'

'Well, then . . . your old woman!' another said, and laughed.

I laughed too. It was so ridiculous I hardly even thought about
it. I knew what it was to be keen on a girl, and I couldn't see
Rudolph sending my mother notes, or buying her chips at interval
with his polo money.

There was no home-game that day, but there was always the
chance of a job for picture money. And I wanted to see Rudolph.
We hadn't been riding for two or three mornings, and when I
asked my mother why she said he was busy. And he hadn't come
down to our place Friday night, as he usually did.

The long shed smelt of hay and kerosene lamps and fresh
manure, and it was cool and quiet: very different from what we
were used to on match days at home, when the stablemen would
be racing around swearing with saddles over their arms and
bandages and mallets, and there would be big flash cars parked all
over the place under the gum-trees, and some of the members
always got drunk and their wives and families brought friends into
the stables and got in the way showing off the horses they owned.

I looked into each loosebox as I passed it, and spoke to my
favorites. Rudolph wasn't in the chaff room, but one of the

131

regular grooms had a stranger in the harness room. They were sitting on piles of folded chaff-bags with a pack of cards and a bottle of beer on an upturned box between them. I thought the groom was taking a bit of a risk, because Rudolph didn't allow the men to drink when they were around the horses, and he never let strangers into the stables at all.

'Where's Mr McKean?' I asked.

'Gorn!' the groom said. 'Gorn back to fuckin Hollywood, that's where!'

I didn't believe him, of course. Nor for a week or so, but by then the way Rudolph had suddenly left South Perth and his job at the polo ground had been well and truly threshed out around our way.

When I walked out into the bright sunshine at the other end of the stables I nearly bumped into a black man sitting on a box: although not a black like the raggedy, skinny ones who traipsed along Suburban Road sometimes, yelling the gum-saplings they sold for clothes-props. Everyone reckoned those blacks were thieves, and that they beat their gins and the little black children with a leather belt if they didn't sell all the props they'd cut. And they stank. One time I heard a lady say to my mother in the shop: *The dirty buggers, Mrs Hungerford! I'd stand under the clothes line all day long and hold it up with my hand before I'd let one of them through the gate to sell me a prop!* and later on when my mother told my father about it he said the old biddy would stink, herself, if she couldn't get soap and hot water, like the poor black people.

This black man was clean, though — so clean his skin shone. His teeth were just as white as Rudolph's — maybe even whiter — and when he smiled at me I noticed that the inside of his mouth was as pink as a geranium. His hair was black and oily, like Rudolph's, only he didn't do the pushback. He parted it over one ear like my father, and combed it right across the top of his head to the other. You could see that it was clean too, and as I smelled his brilliantine I remembered that Rudolph's hair hadn't been all that clean, really. It had had a sort of thick smell to it.

The black was properly dressed, too, in clean grey denim pants like my father's, and a clean grey flannel shirt with short sleeves that showed the muscles in his arms. He had on black sox and shiny black elastic-sided boots with long, pointy toes: you could see where his feet came to in them, and the shape of his toes inside. On the ground beside him, on the dry grass and gumnuts, there was a wide-brimmed black felt hat like the ones Ken Maybard and Tom Mix wore.

'What're you doing with that?' I asked him. He was rolling and squeezing a lump of marri-gum between the pinky-brown palms of his hands. I thought it was strange to see him sitting there so clean and sure of himself, even though he was a black.

'Makin' a woomera.'

'What's a woomera, forever?'

'Little bit hard to tell you', he said. 'When I've finished it, I'll show it to you. Show you how it works, like.'

His voice was so soft it sounded almost silly, coming from a man. But you could see he wasn't any sort of a sissy. It was just the way he spoke . . . as if he had to think for a moment about every third or fourth word, and look at it, and recognise it, before he let it out.

What I really liked about him, straight away, was that he spoke to me as if he was another boy, like me. Or, better still, as if I was another man, like him. Equal. When I asked him what he was doing with the ball of gum he told me. Most people — even Rudolph, sometimes — would have said: *Nosey Parker!* or something like that. At school you thought you were pretty smart when you said: *Ask no questions, tell no lies. Shut your mouth and you'll catch no flies!* 'Making a woomera', he'd said, just like that, and as I thought about it I remembered something else about Rudolph — or maybe only just then would admit it to myself. I'd always felt a bit silly when I first walked into the stables in the morning, and he sang out: *Hi, there! You young son-of-a-gun!* or *Hey — get your cotton-pickin' ass over here!* None of the men around our way would ever have said anything like that — and they only shouted when they were wild. All they ever said was: *G'day, Tommie!* or: *Cold out, eh?*, and they said it quietly.

The black man was looking at me, smiling. I suppose he wondered what I was thinking about. I said: 'Do you work here, now?'

'Yeah. I work here.'

'Where do you come from?'

'Here.' He gazed around at the stables and the marri gums and the old hotel. 'Round about here.'

I looked across the polo ground. I could remember it before, when it had been the old Teagardens Racecourse, and we used to run around the course playing racehorses, and scamper like possums all over the old weatherboard grand-stand: it was still

133

there, falling to pieces under some big gumtrees, and our parents would have had a fit if they'd known we went near it. There was the judge's box and the two big ponds they used to water the horses at, and right down the bottom of the ground, Billy Bew's little plaster-and-board cottage at the top end of his garden, well above high-water mark in the biggest floods.

I couldn't see how the black man could have come from all that, because we played on the racecourse all the time when I was little, and if he'd been there I would have seen him. I turned around and looked at him.

'You can't have come from here. There was a racecourse, before. With a grandstand, and everything.'

'Before that, sonny.' He smiled again. 'I was only a little feller. My daddy used to catch possums in the trees, used to be all over the paddock.' He pointed down to the river. 'And crabs, down there.'

'We still go crabbing,' I said, 'in summertime, after tea. You can get a chaff-bag full.'

'Yeah. I know.'

I thought he must be very old, perhaps even as old as my father, and an awful thought struck me.

'Did you ever sell clothes props when you were a little boy?'

I had the awful feeling that *that* was where he'd really come from: trudging along Suburban Road in the dust of the carts, and being beaten with a leather strap. And of course, he wouldn't want to admit it.

'No. We never sold no props.' He'd been smiling while I spoke, but he'd stopped. 'We left.'

'Where'd you go?'

'Oh — all-about. Up Murchison way. My daddy worked for farmers, and I learned about horses.'

All the time he was speaking he kept on rubbing and pressing the marri gum between his palms. I watched him for a while, and then I said: 'What's your name?'

'Simon. Simon Good. What's yours?'

'Tommy', I said. 'Show me what you're making with the gum?'

He leaned sideways and picked up something I hadn't noticed in the grass beside his hat — a peeled white gum stick about an inch thick. It was a bit flat down one side, maybe three feet long and straight as a ruler. He felt along the band of his black hat and took out a piece of white shining stone about three inches long, shaped to a point at one end. It was the sort my father had told me, once, was called quartz. He said it was the kind you found gold in. Then Simon took a little coil of fine copper wire out of the breast pocket of his shirt — you could see it had been straightened out from a piece of electric-light wire.

'What's all that for, Simon?' I said.

'You'll see.'

He stuck a wad of the gum on the flattened side of the stick, close to one end, and pressed a shaped wedge of wood into it. Then he laid the white stone on the piece of wood so that the tip of the stone stood away, maybe half an inch from the side of the stick: it looked like the barb of a fish-hook. Then he wound a few turns of the copper wire around the stone and the stick, binding them together. He smeared the bind with gum, made some more turns with the wire, and smeared on more of the gum. He kept on doing it until there was a knob of wire and gum around the stone: as big as a pigeon's egg, maybe. Only the very tip of the stone poked out of the gum. Then he held up the stick and looked along it out of one eye, squinting with the other and frowning a bit. The whites of his eyes were a pinky-brown, like the palms of his hands, and the dark-brown part in the middle sort-of melted into them.

'Did the black people have those things?' I asked, and he nodded.

'Then how did they tie them up?' I felt very smart. 'They didn't have any copper wire.'

He smiled again. 'Pulled the strings out of kangaroos' legs.'

'What's it for, anyway?' It all sounded a bit wonky, but I let it go. 'What do you *do* with it?'

'It helps you to . . . throw a spear, maybe.'

Woomera, he'd called it. I said it to myself, in my head, and it sounded wonderful. Old and strange and wonderful.

'Show me how?'

'Not with this one. It's new. The gum's got to set real hard before you can use it. Wait a minute, eh?'

He got up off the box he'd been sitting on and went into the stables. There were two little rooms for the men to sleep in, the ones who worked there all the time. One of them would be his, now, and I guessed he was going into it.

When he came out again he was carrying another stick like the one he'd just made. Another woomera. And he had brought a half-a-dozen of the long, straight flower stalks off a blackboy: I knew them all right, because we used them for spears ourselves, when we played black men out in the bush. He stopped beside me

135

and held the woomera out to me, the little stone hook pointing upward.

'See?' He put one of his fingertips on the stone. 'You fit the end of the stick against the stone — like this.' He showed me how, and I could see that the end of the spear had been hollowed out a bit, so that the point of the stone wouldn't slip off it. 'You hold the spear against the woomera, right at the other end', he said. 'Look — like this. See? Then . . .'

He bent backward into a sort of a curve. It looked like the spring of an alarm clock I'd got from a boy at school. He raised the arm with the woomera and the spear, and pointed it at a kerosene tin against the stable wall.

I didn't quite know what to expect, and what he did next took me by surprise. It seemed as if he let go the spring in his body all of a sudden so that he stood up straight and his arm shot out in front of him straight as a die. The blackboy spear flew at the kerosene tin, harder and faster than I thought anyone could have sent a spear just by hand, without the woomera. The tin went rolling with a clang. I don't think I'd ever seen anything more wonderful.

'Who showed you how?' I said.

'My daddy. When I was a little feller, like you.'

'Can I have a go?' I said.

He handed me the woomera and one of the spears. I stood there staring at them, and my fingers curled around them. It made my back ripple. I felt as if the big trees were still standing all around the racecourse, full of possums for Simon's father to catch. And I remembered they used to come and play in our ceiling, and make wet patches, and hiss and fight, before the trees were all cut down and dynamited and burned, and you never saw possums any more. I thought of those other black people selling their clothes props at our front gate, and how they sounded crying out: like the flocks of black cockatoos that flapped and squawked over our house in stormy weather, on their way to the shelter of the hills. I felt as if I was looking through the window into Simon's room in the stables, watching him sitting on his bunk and making the woomera and the spears his father had taught him to make: now, when really he had no use whatever for them any more.

'Come on,' he said, 'I'll show you how to throw a spear.'

He took my shoulders and turned me about, so that he stood behind me. Then he put one arm around me and guided the fingers of my throwing hand into the proper hold, so that you'd be able to let the spear go while you still held onto the woomera. All the time he talked to me about what we were doing, and the horses, and about the Murchison where he'd grown up and had got to know all about them. Before very long I'd got the knack of it. I could send a spear nearly all the way to the kerosene tin, and usually in the right direction.

I woke up to what time it was when the groom came out of the stables with his friend, and banged the door behind them.

'We're going, Simon', he sang out. 'You got the keys?'

'Yes. I got them.'

They took off through the marri gums toward Suburban Road. Simon gave me his pink-and-black smile. He said: 'Pub!' and shook his head the way my mother did when something didn't please her too much.

Seeing the groom reminded me of Rudolph. I hadn't thought of him all afternoon. I said: 'Where's Rudolph?'

'Who's Rudolph?'

'Mr McKean.'

'All right, then,' Simon said, 'you call him Mr McKean, eh?' I nodded, and he said. 'He's gone.'

So the groom hadn't been pulling my leg. Rudolph *had* gone. And he hadn't even told me he was going, nor said so-long. It was one of his American sayings, and of course we had copied him. Now it was so-long, Rudolph. I reckon I felt a bit like crying.

'Where's he gone, Simon?' I said. 'Back to America?'

'I think, America', Simon said. 'You got jobs to do, at home? It's getting a bit late.'

It was getting late. Most of the bees had left the marri blossom, and Roberts's cows were making their way in from the paddocks to the milking shed, mooing and swinging their udders. Down at the bottom of the polo ground Billy Bew's little cottage got caught in the last of the light, and it looked as if it was on fire inside. Before dark I had to be home to milk our own cow, and cut the wood and feed the chooks.

I didn't miss going out on the horses. Inside of a couple of weeks I was hitting the kerosene tin most times, and once I even hit a beer-bottle.

Down Como

One afternoon when Ernie and I were down the Chinamen's cutting grass for our cow, Ernie said: 'I heeled one, yesterday.' I knew what he meant. Some Saturday afternoons, and even some days after school in the summer, he and I went caddying together at the South Perth Golf Links. When your bloke hit a ball into the rough you pretended to look for it very carefully, but if you got a chance you pressed it into the ground with your heel so that you could come back later on and pick it up. It was called heeling, and all the caddies did it.

If you were lucky you could sell the ball to another golfer. I reckon they all knew where the balls came from but they didn't mind getting a bargain — you couldn't hold out for much because if you couldn't sell a ball all you could do was to unwind it for the elastic. You had to be very careful when you got to the little bag of white stuff at the middle. Everyone reckoned it was deadly poison, and you died if you got too much on your fingers.

'If you're going down Como Sunday we could walk', Ernie said, when I asked him when he was going to pick up the ball. 'We could cut across the links, and get it then.'

Our family went to Como practically every Sunday in summer. I'd been going there for as long as I could remember. When I was little my father owned a carrying business, it was before he bought the shop, and we used to go down on one of the big lorries he kept at the stables in Nash Street, in Perth. He had four or five pairs of beautiful draught horses, gentle as kittens with long manes and tails and plumes of silvery hair behind their hooves that made them look like huge, strange birds. They worked in pairs, always two to a lorry and always the same two horses together — Punch and Judy and Darkie and Snow were my favourites, but we loved them all.

When we went to Como on the lorry we always took the people next door, or down the back, or up the road. There was plenty of room. We'd all sit around the edge of the lorry dangling our feet, and singing and waving to the people in their gardens as we went by. Sometimes a motorcar would come toward us, or pass us from behind, and when that happened my father would hold the reins hard against his chest, pulling back on them, and say: 'Now Punch! Now, Judy! *Whoa*, there! Steady, girl!'

Even when you could hardly see the motorcar in the distance our mothers would begin to cry out: 'Pull your legs in! Pull your legs in! You'll get your legs cut off!'

We all waited for when the lorry turned off Labouchere Road

into Preston Street and sloped on down the hill to the beach. Almost to the start of the long jetty where it ran right out into the deep, with a little red-roofed waiting shed for the ferries at the very end. From the top of the hill you could see where the blue stopped and the white began, and the long rows of waves breaking in the shallows looked just like the layers of crochet my mother did around the bottoms of my sisters' petticoats and pants.

We never left Como until after sundown, so that it got dark on the way home. We'd curl up on the piles of chaffbags my father had thrown on that morning. The others played *I Spy With My Little Eye* and *My Brother Sam Kept Faddy's* and *Bizz and Buzz*, but they were counting and spelling games and I wasn't very good at them: I wasn't very far out of the infants, then, when my father had the carrying business. I'd lie on the bags listening to the others, and to my father singing to himself up on the high seat, and look at the sky. I used to wonder why the stars didn't *all* fall down, and when one did I'd be the first to sing out 'Falling star!' and make a wish. I didn't stay awake for very long, though, and always the next thing I knew I was being carted inside at home, for what my mother called 'a lick and a promise' before I was bundled into bed. I knew I'd never forget the smell of the chaffbags and the sound of the grown-ups talking to each other, and laughing, and someone saying: *My Brother Sam kept Faddy's, and the first thing he sold was B.* And the jingle-jangle of the harness and the clump-clump of the horses' hooves — they seemed to be able to put them down on the road all together, as if they were beating out a tune on a drum.

After my father sold his carrying business and went into the shop we always went to Como by tram. It seemed that nearly everyone in Perth did — tram-load after tram-load of them, often with two trams hitched together to carry the mobs, until when you got there you couldn't find a shed to sit in or a bush to sit under: unless you got in early, so that on holidays such as Boxing Day and even on ordinary Sundays, sometimes, when it looked like being a scorcher, I was sent down first thing with a rug and a few lunch baskets to spread around and grab a good spot. I didn't mind — I'd take a Tarzan book and have a good read while I was waiting for my mother and my sisters to come down. My brother Mickie never came with us, but we often brought Mrs Moodie and her girl Jean, who was my first sweetheart.

There were swings and a merry-go-round and sometimes hoop-la and a coconut-shy, and a man with little donkeys for penny rides on the beach, and fish-and-chips and other shops for everything you'd need. There was even one with a long line of coppers, always on the boil for people buying water to make their tea. Every Sunday was like People's Day at the Show, with crowds running around and sky-larking and just sitting on the grass or the sand, in bathers and pretty summer colours that always reminded me of my mother's cinerarias.

If we went early, we'd swim until lunchtime and then we'd wolf into hot tea and sandwiches. Mrs Moodie called them 'sangwidges'. She'd say to my mother: 'What sort of sangwidges have you brought, Mrs Hungerford? I've got tomato-and-onion.'

'Well, Mrs Moodie — I've got mutton-and-mustard — and I put a few tomatoes in whole. Shall we share and share alike?'

They said that every week, and they shared every week, but they never did it without discussing it first.

After lunch we had to sit around for an hour by the clock, grizzling because my mother said if we went into the water so soon after eating we'd sink to the bottom with the cramps. It was one of her ideas. Another was that she'd never let us go swimming in the river before November. She said there was still too much fresh water in the river before that, and we'd get pneumonia.

After lunch, all afternoon while our mothers sat on the grass and gossiped and watched the people go by, we swam and duck-dived and played games in the water. Our hands got wrinkled — we called them 'washerwoman's hands' — and our eyes smarted and got blood-shot with the salt, and our faces burned red and sore. But we wouldn't think of going out until sundown.

When it began to get a bit cool someone would say: *Last one down the jetty's a black-gin!* Someone else would always say: *Five more dives!* and after we'd had them we'd scramble out and race down that long stretch of rough boards with the cold wind at our backs and the great red sun touching the tops of the trees on the other side of Melville Water. When we'd got dressed we'd line up again for more sandwiches and hot, sweet, milky tea, and every time I buried my face in my enamel mug I told myself there couldn't be anything better in the whole world.

Sometimes, if it was a very hot night, or if it was a holiday next day, we were allowed to go in again for a while after dark. On ordinary nights, I'd just wander around with Ernie — who usually came with us — looking at the side-shows and dodging my sisters. We'd watch the crowds crabbing with long-handled scoop-nets from the end of the jetty, and quarrelling about who should have

142

first go at any crab as it swam sideways into the circle of light. We'd lean on the railings where the yachts tied up and watch the yachties canoodle with their girls, until we got roared at to buzz off or we'd get our bums kicked. We'd stand outside Cassey's dance-hall and watch the lairs in their grey melange Oxford bags doing the waltz and the slow foxtrot and the Boston Two-step, and we'd tell each other which girl *we'd* like to dance with. Sometimes we'd just sit on the beach and listen to someone in a crowd nearby playing a banjo or a mouth organ or a ukulele, and singing *Gundagai* and *Murray Moon* and *Long Long Trail*.

We didn't have watches, but you could tell when it was getting late by the *Merry Widow Waltz* from the hurdy-gurdy. As people went home and the noise of the crowd died down, it got louder, and when that happened we'd wander back to where my mother and Mrs Moodie were sitting.

At about nine o'clock Mrs Moodie would say: 'Well, Mrs Hungerford — time to G?' and everytime she said it I seemed to see a big capital 'G' hanging in the air above her head. We'd pack up the gear and fight our way onto a tram, and in half-an-hour we'd be home again and I'd be telling my father all that had happened during the day. He always had to stay home and mind the shop.

The Sunday after Ernie told me about heeling the ball it was the kind of summer day when as soon as you woke up you knew it was going to be a scorcher: dead calm with a sort of soft yellow shadow in the air, and the river still as a blue glass tray under the thinnest mother-of-pearl haze. I knew we'd be going to Como for sure, but perhaps not until after lunch: or if it turned out as hot as it looked like, probably not until after tea, when it had cooled down a bit.

I reckoned it would be better to go early with Ernie and pick up his golf-ball on the way. I had some bottle money to buy our lunch, and we didn't mind walking, anyway. We knew every cart track and vacant lot and bit of bush for short cuts, and in no time at all we could be on top of Forest Street hill looking down on the links and Como. There wasn't a house anywhere near the top of the hill, and you could stand there looking right down the river to the soft purple cloud where Fremantle was.

I went to the back door and sang out through the fly-wire: 'Mum! I'm going down Como early with Ernie!'

'Oh? You are, are you?' my mother said, from inside the house.

The way she said *are you* I knew exactly what she meant.

'I'm sorry, Mum. I mean, *can* I go early? With Ernie?'

'That's a bit better. Just mind your manners, young man, or I'll soon be taking tea with you. *And* Mr Ernie!' She would, too. She often gave friends of mine a clip under the ear if they annoyed her, and of course their parents did the same for me. 'And what are you going to do about lunch?'

'I've got enough bottle-money for some chips.'

'Then wait a minute.'

I thought: *Oh, Gawd! Wait a minute!* With my mother a minute could be anything up to half-an-hour. All the same it really wasn't much more than a minute — well, perhaps five, or ten — when she opened the door with a brown paper parcel in one hand and my fisher-hat in the other.

'Oh, *no*, Mum!' I said, when I saw the hat: but she took no notice of me.

'This'll fill the corners the chips don't reach', she said. She handed me the bag and pulled the hat down, hard, on my head. 'Wear that all day: *All day*, d'you hear? I don't want you coming home with sun-stroke — and remember what I told you about getting sunburned!'

She was always on about getting sunburned. The trouble was that during the summer we spent the whole weekend out in the sun, and on Mondays kids turned up to school absolutely calsomined with calomine lotion and all sorts of stuff, about as many different sorts as there were people to use them, I reckon — cold tea, olive-oil-and-lemon, milk, starch-water and all sorts of things people thought up. My mother used cold tea for a long time, but then someone told her about olive-oil-and-vinegar and she always kept a big bottle of it mixed ready in the bottom of the kitchen dresser.

I'd got myself badly burned the year before, one time when I was drop-netting for crabs from a boat out in the middle of the river. It was a dull, hot day, but you couldn't even see the sun, so I thought I had no chance of being burned and took my shirt off. My mother sat up by my bed half the night patting cold tea onto my back and my chest, but I still got enormous blisters that hung on me like flat bags of water. Then they burst and I peeled, and every time I'd take off my shirt there'd be a shower of skin all over the place. My father said it was like moths getting out of the government's purse, and seeing the light of day for the first time in years. My mother just made it known that it was the last time

144

she'd be sitting up half the night slopping cold tea on *anyone*, and the next time I lost half my hide she'd take the rest of it off with a strap.

It was bad enough for her to be always growling about sunburn, but what I really hated was the fisherman's hat. It was all right for little kids, but she didn't seem to realise I was nearly thirteen. In two years I'd be over fourteen, and all the boys down the jetty said that was when something very important happened to you. I asked my father what it was, and he told me it was when I would leave school and get a job, and as far as he was concerned that was just what the doctor ordered.

What made me even wilder about the hat, than having to wear it, was the way my mother took no notice whatever of me when I tried to explain this to her. She just went on as if I'd never opened my mouth.

Once we were outside our gate and across the road, and she wouldn't be able to hear me, I said to Ernie: 'Bloody silly hat! Doesn't she know I'm nearly *thirteen*? She thinks I'm still a little kid!'

'They're funny about things like that', Ernie said. 'D'you know what I reckon? I reckon they don't *want* you to grow up!'

'Then bloody to her! I'm *going* to grow up, and bloody to her!'

We were walking under one of the lillipillis by the side of the footpath, so I shinned up it and stuck my fisherman's hat in a crotch. I'd pick it up on the way home, or next day, or some time. When I got down again I opened the brown paper bag my mother had given me. There were two big double doorstep slices of bread and cheese, and two thick slices of shop cake and two apples and two Silver Sammies out of the penny-box in the shop.

I thought she must be the best piece maker in the world, and then I felt ashamed for saying bloody to her over the hat. I felt somehow as if I'd walked away from her and I'd never be able to turn around and go back, even if I wanted to, sometime. I don't really know how I felt, but I reckon it was *lonely*. Then I thought about the hat, and me being nearly fourteen, and I reckoned if that was what growing up was, there wasn't much you could do about it.

One of the first people Ernie and I met when we got down Como was a girl I hadn't known for very long. All our friends used to gather at the end of the jetty, and she was there with them. Her father had a station up Broome, and she'd come to Perth to go to school. She was staying with another station family down the

145

other end, the posh end, of South Perth, and she went to the same convent my sisters went to. That was how I'd met her.

I didn't like her very much. She was skinny and hard and brown, so that when you were playing in the water and you grabbed her it was really just like grabbing one of the boys. She never giggled and screeched like the other girls. She had funny green-coloured eyes and straight black hair cut in a bob at the back and in a razor-edge fringe across her forehead. Her lips were always rather red. I thought she must put something on them until I realised she wouldn't get away with anything like that at the convent: one of the boarders told me they weren't even allowed to use scented soap. She swore, and she could climb like a boy. She could swim almost as well as most of us, and the first day she joined in with us she swam further underwater than anyone I'd ever seen. She told us, afterward, when we were lying on the beach, she'd been taught by a Japanese pearl-diver up Broome.

One of the other girls lying close to me whispered to me: 'Chinky looking skite! Bet she's never even *been* to Broome!'

A moment later the new girl pointed to one of my mates and said: 'You're going to be my boy, Bunny!' It was something new to us. Nobody ever came out in the open and said *You're going to be my boy!* or *You're going to be my girl!* It seemed to put a sort of ring around her.

She and Bunny were real soppy about each other for a couple of weeks, but then she just dropped him and claimed another, and dropped him and claimed another, and so on until I was about the only boy who hadn't had a turn.

When she'd gone about half-way through the crowd she claimed a boy we called Bollocky Bill, and I made up a little bit of poetry about them, starting *Bollocky Bill the sailor bold sailed all the waters blue*, and how when he got back to port again he had this girl he'd met in Africa, and that was why she was so brown, and how although her name was Lily she wasn't much like one. I expected her to be ratty, or even to punch me, but the first time I met her after I passed it around the crowd she just started to cry.

I felt terrible about it. My sisters cried all the time, but that was something else. She looked so different when she cried. All of a sudden I couldn't imagine her swearing or fighting or climbing trees or playing around with Japanese pearl fishermen up Broome. It shook me up.

I was even more shaken up when I realised she was actually very pretty. I couldn't think how I'd ever thought anything else. Her skin looked a deep sort of gold colour rather than just dark, as I'd thought. And her hair seemed to have a lot of shining brown in it, and I liked the way it was cut across her forehead, like one of the dinky Japanese dolls my sisters had had when we were all little. And she wasn't hard and skinny, at all. I thought she looked a bit like a gum sapling, slender and smooth as if you could break it. Although I'd never have told anyone *that*.

We swam and skylarked all the afternoon with the crowd. We played underwater chasey and did cannonballs off the rails to splash the people in the yachts, and it seemed to me that all the time, without trying, I was always near the girl from Broome — chasing her and being chased by her, touching her and being touched by her, looking at her and catching her looking at me.

It really was a scorcher of a day, as it had threatened to be, and it seemed to get even worse after sundown. My mother and my sisters came down in the evening, and we were allowed to go in for a swim after tea — an hour after.

I knew before I put my foot on the land end of the jetty I'd meet her at the other end, in the red-roofed waiting-shed that always smelled of jelly-fish and seaweed and wet bathers.

We swam and dived and showed-off for a while in the circle of green-gold water under the lights. Then, without even telling each other what we were going to do, we paddled together into the darkness under the jetty.

It was all piles and beams, hard and sharp with barnacles. The noise of the people on the jetty over our heads seemed soft and hollow and far away. The water was so still and so black it seemed almost solid, and every prawn and crab and small fish dragged phosphorus fire behind it among the rocks and weed below us. We swept our hands around us in circles, so that every one of our fingers grew a long glittering feather of light. It was so strange, and so beautiful, I could hardly believe it. We whispered to each other: 'Look at *this* one! Look at *this* one!' As we swept our hands around us we touched each other on the shoulders and the back and the chest, and every time she touched me it felt as if the cold fire from her fingers really burned my skin.

After a while Ernie ducked under to join us, and he looked like a million falling stars in the dark water. I don't know how he knew where we were. I reckon he must have been watching us.

'Hey, Tommy!' he whispered. 'You mother wants you. They're going home!'

Straight away I thought about my hat, up the lillipilli tree all day. For the first time I could remember it didn't make me feel wild. Somehow I knew I'd worn it for the last time. All I had to do was to pick it up before my mother missed it.

As Ernie and I ran down the long jetty to the beach the first of the night's real coolness brought up goose-pimples on our burning skin. The Fremantle Doctor had come in, but very gently, and Ernie's teeth were chattering already. He didn't say anything until we were almost stepping onto the sand, and then he said, suspiciously: 'You been muckin' around with that tart a lot, today!'

I didn't say anything. I hadn't even said goodbye to the girl from Broome. I knew she'd be there, at the end of the jetty, next time I went down Como.

The Lady Who
Was Diddled By The Judge

All through my schooldays I had thought, in a vague sort of way, that 'when I grew up' I should become a writer. After all, it was the only thing I could ever do with any skill or satisfaction to my teachers, and from an early age a succession of them had assured me that it was obviously my bent. In later years one of them swore he would get me a job on the *West Australian*, but nothing ever came of it. The in-school careers counsellor was yet to arrive on the scene.

By sheer luck I *did* get a job on a newspaper, eventually, although on the second-stringer *Daily News* rather than on the *West*, and at the printing, rather than at the editorial, end of that long, narrow building on the Terrace, with its front door so conveniently close to the bars of the old Palace Hotel and its back entrance so conveniently close to those of the old Esplanade.

It wasn't my first job, however.

I had got my Junior, then still supposed to open all doors. When no doors opened by the time the new school year came around, I enrolled — just to keep my hand in until some prescient employer should recognise my potential — in the commercial course at the Perth Technical College. You can forget the book-keeping, as I did — I never really got it stuck in my head which side of the ledger was *credit* and which was *debit*. I had my eye on a job on a newspaper, and I knew I would need the shorthand and typing. After I'd been at the Tech for several months the call came — not from any newspaper, but from the Wellington Street address of Aladdin Industries, opposite the Metropolitan Markets.

I was one of five or six intelligent, healthy, eager adolescents weeded out by the headmaster to compete for the position. *I haven't got a chance*, we lied to each other, on the way over to the meeting. You'll *get the bloody job!*

Disposed about the storeroom among boxes and crates of Aladdin lamps and their spare parts and shades, we met the manager, who personally conducted the inquisition. He was a short, slight, nervous man with a very Scottish name and sandy red hair and moustache, and pale blue eyes rather too close for the comfort of anyone who might be going to work for him. He put us through a remarkable succession of written and oral tests, the extent of which might have suggested at least a partnership for the winner. I'm now certain he culled them from some little publication called *How to Sort Out your Office Boy*.

I got the nod. Eight-thirty to five-thirty weekdays with an hour for lunch. Eight-thirty to noon Saturdays. For overtime, no payment apart from one-shilling-and-sixpence for your tea. Twelve-and-sixpence-a-week. *Ten-bob for Mum and two-and-six for me!* I recall exulting. Oh . . . and bring your own bike. Annual holidays weren't discussed.

I lasted, I don't know, some months. It was a lump of time in which I was unhappier than I'd ever been before or, indeed, than I have been since.

Not that I suggest that I was the model office-boy but . . . it was a killingly boring, do-nothing, get-nothing routine job which every day, day after day, began with sweeping out the office in the morning and every day, day after day, ended at the tail-end of the afternoon with making up the orders — mostly from country customers — and trundling them over to the West Perth Station on my little hand trolley for despatch. As a bonus, I could see the row of brothels in Roe Street. In between morning broom and afternoon trolley there was nothing to do but to go on the occasional message down town, or over the road for lunches, or just to watch the clock edging *so slowly* around to knock-off time.

'Work and you'll get on in this job', the manager had assured us, when he was interviewing us. He pointed through the storeroom doorway to the outer office where a thick-set, black-haired Irish-as-Paddy's-Pig boy was industriously scratching something into an account book with his nose. *At his own desk!* it was pointed out to us. 'See that lad? Never late in the morning, never leaves until his desk's cleared. Never *looks* at the clock!' We regarded this phenomenon with whatever reverence we could muster. 'Been with us three-and-a-half years, and already he's getting a *man's wages!*' the manager went on. 'Only *nineteen!*'

At that time a man's wages would have been around four pounds a week, so it was quite a carrot to dangle in front of us. Soon enough, however, I was to find out — quite by chance, from seeing the wages book opened on the manager's secretary's desk, and looking into it — that the Irishman was in fact getting one pound a week. After three-and-a-half years, and for virtually running the daily conduct of the office, he was getting seven-and-sixpence a week more than I — and there didn't seem to be many reasons why I should expect that, in three years' time, I should be getting any more. In fact, since he was still only a boy, and so mightn't be expected to die overnight, and since he looked pretty satisfied with his job . . . where *would* I go from the broom and trolley?

I hadn't been in the job for very long when the traveller

dropped a bombshell on my prospects.

He was a breezy, self-confident young man who, like the manager, wore a very military-looking leather coat but who, unlike the manager, didn't ride a motorbike. He was a real trimmer, my immediate superior told me. Made as much as twelve pounds a week — which was senior bank-Johnny stuff, and more.

While the manager of Aladdin Industries had been studying how to con the office-boy, I'm certain this traveller had been studying how to build up a stable of happy, contented customers. He had a lot of literature on the subject, all of which came from some American address, and he gave me a few single-sheet pamphlets to read. One of them has stuck in my mind — a homely piece of States-side potted wisdom under a page-top illustration in mauve ink of an old man sitting on a rocking-chair on a front porch in some, doubtless Southern, town. It related how a young man came to a strange community, and asked this old rocker about the people he might expect to meet.

'What was they like where you come from Son?' the sage asked.

'Terrible. Mean. Backbiting. Never asked me to supper,' the stranger replied.

''Fraid that's what they'll be like here, Son', said the sage.

A second young man arrived and made the same inquiry — and in answer got the same question.

'Oh — great', he said. 'They were great. Everyone happy and helpful, and kind and hospitable. Always asking me to supper.'

'That's just how they are here, Son', said the sage.

With such advice behind him the traveller couldn't be anything but a roaring success. Because I made up the orders I knew that the bulk of his business was in the whistle-stops of the south-west of the State — fairly predictably, since it was there that electricity had not yet fully penetrated. One day when he came into the storeroom I asked him how he went about selling: he had brought me his leather coat to buff-up with boot polish, and he stood watching me for a while.

'You stop at the pub in town and ask where the best farms are', he said. 'You don't ask the manager. You ask the barman, and you dook him. You make sure you arrive at the farm just about night-fall. You set the lamp up in the kitchen and then you say you've got to go out and rearrange the boxes in your car. They can think about it while you're gone. Give 'em ten minutes, and then when you come back you say some thing like: "Gee — what a nice picture over the fireplace. I didn't notice it before, in the shadow." Make 'em think they've been living in a bloody cave. They're hooked. They just can't go back to the old kerosene job. They're falling over themselves to sign up. Never fails — usually they ask you to stay to tea too, and you pocket expenses for tea at the pub.'

Then he dropped his bombshell. 'You should get out of this dump,' he said, 'you'll never get anywhere here.' He nodded in the direction of the manager's office. 'I make three times what *he* does, and the way things are out there . . .', he nodded at the general office where the Irishman was head-down over his labours, '. . . you'll never get as far as his job, even. D'you know what he gets a week?'

'Yes,' I said, dismally, 'I looked in the wages book.'

'Well . . .'

I thought it over for a whole weekend. Broom-pusher, trolley-trundler and pie-and-sandwich boy for the rest of my life. On Sunday night, just before time for bed, I told my mother and father I didn't want to go back to work the next day. Or ever, at Aladdin Industries.

They had other ideas, of course. A job was a job was a job, and I'd be much better off to stay where I was, *being paid*, while I looked around for something else. And no matter how bad it was, it was better than *being on the street*. And there were lots of boys who'd give their back teeth to have *any job at all*, and here I was thinking of throwing one away.

It looked as if I'd have to take matters into my own hands, and I got my first opportunity very soon. The manager had seen what a good job of polishing I'd done on the traveller's coat, and brought his own to me for similar therapy. It was a nice nigger-brown, so I went over to the hardware store on the other side of the road and got a tin of black boot-polish. I started on the collar, and by the time he came out to the storeroom to see how I was going, I'd progressed half-way down one side of the front. I thought he'd have a fit.

'Black!' he raved. 'You're using *black!* You silly bugger, can't you see it's brown?'

'Brown?' I said. I looked searchingly at the coat. 'Looks like black to me.'

'Oh, *Jesus!*' he roared.

He seized the coat from me, spat on his handkerchief and began to scrub at the blackened area. After a while he stopped, and looked at me with such exasperation I thought he'd grab one of the Aladdin lamps off the shelf behind me and beat me with it. However, he pulled a two-shilling piece out of his pants pocket and handed it to me.

'Go over to the hardware and get a tin of *brown* boot-polish, and a bottle of methylated spirits.' I could see he was under some strain to keep his voice at a reasonable level. 'Come back here. Get some cotton waste from the store and clean that black polish off gently. Do you understand, *gently*? And then put on the *brown!*'

No mention of the bullet. And when later on I delivered his coat to him, a nice glossy brown all over, he was quite amiable . . . probably overjoyed at getting it back in one piece. I should have to start all over again.

My second, and as it turned out, my final chance came within days. I thought it would be better to strike while the iron was hot.

First thing in the morning of The Day, the manager told me to sweep out the display room and to fill and polish all the lamps on show there. He had arranged to meet a prospective big buyer, and he wanted everything to be — as he put it — *ticketty-boo*. I swept the room out and polished the lamps, but I didn't fasten the wick-and-chimney assembly by which, more often than not, they were picked up. I merely placed them on the fancy fuel bowl as if they had been screwed in securely.

Lurking in the doorway of the store-room, I saw the prospective big buyer arrive. The manager ushered him into the showroom, and in no time at all ushered him out again with kerosene splashed all down the front of his grey melange slacks with the sewn side-seams. Within minutes of the prospective buyer's departure down the stairs I had been haled into the manager's office, bitterly dressed-down, given an inkling of how I'd end up, and sacked.

'Pay him off!' he roared to the goggling Irishman. 'I can't *bear* to have him around the place for another *day*.'

It wasn't exactly the way I'd have preferred to end my first job, but maybe it's not too hubristic of me to believe that even then, as the prospective buyer was walking away down Wellington Street and the manager was fuming in his office, and I was clumping down the stairs with my last twelve-and-sixpence in my hand, the three sisters were conniving in their cave on my behalf. One of my Coode Street swimming friends was the son of the printer at the *Daily News*.

Within a week or two of the debacle at the lamp-shop he told me there was a job going at the paper, in the composing room, and that if I wanted it I should go in and see his Dad. He himself was still at college, and in any case the job paid only thirty-six shillings a week . . . *thirty-six-shillings a week!* A *pound* a week for Mum and *sixteen-shillings* for me! Take out my two-and-six for a weekly boat-ticket, and I would be *left* with more than I'd been earning at Aladdin Industries! And if I hadn't been out of work when the job came up he would never have thought about telling me, I should never have gone to work at the *Daily News*, and I should never have got to meet the lady who was diddled by the judge.

My new job turned out to be a revelation, the sort of thing I had never dreamed existed.

An enormous cavern at the river end of the *Daily News* building housed the stereo department, the composing floor and the battery of a dozen-or-so linotype machines, all under the one immense expanse of roof. Light flooded into it from a huge skylight above and tall windows all down the western wall. There was hardly any air at all – it was all the rich and heady smell of hot oil and printer's ink, and a miasma of melting type-metal – lead! – in the big stereo pot, the little stereo pot, and the small pots attached to every lino. At times it got rather difficult to breathe, but nobody seemed to die of lead-poisoning.

In this secluded world I arrived early every morning to light the linotype pots and to clean the spacebands with graphite and generally to prepare for the advent of those princes and potentates of the printing world, the linotype operators. At that early hour the huge room was always cool, no matter how hot the summer, and always warm, no matter how cold the winter. The wooden floors, swept clean on the previous afternoon, gleamed dully with the shine imparted by years of scuffing from slugs and metal shavings.

The solid steel benches were cold to the touch, the pages from yesterday's paper lined up on them in their formes for distribution – the leads saved, the handset type 'dissed' into their respective fonts, the bulk of the slugs consigned to the stereo pot for reincarnation in new news-stories, new articles, new advertisements. At the far end – my end – of the room the four rows of linos waited impatiently to begin their daylong frenetic clatter: you could almost feel their impatience to get going. At the other end the big, solid, stolid stereo plant stood around like circus animals waiting to be put through their routines.

Every day my working hours passed in a constant barrage of consultation, panic, insult, dirty jokes, practical jokes, acrimony, horseplay and profanity — the last of a virtuosity which made me wonder somewhat when I first heard word of 'Chapel meetings' and the 'Father of the Chapel' — although soon enough I found out the terms were a hangover from the day when most printing had been done in monasteries.

That dragonfly interweaving movement of thirty-odd men going about the controlled chaos of daily producing a paper from *go* to *whoa* reached an almost unbearable pitch just before edition time. Then, when the front page got away to the stereo, it collapsed in moments. The huge room cleared of men and movement, the chatter of the linotypes gave way to the subterranean rumble of the presses down there in the basement. Before you'd cleaned up and changed into your street clothes everything but the presses had gone back to sleep until next morning, and to walk through the composing room was almost like walking through a church.

At Aladdin Industries I had been bored stiff. At the *Daily News* I found myself embroiled, in no matter how lowly a capacity, in a daily circus, battle, sporting event and thimble-and-pea game. The challenge of it was that you never knew what the next hour might throw at you. The beauty of it was that whatever *was* thrown rarely survived the day of the throwing: you hardly ever took your worries home with you.

At Aladdin Industries I had rarely seen the manager, and to his secretary rarely said more than *Good morning* and *Good afternoon* and *Do you want a pie or sandwiches?* With the Irishman I hardly ever exchanged more than half-a-dozen words a day. He always had his head down earning his pound a week, and if he spoke to me at all, apart from business, it was usually to impress on me what a humdinger the boss was and what a ripper the traveller was. At the *Daily News* I found myself pitchforked into a bunch of men like nobody I'd ever met before. I don't know whether a newspaper attracts individuals or creates them, but practically every man in the three departments under that one roof — and of course those of the editorial staff who breezed in and out — was someone out of the bag, as individual as Ayers Rock and not to be confused with anyone else on earth.

For me, I suppose because I worked most closely with them, the lino operators were the core of the maelstrom — noisy, demanding, knowledgeable, pugnacious, generous, wild as willy-willies. They in turn whirled around Jimmy Ward, the head lino mechanic, who probably was the most remarkable character of all.

He was also the ex-husband, and at least part present support, of the lady who, according to him, was diddled by the judge.

It's already more than thirty years since I last saw Jimmy — since by chance I met him in Collins Street in Melbourne, and by intent spent the next couple of hours in the bar of the Federal Hotel buying him some of the beer I could never afford to shout him when I was his 'boy' in the linotype department at the *Daily News*. I've rarely thought of him since then, but everything about him is as indelibly stamped on my memory as the tattoo on a sailor's arm. Jiminy Cricket jumps into my mind when I search for a comparison — small, angular, sharp-as-a-tack, jerky, noisy and profane. Add vindictive, kind, maudlin, treacherous, secretive and fairly chronically dedicated to the drink, and you've got a good working mud-map of my old boss.

He might have been a well-preserved seventy-five or a very battered fifty-five — nobody knew for sure. He was perhaps five-feet-five in height and he probably weighed eight stone. Considering the first impression he made, of being leather-and-whalebone, he was surprisingly plump, and his skin beneath his clothes was fine and white. His whole, wizened little marmoset face seemed to implode from the periphery of large ears, grizzly hairline and modest chin to the nose and mouth assembly in the middle. His eyes, peat brown in colour, each had a penumbra of milky-white about the iris. *I'm a Spaniard!* he'd proclaim, jigging about like a jumping-jack, usually toward the end of the boozy Saturday afternoon shift. *I'll show the bastards! You watch me! I come from Spain, where the corridors are!*

Maybe he did have some Spanish blood. His scanty hair must have been jet black in its heyday, and a fine, hooked Iberian nose with flaring nostrils overhung his endlessly champing, toothless gums. Summer and winter he wore the same heavy blue serge pants, never cleaned or pressed. *Only pair I got!* he'd mourn. *I'd have a bloody suit if it wasn't for that old harlot up the Courts!* — an allusion I wasn't to understand for a long time. He never wore anything but a striped, collarless shirt fastened at the throat with a bone stud. He kept his black alpaca jacket until it virtually fell apart, and when once a year he came in wearing a new coat he'd say bitterly it was the cheapest he could get — *and from the Jews, too!* — and that if it wasn't for his bloody old prostitute he'd be able to afford much better.

For as long as I knew him he wore the same mangy old homburg-style hat in heavy greeny-black velour, brim turned up all round. His black shoes pointed skyward at the toes like Persian slippers, and were total strangers to polish. He wore black woollen socks which probably were changed now and then.

None of this mattered, however, in the *Daily News* context. He was a genius with machinery of any kind, and I believe he performed miracles in keeping the linotypes operating at a time when for any Perth company the decision to spend more than a pound on plant — other than the directors' grog cupboard — was a matter for very long consideration.

I hadn't been working with Jimmy for very long when I began to suspect that he could look straight through steel to see what was happening in any part of the fiendishly complicated but beautifully logical mechanism of a linotype. It might well have been, too, that the machinery spoke to him. He would stand with his fingers resting lightly on a bearing, his head cocked on one side like a magpie listening for a worm, his lips folding in and out over his gums like an anemone testing the water around its retreat. He would put up a finger to enjoin me to silence, and say: 'Let's hear what it's got to tell us!' After a while he would nod his head as if in understanding of what he had heard, and then would move straight in on the seat of the trouble.

He certainly *knew*, as he proclaimed loudly ten times a day, but he never voluntarily imparted any of his knowledge. This made it difficult for his assistant to learn anything but the run-of-the-mill stuff which went on around us all day and every day. I would stand watching like a hawk as he, with never a word of explanation or instruction, worked on some more esoteric breakdown or adjustment. When he got to the nitty-gritty he'd say: 'Duck down to the store-room and bring me a three-eighths drill', and when I got back the whole job would be sewn up. There was only one way to find out anything from Jimmy, apart from the routine work you picked up for yourself just by watching the machines: and later on I was put onto it by one of the operators. In the meantime, Jimmy watched me as hard as I watched him, and when he judged that I'd fathomed out some point or other, he'd make a great song-and-dance about showing me how.

'You stick with *me!*' he'd say. '*I'll* teach you. I *know*. Those other bastards don't know *nothing!*'

Before long I found out that *those other bastards* meant specifically Mr Stanley Reid, the head lino mechanic at the *West Australian* — a *bloody pretender*, if Jimmy were to be believed, a know-nothing, do-nothing impostor who couldn't fix a sewing

158

machine. One about whom Jimmy could run rings with his hands tied behind his back, blindfolded. Stan Reid nevertheless managed somehow to keep in perfect running order a battery of linos about twice the size of Jimmy's, and it was through him, in a roundabout way, prompted by the operator, that I discovered how to tap Jimmy's fount of knowledge.

'You'll never learn anything off Jimmy that way', this operator said to me one day. He had been watching me watching Jimmy hide behind his widespread arms some adjustment he was making to the mouthpiece of a pot.

'Then . . . how?' I demanded, in desperation.

'Just tell him what Stan Reid says.'

'I don't *know* what Stan Reid says. I never *see* Stan Reid.'

'That doesn't bloody matter. Just say Stan Reid says so-and-so, and you'll be in like Flynn.'

It worked like a charm, the very first time I tried it. I had been having trouble with the spacebands on one of the machines, and couldn't work out what was going wrong, so I said to Jimmy: 'Stan Reid reckons when the doover hits the doofunny on the spaceband release the dooflunkus should do so-and-so.'

'Bullshit,' Jimmy said, immediately, 'bloody Stan Reid don't know. He's a bloody Jew.' Jews were one of his pet hates. He used to torment the life out of one of the operators, who qualified simply because his name was Obanski. 'He's a Jew, and he don't *know*.'

'Just the same,' I persisted. 'Stan Reid says . . .'

'Stan Reid be buggered,' Jimmy interrupted, '*I'll* show you how the space band works. I *know!*' And forthwith he took me to the nearest unoccupied machine and showed me exactly what I wanted to be shown.

I didn't employ the dodge very often. As another of the operators maintained, my boss was 'as cunning as a shithouse rat', and probably he would have tumbled before very long. Later on I used to take him over to the Palace after work to lubricate the process of learning. It was costly, because Jimmy was famed for his hollow legs: but it was worth it.

That was all still in the future, however, when in my second or third week as the lino 'boy' at the *Daily News* I at last got to meet the lady who was being diddled by the judge . . . Jimmy's ex-wife, whom he was still supporting at the behest of the Courts. I had already met another lady whom I'd mistaken to be his missus. She was a pleasant, softly-spoken Scottish lady whose lovely red-gold

Boticelli-Venus hair had won the nickname of 'Ginger Em' among the printing staff at the *News*.

She used to come in some Friday afternoons, maybe when there was a crisis in their budget, just to see to it that at least part of Jimmy's pay made it safely past the beckoning doors of the Palace bar. One day I was standing with him when she poked her flaming head around the door of the composing room, looking for him. *Look at the poor bitch!* he said, sourly. *Same bloody dress for three years. An' that old prostitute up the Courts gets around like a bloody peacock!*

Jimmy and Ginger Em lived in a little crib over an empty shop in West Perth, although not in the toffs' part: closer to Roe Street than to King's Park Road. It was something else he blamed on his ex-wife, who had half a house to herself *while me and Emmie live in a shithouse!* Despite Ginger Em's self-effacing manner she must have been something of a character herself, because for a time the staple of Jimmy's complaints at work was the baby kangaroo someone had given her. *Brings it into bed with us to keep it warm!* he would roar. *Dirty little bugger pisses all over me!*

They had also a huge sort-of-labrador bitch on whom, he told me, he had performed what to me seemed to be a very unusual kind of birth-control. I had been complaining about our own cocker bitch's being in heat in a street where everyone had a dog and every dog had got to know about it — as they always did.

'Put the poker in the kitchen stove until it gets red-hot, and then just to-o-o-uch her on the fanny with it', he advised me. 'I done it to our bitch years ago. Never looked sideways at a dog since!'

I wasn't left in the dark long about Ginger Em's status. Les, the 'boy' I'd shunted further up the ladder by joining the staff, told me all about it when he warned me that one of the jobs I should inherit from him was to take Jimmy's maintenance over to the Court every Monday afternoon.

'Oh,' I said, 'isn't Em his wife?'

'Gawd, no!' Les said. 'Wait 'til you see his real missus. A bloody bottler. Jimmy reckons she's on the batter!'

On the following Monday afternoon, after lunch, Jimmy beckoned me into a corner behind Louis Obanski's machine. Under the rattle of the matts and the clank of cams he pulled my head down to his level, looking around suspiciously to make certain we weren't being overheard.

'Want you to go up to the Court for me!'

160

'Okay, Jimmy,' I said, 'I'll just wash my hands.'

'No, not now!' He was jigging around like water on a hot stove, agitated and venomous. 'I'll tell you when!'

It was my introduction to a weekly routine as stylised as cake-icing: always the secret beckoning from behind Louis Obanski's machine, always the secrecy, always the delay in parting with the treasure. I never discovered the need for the secrecy, since before long I was to learn that everyone in that huge room knew exactly why I was going out. In fact, every Monday one or another of them would come up to me and say: *When you take Jimmy's dough over to the Court, get me a packet of Three-threes, will you?* or *Going over to see Jimmy's old crow? Okay — drop this watch off at Mazzucchelli's on the way, eh?*

I certainly didn't mind taking a break away from the grind any afternoon. It was particularly welcome in summer when the temperature in the composing room at mid-afternoon might climb as high as the century, and over, and the air became thick with the fumes from the pots.

I got a particularly horrible dose from my Thompson type-casting machine, an archaic contraption of old iron resurrected from somewhere a couple of years after I joined the staff and put in my care. Between us, the old Thompson and I produced all the handset type, the rules and the leads used in making up the pages — with no addition to my pay, of course: it was just added to my work on the linos. It was a cranky, temperamental veteran, with very good ideas as to just when it should start and stop. One false move on my part and it would fracture the arm controlling the plunger which expressed the molten metal into the mould. Before long I developed the hearing of a bat in locating and recognising the litany of knocks and creaks and wheezes that presaged disaster, but I couldn't always head them off. Sometimes the old Thompson would run for days without the slightest tremor, lulling me into a lovely sense of security. At others it wouldn't run at all for days, for reasons which nobody, including Jimmy, could locate. Some mornings it would begin casting the moment I pulled out the starting lever. At others I could set it up twenty times without any luck and then, for no reason that I could unearth, it would begin serenely on the twenty-first. It was a venomous little brute, and I still have on my forearms, and in one spot on the left-hand side of my belly, the scars of molten metal it squirted me with at various times. I got far more wounds from the old Thompson than ever I got from the war.

161

On maintenance Mondays, when Jimmy could no longer put off the dreadful moment of handing over the three-pounds-ten, he would beckon me again from behind Louis Obanski's machine. When I had joined him he would very reluctantly drag the money out of his pants pocket. It was mummified in the coils of an elastic band he had wound round and round it, and as he unfolded it every one of his fingers seemed individually to balk at this last parting. Shuffling and blinking and cursing, he would count it carefully, all four of those precious notes, twitching each one between forefinger and thumb just in case, by some miracle, one of them might have divided into two. Finally he rewound it in the elastic band and handed it to me.

'Take this up to that old prostitute of mine', he said, every Monday. 'Bein' diddled by the judge. You knew that, didn't you?' I didn't at first, but before long it was sufficiently impressed upon me. My only mental picture of a judge was the conventional one, so that every Monday when Jimmy was on about his ex-wife being diddled by one, it presented me with the same vision: of a curly grey wig jigging around on a bedpost while its owner thrashed around on the mattress in his long black robe.

'Bloody old hooer,' Jimmy said, 'I'd have dough in the bank if it wasn't for her!'

Poor old Jimmy. What he sent up to the Court every week was more than half his *Daily News* pay, and he was always chasing his tail to make up the shortfall to keep his West Perth home going. And, of course, his thirst.

He made some money on 'foreigners' — small jobs of fitting and turning he brought in to do on the shop lathe, in shop time, and as far as he could manage, with shop materials. He was always getting cries for help from little one-lino shops around Perth, where the economics didn't warrant maintaining a full-time mechanic, and during his annual holidays he often took jobs in the larger country towns. He came back looking better than he ever did during the year, but he'd say: *Orright for you buggers — you can take your holidays. I got to work mine. I got to keep that old harlot up the Court!*

Also he had his watchmaking connection — although I don't think he ever trapped the same customer twice. It was not that he wasn't an expert watchmaker — watches were machinery, and machinery of any kind was Jimmy's meat. It was just that whenever he got his hands on a watch — *so the Daily News said* — it went into hock until some windfall, or another job, permitted him to spring it, fix it, and return it to its anxious owner. Later on he devised the plan of biting me for a pound or ten-shillings on Monday or Tuesday, repaying it meticulously as soon as he got his pay on Friday, and then putting the hips in again on the following Monday: so that in effect he added to his own income by siphoning off mine.

Still, with all his lurks and dodges I suspect that things must have been pretty difficult at times for him and Ginger Em, the dog and the kangaroo.

As I walked away from him with his precious three-pounds-ten, he would whisper after me, hoarsely: 'Have a good look at the old prostitute. When you come back, tell me how she looks. Don't forget!'

On my first visit to the Court I didn't see the lady who was being diddled by the judge. There was nobody at all sitting on the long, polished bench of hard jarrah against the wall.

'For Mrs Ward', I said to the clerk, as I pushed the notes across the counter. 'Where is she?'

'Don't show up every Monday,' he said, 'maybe tomorrow, Wednesday, before she comes in. Depends.'

'Can't be too hard up?'

'Why should she be? Wish I had some silly bastard slipping *me* three quid a week for naught.'

'Naught!' I scoffed. 'She's on with the judge. Maybe the Clerk of Court, too.'

'Wouldn't go around saying that too loud if I was you', he said, looking about him nervously.

When I got back to the *News*, Jimmy and I retired behind Louis Obanski's machine. I handed him his receipt.

'Bloody old prostitute', he said, morosely, when I told him she hadn't turned up. 'Off somewhere, bein' diddled by someone.'

She was there the following week, and on nearly every Monday during the couple of years when I was Jimmy's courier. She was small and plump and dark, with the vivid colouring — helped along a little, even I could see that — which pointed to some possible Dago ancestry: even, perhaps, to origins somewhere in the land of the 'corridors', like Jimmy's.

She wore a pretty brown straw hat, very feminine, with a big rose of deep yellow velvet. Over the years I was to see it replaced seasonally with bows and ribbons and little bunches of artificial flowers, but always the same hat. From under the brim her dark brown hair looped artistically over her forehead and ears, and from under the loops her cheeky brown eyes twinkled with what might have been the joy of living, or anticipation of getting her pudgy little hands on Jimmy's three-pounds-ten, or mischief or malice. It was hard to tell. She had an indiscriminate nose, very discriminately powdered, and rather thin lips, lipstick red, under the ghost of a moustache. Below her lips there was a soft chin, and below the chin she had arranged three rolls of soft pastry liberally dusted with flour. Below those there were two much larger buns, the division between which could just be seen above the neckline of her flowery frock. I think I never saw her dressed in anything that wasn't floral in pattern, in winter beneath a topcoat of heavy brown material with a good collar of something that certainly was not the ubiquitous rabbit of those days, in summer under a light coat of black marocain exactly the same as the one my own mother wore. Between her and the hard jarrah bench she sat on there were two more, much larger buns, which stretched the material of her dress as wrinkleless as a starched dinner-shirt. Her legs were short and plump, and her silk stockings ended in neat feet in good shoes with what my mother called 'sensible' heels.

From the moment I saw her I fell a little in love with her. I knew that if I were to get close enough to her she would smell of 4711 Eau de Cologne and the very same pale pink *poudre de riz* my mother clouded the house with every time she went to town. She was in fact a very nice looking, ordinary lady who, I decided, probably didn't even *know* any judges. And yet . . . there was something about her. It was as if, as she sat there on that hard jarrah bench, against the green wall of that Government office, there hovered somewhere behind her a frieze of merry-go-round horses, rolling their eyes and tossing their wild manes to the music of the Merry Widow Waltz.

After a few visits we began to exchange guarded smiles of greeting. Hers never went beyond a lifting of the corners of those gently reddened lips and a crinkling at the corners of those twinkling prune-seed eyes. Still, as I leaned against the counter watching the clerk filling out Jimmy's receipt for the three-pounds-ten, I could feel her eyes on my back in a way that made me twitch. As I walked out they slid around to follow me. It was as if she were measuring me up against someone else. The judge? Of course not! I could never even think of her carrying on in the way Jimmy maintained she did. Not that comfortable, smiling, nicely-dressed, plump lady who — drop a year or two and a pound or ten — might have passed for my own mother. And in any case, she was too old: I was at the age when you believe that nobody beyond the advanced age of forty could be capable of sex.

In time another boy joined the lino staff, and just as Leslie had done before me, I handed over my courier run to him. One Monday when he was not at work I made another visit, my last, to the Court with Jimmy's three-pounds-ten.

The lady was there, and as soon as she saw me she smiled with an instant twinkle of recognition in her brown eyes. As I propped against the counter I was more than ever conscious of them boring into my back. When I turned around to go she broadened her smile and for the first time revealed her teeth.

I got the shock of my life. They were small and sharp like a dog's, and their appearance changed entirely the expression of her face. What had looked merry and mischievous became plain malicious, and what had looked like a smile became a sneer. The frieze of merry-go-round horses in their gay and shining paint became prancing goats. For the first time she looked to me like someone who would enjoy being diddled by the judge — and I think something of what was going through my mind must have shown on my own face.

I know I blushed. She laughed outright, and as I passed her she leaned forward.

'How is my dear old Jimmy?' she asked, and her voice was rough as bags. I had got to the doorway, but it pursued me into the corridor. 'Give the old darling my love!'

As I clattered along the shining brown Government linoleum toward the outer door in Beaufort Street — a mile from the brothels I used to inspect so avidly when I was dragging my load of Aladdin lamps up onto the West Perth station — I heard her laugh. And what was worse, I heard that clerk join in with her. I don't think I have ever felt more humiliated. Laughing at me, that old bitch with her dog's teeth! And that silly fat-arsed clerk, laughing with her! Probably had been laughing with her as long as I'd been going up to the Court for Jimmy. I burned all the way back to the *Daily News*. And it wasn't for myself only. I kept on thinking about poor old Ginger Em, who was so soft with the kangaroo, coming in to the *News* on Fridays to get a bit of what was left after Jimmy had put aside the three-pounds-ten for the maintenance.

'Was she there?' Jimmy demanded, when I handed him his receipt. 'How did the old hooer look?'

He had asked me the same question every Monday since my

first return from the court — every time, I'm certain, in the hope of hearing me say: *She died yesterday, Jim*, or *Bloody crook!*

Because I knew what he wanted me to say, but in part because I'd been primed by the operators, who loved to tease him, I used to send him up the wall.

'Great, Jim!' I'd say. Or: 'Had a nice new hat on, Jim. Must have cost her *quids!*' He climbed even further when I did a little embroidery. 'Had a real well-dressed bloke with her, Jim. Would that be the judge?'

Not this time, however. I'd teach her!

'Terrible, Jim! Face all sunken in, thin as a rail!' I almost convinced myself I was telling the truth. That old bitch, with her big fat arse and her dog's teeth! Laugh at me! 'You won't be paying out for her much longer. Couldn't hardly drag herself up to the counter to pick up the dough!'

Jimmy stood there staring at me, his receipt in his hand, the matts clacking down into the magazine on Louis Obanski's machine, just above his head. I think he believed me, but I don't think he could take it in. It was as though the town had been relieved after everyone in it had died of starvation. I began to feel a bit of a shit for having him on.

'The bloody old hooer,' he said, eventually, 'the bloody old prostitute. If it wasn't for her I'd have dough in the bank!'

For the first time I had the feeling he was saying it because it was what he always said. That he wasn't really looking forward to a future when there'd be nobody but Ginger Em and the dog and the kangaroo. When he couldn't be able to blame everything on the lady who was being diddled by the judge.

Professor Murdoch
And The Old White Road

It was the afternoon of my day off. I sat at the table in our kitchen staring at the sheet of paper in front of me, wondering what I should write on it. I was at that age — about seventeen will do — and at that stage of my flirtation with writing, when no virgin page I encountered had much chance of remaining virgin.

I had been working for about a year in the linotype department at the *Daily News* in Perth, and had fallen easily into the routine of work all day Saturdays with one mid-week day off every two weeks. I'd done the lawns and edges and had cleaned out the old wood-burning copper for my mother. It was a warm day, but cool in the quiet, sweet-smelling house, which she had 'done' from front to back before she went out to do her shopping.

I was still hooked on the poetry which I — like most young writers — had become embroiled with very early on. I can still remember my first effort, done when I was about eight. I used to spend a lot of time with my nose in my father's big atlas, looking for words to make my skin tingle — Nijninovgorod, the Kalahari Desert, the Coromandel Coast, Barbados, Samarkand, the Sea of Azov. This time I'd come across the Friendly Isles.

Friendly? Islands?

I asked my father why, and he told me it was because when the first white travellers had landed there, the ladies had been so neighbourly: looking sideways at my mother.

'What about the fathers, then? Weren't they, too?'

'Crikey, no', said my lying Irish father. 'They'd jolly soon have you in a pot to cook you up with potatoes!'

'*Now*, Arthur!' my mother chided him, and I knew it was a story.

I asked the nun who was my teacher then, at the convent, and told her what my father had told me. She ignored completely the intelligence about the ladies, but assured me that the natives really were friendly. They no longer ate visitors. The missionaries had worked miracles. The Friendly Islanders wore clothes now, and sang hymns, and loved Jesus. *As you do, don't you?* At the time I was still able to gabble, without lying: 'Oh, yes, Sister! I do! I do!'

In the way of things, it all had quite an effect on me. I assembled for myself a very clear picture of a little island in a vivid blue sea, with palm trees, as in the illustrations to one of my story-books, and a white beach as at Como, where we went swimming, and black people putting wood on a fire under my mother's big iron preserving-pan. And having assembled it, I sat down one day and wrote my first poem. I have never forgotten it, and think that I never shall.

> There was a man from the Friendly Isles,
> He was full of frowns, very seldom smiles.
> He was by the natives got
> And put into a cooking pot
> Where he found it very hot.
> So he hopped out and ran for miles.

I showed it to Sister Gervase, who smiled and patted my head. My father roared at it. My mother studied it briefly and snorted. 'Go and see if there's any eggs in the nests!' she said. 'Wasting your time with that rubbish.'

Things improved, of course. I wrote more and more poems, and longer and longer ones, and in time transcribed them from their random bits of paper into a half-used autograph album discarded by one of my sisters. I called it my 'poetry book', and had some vague sort of idea that when I'd filled it I'd get it published. Anyone who's been bitten will readily recognise the symptoms of the disease.

Not long before the day when I sat at the kitchen table staring at that sheet of paper, my mother had brought home a new rose for the garden. It was called *Nigrette* — a beautiful dark red bloom with the dusky blue tinge you see on some negroes.

Nigrette. For some reason or other it fascinated me, set me alight. A *lambent* word, I thought. Lambent was very big with me just then. *Nigrette*, I wrote on another virgin sheet. *I feel your kisses yet, Nigrette* / (Kisses were, too!) *Your lambent eyes of darkest jet* / *the night they stained my pillow wet.* / *I know that I will ne'er forget,* / *Nigrette!* and kept it up for six or eight stanzas with only "ette" rhymes: regret, cigarette, abet, se*cret*, your cunning net, I've paid my debt, and so on.

I liked it, and transcribed it into my permanent collection. It wasn't until some time later that I noticed what had been written on the facing page, in the lovely, round, plump and curly hand of mother's lovely, round, plump and curly friend Mrs Moodie:

> A wise old owl lived in an oak.
> The more he heard the less he spoke.
> The less he spoke the more he heard —
> Why can't *you* be like that wise old bird?

Carefully, I printed across the top of my new virgin sheet the title of my new poem. THE OLD WHITE ROAD. I'd got so far, and as always I felt quite confident that the rest would follow. After all, 'Nigrette' had started out as just a word, the name of a rose — and look what had happened.

In this instance, however, I had far more than only a word to go on, and what I had to go on had been bumping around in my head all morning. On the previous evening, I'd been out along the old white road in question.

We often went out there on summer nights, boys and girls, on our bikes. One carried the billy with the tea and sugar and milk packed in it. One brought the sausages and the potatoes for cooking in the coals, someone else the crabbing nets, someone else the sugar-bags to carry the crabs home in. We gathered at our place after tea, bikes leaning against the front fence while the provisions were being assembled, and as we began to pedal away someone always sang out: *Has anybody thought of matches?* Believe it or not, none of us smoked.

We Indian-filed along Canning Highway, crossed Canning Bridge, turned left and bumped along the old white road, every now and then hidden from each other in the dense shadows of the overhanging paperbarks.

We always made for the same spot — a natural clearing grassed with couch about a mile or so in from the highway. It was close to the water, surrounded by bush, not a house within cooee in any direction. Once there we piled our bikes and separated ('Look out! I've brought me torch!') to different sides of the clearing to change into our bathers.

Some stayed ashore to light the fire and cook the potatoes and sausages. The rest went crabbing, and after an hour or so wading hip-deep up and down the shoreline, returned with as many as we would be able to carry home on our bikes. Sometimes we carted a kerosene tin with us and cooked a couple of dozen in river-water, and ate them hot: *Very bad for your digestion!* my mother said. Of course.

The feast over, we'd sit around the dying fire for a while, singing songs, telling yarns, gossiping, arranging future outings, sneaking a few cuddles — until at about half-past-nine somebody would say: 'Well . . . getting late!' or 'Bloody work tomorrow!' It was the trigger. We'd pack up the gear, portion out the cooked crabs for easy carrying in our sugar bags, and pedal off homeward.

I don't know whether the old white road had a name — if people then called it what they call it now. Somehow *The Esplanade* seems a bit pretentious for that lovely, winding strip of pearly white coaxed out of the crushed limestone and oyster shells by the moons of those softly-beating summer nights I think I remember.

It was so still. Motor traffic was then no more than the echo of somebody else's coughing in another part of the hospital, and houses hadn't yet come to obliterate the bush on the heights overlooking the Canning River. The little bays the roadway skirted between the bridge and Mount Pleasant had forgotten the long-ago invasion by Roads Board men in grey flannel singlets and bowyangs, and huge Roads Board draught-horses between the shafts of lumbering Roads Board drays. The paperbarks and ti-tree and gums had come back to dump their shadows on the crushed shell, and the water-rats had come back to the dense mat of rushes between roadway and shoreline. On those nights it seemed that in the whole wide, dark world there was only us — and the professional fishermen ghosting along through the dark-brown shadows just off-shore, soft rattle of rowlocks and thump-and-splash of nets played out behind to harvest the fat mullet feeding in the shallows.

It wasn't about fishermen and water-rats that I was thinking, however, as I sat at our kitchen table staring at the title of my new poem.

On the previous evening I'd been pitchforked, almost without trying, into the culmination of a sort of plan I'd been nudging around for a while, tentatively, in regard to a very pretty girl who had come to live nearby. She was what we were learning to refer to as a real eyeful, plump little figure, brown hair and brown skin and very cheeky brown eyes ('Come to bed eyes!' we told each other, hopefully) and the sort of laugh that touched every knuckle in your spine. She had joined our tennis parties, and then our crabbing parties, and before long she was much a part of our social scene as our bikes. And she got tangled up in my thoughts in a way I couldn't recall having happened before.

We had already been wised-up about the joys of sex by the first among us to experience it. He was the one who, several years before, had come from the other side of the river to live in our street, and promptly had set about putting us right on a number of things. I suppose we more-or-less expected he'd be the first to crack it for a stuff, as he put it.

'What's it like?' someone asked him, breathlessly.

'Well . . .' He considered it for a moment, obviously trying to sort it out for himself: and then, eventually, 'it sort of . . . makes you want to stretch your legs.'

It hadn't seemed very exciting to me at the time, but that didn't stop me from listening quite attentively to the advice passed around so freely every lunchtime at work, where it shared the bill with horse-racing. No sooner had the last mouthful of sandwich, pie or sausage-roll been disposed of than someone threw the conversational ball onto the table, and it bounced along most happily until it was time to go back to work. One of the stone-hands from the composing-room had what he advanced as an infallible technique: he worked it in every day, and it always got a laugh.

'One way you'll never miss', he used to advise. 'Just put it in her hand and say, "Here, Mary — hold this 'til I call a cop!" In like Flynn!'

That is exactly what I'd done the night before.

While everyone else was still sitting around the fire, yarning and singing, I'd edged the real eyeful into the shadows of the ti-tree scrub. I'd teetered around on the edge for a while, and then had done what Charlie Tory had so often advised: although of course I didn't say a word about holding anything until I'd called a cop. She nearly shot up into the paperbarks, and I nearly followed her.

It was enough to make you sit in the kitchen staring at that virgin sheet of paper, and more than enough to want to write a poem about that lovely spot down by the Canning River.

But how to proceed?

I closed my eyes the better to see, but the only images which materialised were of the soft, luminous white of the road and the deep velvety brown of the shadows, and the shining path the moon had laid between our little clearing on the Mount Pleasant side of the river and the black, bush-covered cliff of Mount Henry on the other: so hard and bright you felt you could have walked to the other bank on it, dry shod.

At that point my mother walked in, home from her shopping, and planked her basket on the table beside me.

'What're you doing inside the house?' she demanded. She had a way of shattering poetic contemplation. 'It's a beautiful day outside. I'm dying for a cup of tea. Do you want one?'

'Yes, please, Mum.'

'And then get outside, and *do* something! *Sitting inside!*' She dropped an envelope on the table beside her basket. 'For you — are you too damn tired to look in the box?' She filled the kettle, put it on the stove, lit the gas under it, and turned to me. 'What is

Professor Murdoch writing to you for?'

I hadn't even noticed that the envelope had been opened, but it didn't surprise me — didn't even worry me. I didn't get many letters, and what I did get were harmless notes from uncles and aunts, or friends on holidays somewhere outside Perth: in those days Rockingham was sufficiently far afield to warrant one. I'd bucked about it once, but I'd got short shrift. *While you're in this house, me lord, I'm going to know what you're up to!*

'Dad doesn't', I ventured.

'*Dad's dad!*'

I should have known better than to have broached the matter in the first place.

'I wrote to him and asked him if he'd advise me about my writing.'

'You've got a hide! What's he say?'

'He's asked me to go up to his place next Wednesday, after tea.'

'Then make sure you clean your shoes', said my mother.

For some time I'd been wondering if what I was writing was good or bad, if I should persevere or give it up. I wanted someone to advise me, and Professor Murdoch's name occurred to me because he had written the foreword to the poetry book — *The Poet's Commonwealth* — which had been set for my Junior year: by examination time we had to be able to relate poem and poet to any line selected at random from among the thousands between its dark-blue covers, and while it was probably a splendid training for the memory, I still doubt if it really could have been the best way of instilling a love of the subject in the young.

I was looking for advice, and Professor Walter Murdoch of the Department of English at the University of Western Australia looked like a good source of it. It didn't occur to me to wonder — I was only seventeen, after all — that with so much on his own plate that busy man should have undertaken to help me clean up my own. He lived not very far away, nicely balanced between 'our end' and 'the other end', just at the turn of the road where the Zoo begins: in fact, opposite where the old South Perth Fire Station used to stand.

On the night of our appointment I raced through my tea, spruced myself up, put my transmogrified autograph album in the side pocket of my only sports-coat, and set off up the long slope of Suburban Road.

On my right, as I walked up the hill, the ground fell away sharply to the vegetable gardens between the road and the river.

The Chinamen were still hard at work on the last watering of the day, each man's passage up and down the parched beds marked by luminous plumes of water cascading from the roses of big watering-cans at the ends of the wooden yoke across his shoulders. The warm, humid smell of recently-watered cauliflower and cabbage drifted up to me with the huge, night-flying moths, and mingled with the perfume of recently-watered stocks and phlox in somebody's garden on the other side of the road.

On the farther side of the garden the dark-brown ribbon of riverside swamp squawked and hooted with the noises of birds settling down for the night — every evening, in the last light, you could see long lines and skeins of them wavering in to it from all directions. Beyond the swamp the slate-grey river stretched to the front fence of the city on the other side, gently-lit violet and lavender, with only here and there the flash and glitter of electric signs. Away to the east the hills were no more than flecked with yellow chips of light, a pale blue line against the darker blue of the sky. The moon hadn't yet risen behind them.

Two hours later, when I walked back down Suburban Road toward our end, it was well up. It stood, white as an egg and seeming almost transparent, directly above the third channel post, and as I watched one of the Coode Street ferries ploughed through the silver swathe it shed on the water. The Coode Street jetty was a tiny, glowing island where I knew at least some of my friends would be fishing for cobbler or drop-netting for crabs, or trying to lure someone into the rushes.

I didn't take in all of this immediately. As I reached the roadway at the end of Professor Murdoch's long driveway the lions opened up in the Zoo opposite. They disturbed the peacocks, and their unearthly screeching triggered off the baboons, and a dingo or two. It was a terrifying sound even when you were accustomed to it, and we used to love watching our after-dark visitors staring unbelievingly at the curtains. A bit of a night breeze off the sea, and it sounded as if it was all happening just outside our living-room windows.

Professor Murdoch's place was at the top end of a row of some half-a-dozen on that side of the road, going downhill from the Zoo. The last of them, a solid mock-Tudor two-storey place, had been built by a Perth businessman. 'Two thousand quid, just for the *house!*' we told each other, incredulously. 'The Batemans've gone *mad!*' The huge old trees that surrounded them shut out the world on the river side, and before I came out from under their shadow, and saw the moon, I'd had time to think over my meeting with the Professor.

It hadn't gone quite as I'd expected — for instance, the man himself. I'd never met him, and I'd imagined a large man in tweeds. Condescending, maybe — he was used to dealing with students. A businesslike manner and a mean eye, like most teachers I'd known.

When Mrs Murdoch showed me into her husband's study he was wearing tweeds, certainly — but there my crystal ball went cloudy. Sitting in a big armchair — a very shabby armchair, I was surprised to notice: it would have looked right at home in our own living-room — was a tiny, stooped man with tousled sandy hair and a sandy moustache. Still with his collar-and-tie and jacket on. Before a small wood fire, although the evening was so warm. Surrounded by more shelved books than I'd ever seen before outside a library.

He didn't get up, but he smiled, and when he did his eyes reminded me instantly of the Pied Piper of Hamelin — like candle-flame where salt is sprinkled. When he spoke his voice was soft and dry. He looked to be about forty-five — a lot younger than my father, whom I always used as benchmark for the years. *So old!* I thought, with sinking heart. He'd *forgotten* he'd ever been as young as I was, and uncertain of what he was doing, and diffident about asking advice of anyone for fear of being laughed at.

It was some time before we got around to what I'd visited him for. He quizzed me endlessly about myself and my friends and what we did, and how other young men of my own age (and station implied) filled in their time. I felt like one of the asphyxiated frogs we'd pinned out on wax trays in the science room at school, and took apart to see what made them tick.

He was interested in absolutely everything. At the time I didn't realise it was what had made him what he was, and I thought we'd never get off crabbing and prawning and the Chinamen's gardens, and my boyhood egg-collection and heeling golfballs at the links. It wasn't all one-way, of course. He told me he'd been born in a small Scottish fishing village called Rosehearty, and the way he spoke the word I knew he still felt about it the way I felt about South Perth. In 1874 — I couldn't believe it. Less than fifty years after our State was founded! He was even older than I had imagined. How could he even *begin* to know what went on in the head of a bloke as *young* and *vigorous* as *me!*

He told me how he used to watch the herring boats land their catches at the jetties of the town. That led me fairly naturally into telling him how I used to help the fishermen haul their nets in the shallows on the South Perth side: and we were off again. How many families of fishermen were there? What did they catch, mainly? Did they hawk their fish, or take them to the market in Perth? He had been told there were sharks in the river — did the fishermen ever net any? I told him how once, when I was crabbing during the day, a shark had swum by not ten feet away, close to the bottom, without even looking in my direction. But how would it have known that you were around? Did a shark see you, or smell you, or taste you on the water? Or hear you, or just feel the vibration of your movement on its skin? Had I heard that if a shark attacks you and you punch him on the nose with your fist, you can knock him out just as you would a man? Did I know that shagreen (I'd never heard of it) was sometimes made of the skin of sharks? That the sand-papery feel of shark-skin was actually millions of tiny teeth?

When I'd begun to despair of ever getting down to the business in hand (*my* hand!) he settled back into his chair and said, abruptly: 'Now, Mr Hungerford! Let's have a look at this poetry of yours!' As if *I* had been holding *him* up.

He seemed a little nonplussed, for the shortest moment, when I dragged out my autograph album and handed it to him. He probably thought I wanted his signature. He immediately began to flip over the pages, however, and straight away began to talk about what he found. He must have read incredibly quickly.

'Don't use words like "athwart" was the first comment he made — and it is still probably one of the most valuable ever offered to me. 'You don't ride a penny-farthing bike, do you? H'm . . . m'm. When through the grass the dusky ripples sweep *across* a sunny hillside. Nothing wrong with that, is there?'

'Well . . . no', I agreed. I loved words like "athwart" in much the same way as I then loved strawberry milkshakes, — but I reckoned it might have been unwise to begin an argument so soon after we had got going.

'Poor butterfly', he said, so conversationally that for a moment I didn't realise he was reading from one of my own poems. '*Poor butterfly, you dance in the sun and die.* That's nice — they do, of course. *And yet, you know no vague regret, nor tremulous sigh.* H'm. A butterfly, sighing?' He didn't say it in a way to make you squirm — as so many of my teachers had, particularly about mathematics. He simply asked the question, and more than all the sarcasm in the world it made me see how silly it was to write of a butterfly's sighing — even if it *weren't* tremulously.

'Nigrette', he said. 'Oh, dear!' While I'd been thinking about the sighing butterfly he'd raced on through several pages. 'You feel her kisses yet, do you? H'm . . . m'm. *Stained my pillow wet?*' He looked up from the page directly into my face, the salt sparkling in the candle-flame. 'Have you ever been to bed with a girl, Mr Hungerford?'

'Well . . . no', I said, again.

'Then don't write about it until you have. It's something you really can't imagine, and most things you *do* imagine about it are wrong.' He tapped the page with his fingertip. 'I shouldn't like to see this sort of thing published here. Send *Nigrette* to Mr Bing Crosby. He'd love it.'

He flipped over page after page, his glance flickering backward and forward, up and down. The minutes passed, the clock ticked, the fire hissed and crackled, my heart thumped.

'Why, that's lovely!' Professor Murdoch exclaimed suddenly.

'So much in such a small space! *Here's to the swan, the lily-white swan . . .*'

I had been studying my shoecaps. I looked up expectantly — I couldn't place the quotation at all.

'Which one is that?' I asked.

'Oh, not one of yours.' Professor Murdoch turned the book over and pointed to the florid AUTOGRAPHS stamped in gold on the mock-morocco. 'Something someone's written in it.' He held the page closer to his eyes. 'Phyllis. A friend of yours?'

I knew who it was. A very tall girl who was frightened out of her wits by our old white cocky. She'd played in the same basketball team as my sister, at school.

'My sister's', I said. 'It was her book. She'd finished with it.'

'H'm . . . m'm', Professor Murdoch said. 'Swan . . . *may she never lose a feather. If I can't have my own true love, I'll go without forever.* Lovely.' He began flipping the pages again, talking as he went. 'Almost Elizabethan. It makes one wonder just how many little books it's been written in, eh? That's the wonderful thing about poetry — it just keeps on and on, and most of it fits into whatever age it's said in. Oh — *Talk of War.*' He read on for a moment. 'Well . . . I expect young chaps like you are thinking about it, eh! Those madmen in Europe! *Must I then leave this quiet scene . . .* h'm. m'm . . . well, yes, yes. *This lucerne tree so green and dense that hangs above our litchened and weeps pale petals . . .* why not *drops* pale *flowers? . . .* on the grass. Nice and direct. You've seen that lucerne tree, haven't you? Oh, dear . . . *the sweet hot scent of blood that drips*, etctera.' He looked at me with one of his salt-and-candle smiles. '*Does* blood smell sweet? And *hot*? Have you ever actually *smelt* blood, Mr Hungerford?'

'Well . . . no', I was obliged to admit, miserably, for the third time. It had sounded so *right* when I'd written it to describe the blood I'd practically *seen*, dripping from — of course — my own sweet, hot heart; *too young to die*, as I'd noted later on in the same poem. Now it sounded rather silly.

'Always remember . . . a poem must be a statement of fact', Professor Murdoch said. 'No matter how much you pretty it up. *A statement of fact*.' He read on for a while without comment, then snapped my autograph album shut and handed it back to me. 'Keep at it, Mr Hungerford. You've got a long way to go, but . . . keep at it. Dear me! Half-past-nine!'

It was as if his words had set off an alarm in the kitchen. Mrs Murdoch opened the study door with a supper tray, and while she arranged biscuits and cups and milk and sugar on the table he said: 'Oh — by the way. You must get yourself a typewriter one of these days. Copy every one of your poems onto a separate sheet. And *never* leave yourself with only one copy.'

Within ten minutes I was trudging back up the long, tre-shadowed driveway to Suburban Road, the hullabaloo from the Zoo echoing in my head and that sweet, hot young heart of mine full of a kind of resentment. I don't know what I expected of the meeting with Professor Murdoch — maybe some sort of pillar of fire to guide me through the desert, a *Sesame* sort of word to open it all up for me, magically, in a flash. What I'd actually wanted was not so much advice as just someone to tell me I was as good as I thought I was — like most writers. And what I'd got was that stuff about poems being statements of fact. That dopey old bugger in his shabby old armchair in his musty old study!

'A waste of bloody time!' I fumed to myself as I negotiated the dark footpath toward the open moonlight at the end of the Professor's row of houses. The lions roared their agreement.

It would be a long time before I'd dispose of sufficient common-sense to realise the nature of the lesson that diffident, smiling, sandy little man had given me even by only pulling 'athwart' out of my grab-bag of favourites — even if he hadn't pointed out also that blood really doesn't smell sweet and hot, and that butterflies probably don't sigh tremulously, and that until I'd had ladies crying onto my pillow — with me along, I suppose — I shouldn't presume to write about the experience.

I passed the Batemans' two-thousand-pound mansion, and the last of the trees, and stepped out into the full glare of that South Perth summer moon. Immediately I stopped thinking about what Professor Murdoch had tried to tell me.

My whole world was dusted with silver, on the dew-touched trees down by the river and the tin-roofed houses all about me, and the drenched vegetables whose spicy breath rose to the road from the gardens below. The blue of the sky was now frailer than that of the distant hills, where the jealous white brightness had melted the few pinpoints of light glistening among the gullies before moon-rise. My brain was pierced, with almost a physical thrust, by the lance of solid silver the moon had laid across the river; from my feet, it seemed, to the parklands and the glistening roofs and towers on the other side, where early-to-bed Perth had already begun to douse its lamps.

Inevitably, it recalled that lance of silver across the Canning River a few nights earlier, and the recollection came on a mild tide of panic. Professor Murdoch hadn't been at all surprised that I should be thinking about the possibility of war. What if it were to come, suddenly? What if I were never to go out there again — or at least, never again until I was old? As old, even, as Professor Murdoch? Perhaps, one night, I'd walk by myself down the old white road . . .

'I walked by myself down the old white road', I said aloud, but softly. I could feel it beginning to happen: that sense — unexplainable to anyone who hasn't experienced it — of something locking into place, like a balky screw at last biting into the thread and moving in silkily until you give it the last hard turn that makes it stay put forever. The footpath ended just past the Batemans', so I ploughed through the sand to the bitumen. Its stored heat rose about me with the smell of dust and rubber. 'The road where we've often strolled', I whispered.

We hadn't, of course — we always went on our bikes. Professor Murdoch's *statement of fact* materialised like the ghost of Hamlet's father on the battlements of my mind, but I was able to ignore it. Such a small thing! Road, glowed. Strolled, gold. *On moonlit nights when the water glowed like a river of molten gold* . . . I offered two more lines to myself, feeling more certainly than ever the smooth turn of the screw against my own jubilant thread, feeding on the pleasant melancholy flooding through me from the contemplation of my older self lonely by the shining river, lonely in the scenes of my happy boyhood: maybe, even, after I'd been around the world and had seen Samarkand and Barbados and the Coromandel Coast, all those far and fabled places.

'I've wandered far from the rough white track', I whispered to the hollow clunk of my shoes on the bitumen.

Another furphy, of course — I'd never been further afield than to Wickepin, the other side of Narrogin, where one year I'd spent a couple of weeks of the Christmas holidays on the farm of the brother-in-law of my mother's friend, Mrs Moodie. Such a small thing! I thought, again. What's the good of being a poet if you can't take advantage of the license?

South Perth was asleep and Perth was dozing, but I was wide awake. So were the tireless Chinamen, still. A couple of hundred hards ahead of me, down on the flat, the big hooded cart of one of them bounced across the sand from his gateway and onto the road. Loaded to the plimsoll with fruit and vegetables for the market in Perth it swayed off away from me like the high dark poop of some storm-tossed galleon hung with lanterns. Not long before, one of them had been hit by the one-an-hour late-homing motor-car — produce all over the road, and a judgement that the Chinaman's vehicle had carried insufficient illumination. Now every cart on its way to market moved through the night as if, in prosaic old South Perth, some fabulous colony of fireflies had settled on it for the ride.

The swaying dark shape moved on my sight like a metronome, and words formed in my mind to the receding clip-clop-clip of the horse's hooves.

All about me, still but singing, I could *feel* the night listening for my next line.

I was away.

Milly, Mollie and Mae

The night I met the three girls from Carnarvon I'd been on my holidays for the better part of a week. It was hell to have to leave the beach and go in to the studio.

I'd been surfing and sunbaking all day — only raced up to the flat at lunchtime for a tomato and a slice of polony and a swig of tea, then back to the beach again. I was a bit sunburned, although I'd covered myself with coconut oil. I was tired, too, from the surf. I'd rather have gone up to the pub, in my shorts, for a couple of beers, and then down to the surf for another swim. Instead, I had to climb into my grey melange slacks, coat-shirt-and-tie, and trek right in to Perth by bus.

'Be a scorcher in town, tonight!' the driver warned me as I boarded — as if I didn't know already.

There'd been a picaninny sea-breeze during the day, but it would never have reached the city. Just about sundown, it had fallen back into the Indian Ocean, exhausted. Now the big red Santa Rosa plum was balanced nicely where the smoky blue of the sea met the smoky green of the sky: As I watched, it flattened a little on the underside and began to drop away into the deeps, creeping up on Africa. You almost expected it to sizzle and steam.

'Be a bloody scorcher tomorrow, too!' the driver prophesied, as we pulled away from the curb.

I was the only passenger going in. Everyone else was coming out. Shoals of cars were already arriving on the promenade, crammed with people already in their bathers. It would be one of those nights when the white beach would be crowded until late, trembling with the thud and hiss of the surf and the tinkle and strum of gramophones and the occasional portable wireless; and the people skylarking at the edge of the floodlights would glow phosphorescent like the fish in the black water further out.

I didn't relish the prospect of the night ahead of me, of pushing a mob of four-footed girls around the floor from eight until eleven. Although, of course, the five-bob came in handy: I had to put in at home as well as pay my way out at the beach flat.

When I got up to the studio Mary was standing by the gramophone scoffing a sandwich and a cup of tea. A little Pommie woman who ran the greasy-spoon over the road brought them up for nothing extra. Mary looked worked over — she'd probably had a couple of private lessons during the afternoon. They were the gilt on the gingerbread for anyone running a studio, but they could be tiring. Especially if the student happened to be some old codger with a breath like an open garbage-can who didn't care what he did with his flat feet so long as he could trundle a couple of boobs around the floor for half-an-hour.

When Mary had finished the tea she began to run me through the slow-foxtrot step I was going to give the girls that night. I was only one step ahead of most of them, and I had to work the changes to keep it that way.

A lot of the girls — and the boys, too, although I didn't have much to do with them — made the classes the big social event of their week. For some of them, I think, it was the only contact with anyone outside work and home. *Gee! I been looking forward to class all day!* A chance to snuggle up against some bloke's chest for a few minutes, and dream of being belle of the ball.

'Double reverse spin tonight, isn't it?'

'Yeah.'

'I'll never be able to do it!'

'Easy as falling off a log.'

'How d'you think I'm going? *Really?*'

'You're a natural. Okay, now — I'm going to reverse. Right foot back and *drag* that left heel . . .'

'That new piece in the blue dress!' The preliminaries over and into the dirt. 'She's been going up to Ethel Philp's for *years!* They reckon . . .'

'Okay — watch your heel turn.' You had to head them off. '*Drag* your heel hard — you know? *That's* better! Gives you more balance for the turn.' You knew that the minute you sat this one down she'd start magging to the one next to her, and by the time you'd worked along the bench to the girl from Ethel Philp's it would be what *I'd* said about her. You picked her up and it was like dancing with an ice-cube.

You had to get pretty thick-skinned. The girl from Ethel Philp's — or from Johnny Paranthoiene's or Sammy Gilkison's, or any of the dozen-or-so studios around town — usually had been dancing for years. She probably knew a lot more than I did — although that didn't necessarily make her any Isadora Duncan. They liked to take you by surprise. Just when you'd got into your spiel: *Oh — I had the cross chassis-and-lock a long time ago — up at Wrightson's*, and they'd stand there waiting for you to pull something out of the hat.

I didn't often get taken by surprise, just the same. We had a free dancing period for a quarter of an hour before instruction began, and while you were piloting a few of the hopefuls around the floor you kept your eyes peeled for anyone who looked as if she might be a snag.

I had a couple of disasters, early on, when one or two of the pupils began to instruct *me*, but I'd worked out a simple routine to bring them back to the field. You'd just kick the hell out of them, mark up their nice Silvafrosted shoes, and then say something like: *Well . . . don't worry. You'll get the hang of it all of a sudden, one of these nights.* A few more stumbles and then, just before you sat her down, something for the other girls to hear — something she wouldn't be able to cotton on to in a hurry: *Watch that right hip — or maybe it's the way you swing your left ankle?*

It was an awful thing to do, and even while I was doing it I knew it might cost Mary a pupil. Anyone I pulled it on was quite likely to shoot off to some other studio and sit on the bench against *their* wall and tell the girls there about me: *That red-headed cow up at Mary Shaw's!* But when it was eighty in the water-bag and your tie was strangling you, and you were only half-way through the quickstep, with the waltz and the slow foxtrot yet to come . . . and when you knew that even if you broke your leg everyone of the dozen or so sitting along that bench like crows on a butcher's fence had to be danced with and jollied and bullshitted to: and that even while they sniggered and gossiped and sniped everyone of them had her eye on the clock like a gimlet to see you didn't give her a second less than you gave the one next to her . . .

While I was being run through the steps for the class by Mary, Leo and Bonny came in. They trained all through the summer, to be ready for the first competitions of the winter dancing season. They taught for Mary, and in return she coached them in very advanced stuff — it was the way the studios ran. They were the top pair at our studio, they'd won the previous winter's Tango Championship, and they'd been runners-up twice in the State championships. They had to be good, because they didn't have looks going for them. There's something about being tall and dark and good-looking when you're wearing tails — which most of us did when we were dancing in competitions, even if they weren't our own; tails went around like the common cold, between dancers in the same studio and between studios. There's a thing about tails fitting anyone, and I've proved it. For one competition I was in, before I got my own, I wore the suit of a little bloke about five-foot-three with broad shoulders and fair hair, and I'm nearly six-foot with red hair and shoulders like a sauce-bottle.

Leo and Bonny moved like machines — like a machine, in fact. They were small and mousy, but when they took to the floor you forgot all about that. I used to wonder if they really enjoyed it — you couldn't expect a clock to get a charge out of striking. But even if they didn't enjoy it, they made it look as if they did, and that was important. Every studio had a crowd of one-eyed followers who'd vote for the studio's representative even if they were a couple of two-headed cripples, but there were a lot of swingers who'd just go for looks and tip the balance this way or that in the popular vote. Everyone said that had no influence on the judges, but I hadn't been in the business long before I'd seen competitions when couples who'd done everything by the book had been rubbished by the judges simply because it stuck out like a dog's balls that they didn't please the crowd.

When Leo and Bonny came in they went straight to the record rack and picked up the practise-record — we called it that because when we were training we had to hold a record clamped between our pelvises, excepting for open variations. If we dropped it and broke it we were expected to replace it: technically, that is — we always picked some clapped-out old platter they'd worn down to the welt, and nobody really cared what happened to it.

I watched them take off, doing the slow foxtrot the same as Mary and me. They were concentrating on nothing but moving across the floor, corner to centre and centre to corner, round and round like those little carved figures on Swiss barometers. Springs in their heels, all right. After a while Leo piloted Bonny over to Mary and me, and danced along beside us for a while.

'You opening a boong's camp, Shaw?' Leo said. 'Saw three gins as we came in. Down the bottom of the stairs.'

Mary stopped, and we stood staring at him with our hands on each other's shoulders — the way we danced when it was for business rather than for pleasure.

'One of them asked if this was Mary Shaw's', Leo said.

'Spoke quite good English she did, too,' Bonny said, 'like a lumper.'

'One of them had a goanna by the tail', Leo said. He was that kind — always the humorist. 'Probably got a bit of a fire going down in the lobby right now — cooking it for tea.'

'Don't be so bloody silly', Mary said. She dropped her hands from my shoulders and walked over to the gram. She flipped the arm off the record, and *I'm In The Mood For Love* came to a stop.

It had been the tune for that year's slow foxtrot competition

My partner had worn a blue taffeta dress with a shoulder-spray of pink camellias I'd shouted her for luck. It'd worked, because we'd won our heat. I'd gone around for days whistling the tune, in my head or out loud. Me, feathering beautifully down the Town Hall dance-floor, rise-and-fall, contra-body-movement, hip-contact. *Keep smiling!* The lovely hailstone patter of clapping as we swayed into an open telemark and outside-spin in the middle. I swear I could see how good it looked, as if I'd been up in the balcony watching. We got beaten in the next round, though, and my partner got herself another pilot. I was good to dance with, she said, apologetically, but I was poison with the judges.

'Only be a mo', Hungie', Mary said to me, as she passed me on the way to the door.

She had spectacular legs and bottom, and tiny feet, and her shoes and stockings were always impeccable, no matter how hard up she might be: which we all were, always, chronically, eternally, broke to the wide every Thursday. I watched her cross the floor. The insides of her knees just brushed as she walked, and it gave her a very sexy sort of movement.

'I bet she's gone down to nab those three for the class', Bonnie said.

'Blame her?' I said. 'Three one-and-sixpences just about pays one of us.'

'Jesus!' Leo said. 'Can't you just see them standing in the doorway as the mob comes in?' He held out a hand, cringingly. 'Gib'it chickpen', boss?'

Bonnie and I laughed. Even in his grey suit and white shirt and blue tie, neat as whiskey — he worked in one of the big stores, and he always dressed beautifully — he somehow managed to look just like one of the raggedy aboriginals you saw begging up and down the line of carriages when your train stopped at some of the country sidings.

Although you wouldn't expect the three down in the lobby to be like that, I thought — and then realised I had no idea at all what to expect if Mary *were* to lug them up for their one-and-sixpences. You didn't see many blacks around Perth — they were a bit of an oddity. About the only picture I had of them was from the arty sorts of photos they put on the front of writing-pads. Of some naked warrior posed on a rock with his spears placed strategically to hide his genitals, or white-toothed smiling gins picking blue water-lilies in some Northern Territory billabong, and no holts barred about showing what they disposed of above the water-line.

186

And there was the cartoon aboriginal, too. We'd been getting *Smith's Weekly* at home for as long as I could remember, and I'd been brought up on Stan Cross's splay-footed, splat-nosed black no-hopers and their stick-legged gins doing something stupid — like badly trained dogs — outside some wheat-cocky's bark hut.

'Pity we weren't still running the concerts,' Bonny said, 'they might come in handy — big corroboree number.' She shook an imaginary spear above her head and stamped her foot on the floor. She was a perfect little soubrette type, dainty and pink-and-brown, with exquisite ankles.

'You be careful, Bon!' Leo said, grinning at her. 'Skiddy-widdy!'

While they'd been rehearsing the last concert Bonnie had burst her halter-top and brought the house down. At the finale of one number she'd had to jump in the air with her arms stretched out in front of her, and wiggle her shoulders and bottom while she yelled: *Skiddy-widdy way-y-y-y-oh!* and — boom! Or, I guess, boom-boom!

Since then I'd never been able to look at her and see her fully clothed. I'd had a spear-carrier part in that same show — me and another bloke from the studio. Blackened all over — where it showed anyway — in bright loin-cloths and turbans, our arms crossed on our chests with the fists under our biceps to make the most of them, between a couple of papier-mache palm-trees to make up the scenery: for a terrible little precocious four-year-old all permanent-waved and made up like one of the girls down Roe Street, who waggled her raffia skirt and sang *I Wouldn't Leave My Little Wooden Hut for You-oo-oo.*

The act didn't require much practise by the spear-carriers, and the main reason why I attended rehearsals at all was because I'd written the lyrics, and changes might be required *en route*. For instance, one of my lines went: *Remember when Mother Eve met him, handsome Adam wore only a smile!* and the mothers of the girls in the number formed a deputation, bristling, and had the line cut. Until you've met a stage-mother, you've no idea of what a dragon can be like.

Rene, the girl who put the concerts on, taught every known sort of dancing — ballroom, classical, tap, stage-routine, national, you name it — and her pupils supplied the cast for her yearly revue at His Majesty's. She reckoned she was too hard-up to pay me for writing the lyrics, but she offered me ballroom lessons instead.

Overnight, almost, my life-style took a complete somersault. I'd been going along every couple of weeks to the old-time dance in the Swan Street hall, in South Perth: now, suddenly, I was an out-every-night sort of stage-door Johnny, racing home from work, showering, jumping into my suit, wolfing my tea, dashing back to town, crawling home to bed, often after midnight — never before the last ferry, in any case, sitting on that deserted jetty watching the enormous cockroaches clatter around like rattlesnakes. My mother had a great deal to say about it, of course: *using-the-house-like-a-hotel-look-at-you-wearing-yourself-out-never -see-any-of-your-old-friends-now-all-that-dancing-riffraff!* and so on.

Her grip was loosening on all of us, and I was the last. I guess she hated it. She'd still haul off and give me a clip under the ear when she thought I deserved it — until one evening when I was picking at the plates while she was dishing up tea, and worrying her to hurry because I wanted to get back to town, she lashed out at me — for the last time. I caught her hand just before it landed. 'Mum', I said, *'don't ever hit me in the face again!'* I think it might have sunk in then that my most recent birthday had been my twenty-first. In any case, she didn't have to stay her hand for long. She was dead within two years, and I was wishing she was still around to belt me.

When Mary came back up the stairs she had the three black girls in tow, all right, but she was half-way across the floor before she realised they hadn't followed her in. They'd propped in the doorway, and were looking around the studio as if they suspected some sort of trap.

There was a big one and two small ones, and as Leo had said, they were really black. The only one you could really see was the big one in front — the other two stayed right behind her, peeping around her. She was right out of *Smith's Weekly*, almost blue-black with massive shoulders, box-shaped almost to her knees. Her legs were the skinny-gin sort, and from across the room, even, you could see that the salesman at Ezywalkin must have had a bit of bother fitting her with the black patent leather shoes she was wearing: probably would have wanted to sell her the box rather than the boots.

The three of them stood there in the doorway peering about them, and looking at them I remembered three kangaroos we'd surprised in a swamp down by Narrogin, one weekend: standing there with their backs against a quandong tree, their ears and nose twitching as they tried to identify the sounds and the smells we'd sent on ahead of us.

They took it all in as if they wanted to remember it forever. The wooden benches along the walls, with the few boys and girls who'd already wandered in staring back at them. The green cotton curtains at the windows, a few cheap wooden pot-stands with ferns on them, the cheap glass shades hanging from the ceiling above their own reflections in the shining floor. In the corner where Bonny and Leo and I stood, just the gramophone on a little second-hand table, our stack of records on one of the benches, Mary's desk with her appointment book and the phone. I wondered what they thought of it — I'd never been north of Geraldton. Maybe the old Modern Studio, about which Mary was always saying: *I must do something about this dump when I get some dough!* looked like a palace to them.

'Come on, girls!' She smiled and held out her hand toward them.

It occurred to me that it was the way you'd coax children, or dogs. 'Come on, Mae! Bring the girls in!' Out of the corner of her mouth, without disturbing her smile, she said softly to us: 'They reckon Dad used to know their father, in Derby.' She lowered her voice even further. 'White!'

It was mostly girls sitting on the benches along the walls — the boys usually stayed out on the landing until the music started, skylarking and telling dirty jokes in a cloud of cigarette smoke and Californian Poppy. The girls came straight in — they knew where to go, and went there, sat down and began showing each other crochet patterns and pictures of evening dresses they'd cut out of magazines to have made up for the winter ball season — we were usually dragged into it, later on, for an opinion. *Like the diagonal ruffles across the front? That girl from Sammy's won the tango comp last year, she had them. Remember? Christ, yes, you'll knock 'em for a row in that, all right!* Some of them got up together and went over steps they'd learned in last week's class, or tried out some variation they'd seen someone do, some time. It was the part of the evening I liked best, before it got roasting hot, when the tiniest breeze fluttered the curtains and the gramophone muttered to itself in our corner and the floor shone like red silk, and the studio was full of the scent of girls; that year everyone was wearing something called *Soir de Paris*, in a little dark-blue bottle, and you'd have thought you were walking through an orange grove.

The big one — Mae: she'd nodded and smiled when Mary called

out to them — started across the floor toward us. The other two hesitated for a moment before they followed her — probably thought whatever happened they'd be safer close to her than standing by themselves in the doorway. Everyone stared at them, as if they'd just escaped from a zoo. I suppose it was understandable. It wasn't every night you saw three authentic black women at a dancing studio in Perth.

'Clean and tidy, anyway!' Bonny whispered to Leo, as if she'd expected them to be wearing Stan Cross flour-bags.

The big one — Mae — didn't show any of her white blood at all, that I could see. When she got closer to us she smiled — and not out of nervousness, either. You could see that. She had magnificent teeth, and for some reason when I saw them I thought of pomegranate seeds, even though they were so white. It must have been because of the pink gums and tongue you could see behind them.

The other two were different altogether. In their plain cotton frocks they were slender. Not skinny — young-girl shapely. They were pretty, too, their heart-shaped faces broad at the forehead and narrow at the chin. They didn't show any white blood, either. If they showed any cross at all it was in the high cheek-bones some wily old Malay trader had left behind him somewhere on the northern coast a couple of hundred years ago. My father used to say the mixture of aboriginal and Malay blood up in Arnhem Land produced some of the most beautiful women he'd ever seen — and didn't my mother snort. All three of the girls had beautiful brown wavy hair, cut short, but the heads of the second two were so small and elegant I felt that if I were to place a palm against each ear and press inward I could crush their skulls like egg-shells. When they got close enough I could see their eyes were large and brown and soft, with the pink whites that look so terrible on us but so right on them.

I was prepared for all that, but I wasn't prepared for something you couldn't really see until they were close up to you — their long, dark, thick lashes, top and bottom. Just as it seemed they'd realised what was happening, and had inclined gently forward, the way they do, to bound off, we'd shot them.

I thought it strange that none of the three showed anything of their white blood. There was an opinion going around among us at the time that the sex of a child was decided by whose passion, the mother's or the father's, was in the ascendant at the time of conception — very scientific, our discussions were, right out of

Readers Digest. Maybe it was the same with looks, I thought. If it was, the girls' mother must have been in the driving seat every time the balloon went up. In any case, the father might have had a touch of the tarbrush, too. They reckoned you could never tell up north.

Mary introduced them, and when she said: *Millie, Mollie and Mae* I was afraid she'd burst out laughing. I didn't dare look at her — Bonny had three aunties called Lily, Millie and Tillie Hill, and we were always on about them.

'Are you holidaying in Perth?' Bonny asked. She directed the question at all of them, but it was the one called Mae who answered.

'Few weeks.' Her voice was deep and rough as chaffbags, but not coarse. It was the sort that would comfort children. 'Dad won a packet at the picnic races, Christmas time. Reckoned we should see Perth before we died!'

She laughed, and it seemed to fill the whole studio. People sitting half-way along the walls on either side turned around and looked in our direction — those who weren't already staring at Millie, Mollie and Mae as if they were dressed-up platypuses, and straining to catch what we were talking about. Most of them smiled as if she had let them in on a bit of fun — I didn't know her for long, but the way she laughed was one thing that stuck in my memory. Her eyes nearly closed, her mouth wide open, her tongue lying like a bright pink oyster inside the shell of her perfect white bottom teeth.

'How did you come down?' Bonny asked. I don't know if she really was interested, or if she was just playing ladies. I'd been wondering about it myself — Carnarvon was a long way up the coast, and there was no train.

'Boat — didn't you, Mae?' Mary said. 'The old *Koolinda?*'

'*Koolinda*, all right', Mae nodded agreement. 'Goin' back on it, too.'

'Good trip?' Leo asked.

'Bonzer.'

'Plenty of fun on board?' Leo persisted, about as subtle as a cock-eyed-bob. He winked slyly and swiftly at Bonny, and I knew what he was thinking about. I was too — how the three black girls got on with the white passengers, and if they got invited to the parties.

'Tucker was beaut', Mae said.

'What does your dad do?' Leo asked. 'Apart from win dough at the races?'

'Looks after the mills on Howlong', Mae said. Neither of the other two made any attempt to butt into the conversation. In fact, until I got them in my class later on I thought maybe they didn't speak English too well: they spoke it all right, but seemed just not to bother. They stood there, half-hidden behind their big sister, still and watchful as if they were balanced to take off at the first hostile move. Like the kangaroos.

'Oh?' Leo said. He slipped another sideways wink at Bonny. 'And how long is Howlong?'

The black girl paused a moment and flickered a glance around us. I got the feeling she knew Leo was having her on. I think I'd never disliked Leo more. He was a good bloke in many ways, but he could be a regular shit if he wanted to.

'Just outside Carnarvon', Mae said, after that little wait. I suppose she was used to skating around smart alecs trying to take a rise out of her, and had decided to pretend to mistake the question. 'Three weeks we'll be back there.' She laughed again. 'Got to get a job.'

'What'll you do?' Bonny sounded as if she'd made a lightning survey of the possibilities and just couldn't believe there'd be any sort of job for her to do.

'Oh — somethin'.' Mae shrugged. 'Maybe work on Howlong, like Dad. Might cook at the convent. I dunno.' She didn't seem very interested, and I remembered what one of the blokes at work had said, one lunch-time before we got around to the inevitable *met this sheila in the lounge at the Bedford* or *A mate of mine said his missus was knockin' it off with the bloke that reads the meters* or *so on me day off I took her down Scarborough an' rooted her up one side of a sandhill an' down the other*. Somehow the talk had got around to aborigines and what to do about them, and one of the stereotypers reckoned: 'Do this, do that. You don't know what you're talking about. I've worked with the hooers. They don't give a *stuff*. They don't *want* to do *anything!*'

Millie, Mollie and Mae came up to the studio for three weeks all told — three Tuesday nights and three Fridays. I don't know how much they enjoyed it — you couldn't really tell. I do know they didn't learn much. They just didn't seem able to take it in and remember it from one class to the next.

After the first night or two they seemed to get on well enough with the other girls, and the blokes danced with them a lot: maybe it was just the novelty. Mae was usually the centre of a lot of chatter and laughing, with Millie and Mollie hanging on to the edges, smiling shyly into their shoulders. I don't know what they talked about, but I think it was me, sometimes. I'd taken a few of the girls out from time to time, and once or twice when I looked up quickly from some pupil's feet I'd catch them staring at me the way they do when one of them has just said something and they're all thinking about it, and I felt pretty sure that whatever had been said had been said about me.

One night when I picked up one of our regulars she was still laughing her head off, and she wouldn't look at me.

'What's the joke?' I asked.

'Gawd!' she said. 'That Mae! They don't half have themselves a time up there!'

On their last night at the studio — at the time, I didn't know it was their last night — I breezed through Millie and Mollie first. I'd really given up trying to teach them anything. I'd start off by saying: 'Now . . . remember what I showed you last night? The natural turn in the blues?' — about the simplest step in the world. The result was the same with both of them — as if I'd been speaking Chinese.

'Come on!' I'd say. '*You* remember! That step in the corner, back on your left foot, around with the right, bring your left up to it, close with your left, back with your right, sideways with your left?' I'd demonstrate, but it was plain they just didn't know what I was talking about, so after the third night I only went through the motions — shoved off onto the floor and piloted them around with as little trouble as possible.

Millie and Mollie moved well enough, and they were nice to hold. They fitted neatly under my chin, so different from the breath of *Soir de Paris* wafting up from the white girls. I'd like to have heard what the boys had to say about it out on the landing at half-time.

I'd give Millie and Mollie as much time as I could, doing my best to avoid treading on their feet, and chatting them up and smiling encouragingly. They rarely said a word — just a shy smile, sometimes, or a bit of a giggle into their shoulders, eyes on the floor. I suppose they enjoyed it all — the music and the other girls, and dancing with the different blokes. I guess it *was* a million miles from what they'd been used to up Carnarvon.

Mae was different. She really enjoyed herself, and showed it. She learned a few things, and she talked a lot. It was she who told me each of them had had four years at the convent — their Dad had insisted on it. When I asked her what they'd been taught, she said: 'Oh — cookin', cleanin', sewin', washin' — that sort.'

'What about schoolwork?'

'A bit.' She frowned the way she did when I was coaxing her into remembering what I'd given her on the previous class-night. 'Sums an' spellin' ', she said, eventually, but she kept on frowning as if she was trying to remember whether there had been anything else.

During the past couple of classes I'd bulldozed her through the quarter-turn, and had made it stick. It made progress around the floor a bit less monotonous if you could fit one in half-way along each wall, between the natural turns in the corners. Then, on the previous night, I'd got her onto the cross-chassis — it follows the quarter-turn as night follows day. If she'd remembered that all right, I was going to hit her with the lock — which follows the cross-chassis as naturally as the cross-chassis follows the quarter-turn. She'd really be able to dazzle the mob at Howlong, I thought — that's if there was anyone up there who could do it with her.

'Okay, Mae', I said. 'I'm going to give you the cross-chassis and lock tonight. Big time!' I grinned at her. 'First we'll just run through the cross-chassis, though.' She stared at me as if she'd been poleaxed, and my spirits began to slide again. Maybe I'd reached her limits with the cross-chassis. 'You know? I gave it to you last Tuesday?'

'Cross-chassis, Mr Hungerford?' The familiar furrows appeared in her forehead, and my spirits fell still further.

I hadn't got into teaching ballroom because of any burning ambition to change the world. Actually, it was something of an accident. Mary had taken over the studio when Rene decided to try her luck in London, and she was absolutely skint by the time she'd forked out for the good-will and the bits of furniture and the gram — which was going to pay Rene's fare. Several of us had volunteered to teach for Mary until she got on her feet, and I found I enjoyed it. I got interested in it, and took a couple of exams, and I reckon I was a good teacher. To have a pupil just blank out on me in something as simple as the cross-chassis bashed my ring in.

'Oh, Jesus, Mae!' I protested. 'It was only a couple of *nights* ago!' I looked at her, waiting for some sign that she remembered. When I could see that she didn't, I said: 'Okay. Watch. After the quarter-turn . . .' I raised my hands to shoulder level for balance and went into the girl's part. 'Back on the *right*, side on the *left*, feet *together* — remember?' I could see it wasn't sinking in, so I said. 'All right, then, we'll have a bit of a dance and it'll come back to you.' As we moved off, I thought: *What the hell am I doing in here, messing around with these mugs, when I could be out the beach?*

Mae must have known I was a bit shirty. She didn't say a word for a couple of rounds, and then, abruptly: 'Seen your picture in the paper, Mr Hungerford.' She took her hand from my shoulder and fished a bit of newspaper from the front of her dress. As she handed it to me I caught a whiff of that body-scent of hers. It was me, all right — between two women in evening dress, one of them an honest-to-god crinoline. Gigolo and friends.

The previous winter Johnny Paranthoiene had asked me to go to the Post Office Ball with the daughter of his only private lesson. Johnny's studio hadn't been going very long, and he was battling, and this bloke was practically his rent every week: he was some big wheel, a Director, in some government department, and naturally Johnny wanted to fit him.

'Why me?' I asked.

'She's a tall girl. And you've got tails — he stipulated tails.'

I didn't want to be in it. We'd be going to the ball anyway — we went to just about every ball — and I couldn't see myself hob-nobbing with a lot of stuffed shirts while the studio mob were living it up. But Johnny seemed to think that if the deal fell through there'd be no more private lessons, and he'd be scratching for the rent for his studio.

'All right', I said.

'He'll provide the ticket.'

'Fair enough', I agreed. They were a quid each.

'And of course, there'll be a fee for you.'

'Bloody hell, will there!'

I think my hair stood on end. I didn't mind taking a quid for an exhibition, because you worked for that, and damn hard. But a *paid partner!* It was bad enough to be accepting the tickets, without going the whole hog and accepting payment as well. A bloody *gigolo!* I'd seen one in *The Gay Divorcee*, playing fast and loose with Ginger Rogers. A black-haired, currant-eyed *Dago*, sleek and greasy, who made dough out of going around with women. *Never!*

I thought I'd settled that point, but as it turned out I hadn't.

'They want you to go to tea at their place, one night before the ball', Johnny said.

'What the hell for?'

'To look you over . . . meet you, sort of.' I know poor Johnny wasn't enjoying it any more than I was. 'You can't just . . . meet them outside the Embassy.'

The upshot was that I went to tea, met some nice people, had a slap-up meal, sat around afterward in a very posh lounge and knocked back a scotch or two, and left. Mr Director accompanied me to the front gate, and as I closed it behind me, he handed me an envelope.

'The tickets', he said, 'and your fee.'

I don't think I'd ever felt lower.

'Oh', I said, 'I couldn't take that, thank you.'

He just stood there, holding the envelope out toward me. He wasn't a Director for nothing — you could see he was used to chivvying the workers around.

'It was the deal with Mr Paranthoiene', he said. 'It'd be a pity if it fell through. We like you, and Opal's looking forward to the ball.'

Between him and Johnny and Opal — she was the daughter, and I couldn't imagine why he would have to be paying partners for her — I finished up taking the envelope. There was a guinea in it — that snobby figure which in our world indicated a really classy, professional transaction.

Just the same, I was to discover that the job was worth every penny of it, free meal thrown in. Opal and I were the only young people in the Director's party. Everyone else was practically over the hill — probably as old as forty or forty-five. None of the ladies could do anything but the circular waltz, and the wife of one of the Director's colleagues had on a genuine crinoline, wire hoop and all: it was like dancing with our old cocky's cage draped in gold satin. To make matters worse, the Director's *loge* was at floor level directly beneath where our studio crowd were sitting, on the balcony. Every time I glanced up there would be a couple of my friends smiling down at me, elaborately mouthing silent messages of advice or condolence.

I had made up my mind that none of the tainted wage would remain with me, but I needn't have worried about that. After I'd bought Opal a shoulder-spray, and I'd shouted a few drinks, there was little enough of it left: but, as well . . . girls you took home from balls always live in the most distant suburbs, and although we went home to Mt Hawthorn in the Director's car, I had to get a taxi from there back to South Perth. By the time I got home, well after two in the morning, I was well into my own resources.

'Where the hell did you get this?' I asked Mae, staring at the press photograph: taken only, I'm certain, because of the association with the Director.

'One of the girls told me when it was. I got a copy of the paper.'

I didn't know what to say. I handed it back to her, and she folded it and stuffed it away where she'd got it from, into that warm, dusky little valley that just showed above the neckline of her cotton frock. After we'd done a few more rounds of the floor, she said: 'Nice to go to a ball?'

'Beaut,' I said, 'but . . . don't you have them in Carnarvon?' As soon as the words were out of my mouth I felt their place taken by my own foot.

'Sometimes,' Mae said, 'at the pub. New Year, race time. Everyone comes from the stations. None of us ever go, though.'

There was nothing in the way she said it, none of the hostility you might have expected. *None of us.* It was as if she'd said: *In Carnarvon, Sunday comes after Saturday.* It was the way things were where she lived, and I don't suppose she could see any reason why they should change just to please her. She smiled, the point of her pink tongue running backward and forward along her white bottom teeth. 'Last year I worked in the kitchen of the pub where it was held. It was bonzer!'

When the class was over and the last of the stragglers were clattering toward the door, I was sitting on the bench by the gram with Leo, staring at my feet. I was buggered. Mary had tidied up her desk and gone to the toilet, and Bonny had shot off before the last record was finished: reckoned she had to wash her hair before she went to bed. I didn't know Mae was there until I heard Leo say: 'Hello, Mae. You want something?' As he spoke he leaned over to the gramophone and dropped the arm on the last record we'd had on — an old one of Rudy Vallee's resurrected. Just to make sure nobody went home anything but exhausted, Mary'd put on a Boston Two-step at the end. My shirt was still sticking to my back, and the little breeze from the window behind me was like a breath of heaven. I looked up, and there was Mae.

'Come to say hooroo', she said.

'Hooroo?' I echoed.

'Going back to Carnarvon tomorrow.'

'To Carnarvon?' I was so tired I couldn't take it in. She'd

seemed to have become one of the fixtures at the studio. 'Tomorrow?'

She nodded. 'Do something for me, Mr Hungerford?'

'What is it, Mae?'

She fished the piece of newspaper out of her front again, unfolded it and handed it to me. The photograph of me with Opal on one side of me and, on the other, the wife of the Director's colleague, crinoline and all. She handed it to me.

'Write your name on that? Write . . . for Mae Murphy, from Mr Hungerford?'

'All right, Mae. Glad to.' I turned to Leo. He was staring at us questioningly. 'Lend us your pen, Lee.'

He got up to hand it to me, and looked over my shoulder at the picture. They'd all seen it before, of course, and I'd taken a shallacking about it.

'Cripes. Autographs, now!' *Betty Co-ed is loved by every college boy*, he hummed, in time with the gram. *But I'm the one who's loved by Betty Co-ed!* 'You and Mister bloody Vallee!'

I signed the photograph and handed it back to Mae.

'Not with a 'Y', Mr Hungerford', she said, when she'd looked at it. 'M-a-*e*.'

I felt stupid, as if in a way I'd insulted her. I'd never even known her name, properly.

'I'm sorry, Mae.' I took the paper from her, botched the 'Y' into an 'E', and handed it back to her. She looked at it again before she folded it and stuck it down the front of her dress.

'Well . . . hooroo.'

'Hooroo, Mae', I said. 'I hope you . . .'

I really don't know what I hoped for her. That she'd remember the quarter-turn?

She turned around and walked across the shining floor, her heels clack-clacking on the bare wood. Millie and Mollie poked their heads around the door, grinning at her as she approached them. Millie waved to me, and they were gone.

'What the hell will she *do*, in Carnarvon?' I said, to Leo.

'She'll be on the batter this time next year', Leo said. 'They all are.' He lifted the arm from the record. 'Come on. We'll wait for Shaw out on the landing.'

He took off toward the door, pulling the light cords as he went: funny — Mae stomped but he pussy-footed so you didn't hear a sound. I stood watching him for a moment as the studio got darker. *On the batter*, he'd reckoned. Mae, hanging around in the shadows outside one of the Carnarvon pubs, waiting for some stockman or commercial traveller up from Perth to come out and offer her a couple of bob to go around under the tank-stand. Maybe a bottle of bombo.

I lifted my hand to my face.

The strange, musky smell of her sweat was still on my fingers. It crept up into my nostrils like the smoke of burning gum trees.

The Day It All Ended

That weekend I had the Saturday off. Usually we worked until the last edition at about six o'clock in the evening. It got us a full day off every fortnight, mid-week, and once in a long while a whole Saturday.

We were going out to the beach shack that weekend, at Scarborough. I would be able to go straight from the studio with the others on the last bus Friday night. Ordinarily, after I'd cleaned up at work and got out to the beach everyone else would be either up at the pub or gone to the dance. If there was a party on at our place they'd already be feeling no pain, and there's something unsatisfactory about arriving home dead-sober to a crowd half-way toward being dead-drunk.

All the afternoon I'd been taking pulls off the galley spikes to check up on how the war was going in Poland, or looking over the shoulders of the operators as they set up the copy. I'd just read where the British and French Governments had warned Germany to lay off Poland when old Jimmy Ward, the head linotype mechanic, propped behind me to look at the same piece of copy. His breath nearly flattened me. He'd been ducking across to the Palace on-and-off all the afternoon for a taste.

'That bloody Hike-ler!' he said. He could never get his tongue around a name, especially at the end of a long Saturday afternoon: he called me *young Unkersfoot*. 'I'd string him up by the balls!'

I suppose it was how everyone felt about Hitler, but — how did you go about stringing him up? For one thing, although it really looked as if it was on for us as well as the Poles, you just couldn't bring yourself to accept it. We were like people in a run-away car charging downhill toward a precipice: knowing we were done for but still hoping something would happen to make the brakes work. And in another way you hoped that after so long mucking about it would *happen*, and one way or another get you off the hook.

By the time we got out to the shack Friday night it was near enough to midnight, and when we'd had a cup of tea it was well into Saturday morning. It was a beautiful, sharp and silver night with a bit of an off-shore wind rattling the loose sheets of iron on the roof. We'd had a middling-heavy blow during the week — the September Gales coming a bit early — and a land breeze to top the waves off meant that there'd be good surf in the morning.

Mary and Bonny and I all had the Saturday off, and although the others had to go in until lunchtime, nobody really wanted to go to bed for a while. Mary suggested going for a walk up to

Triggs, and we all agreed. There seemed to be a necessity — I felt it, anyway — to make the most of every minute. Maybe there wouldn't be another summer at Scarborough for any of us, though of course nobody put it into so many words.

It had been creeping up on us for years, and now — here it was. People saying in the bus and the pub, in letters to the papers: *This is it!* and *We can't give away any more!* and *He's got to be stopped somewhere!* The big question in the papers was what the Yanks would do. Would they come in? Would they stay out altogether? Would they hang fire long enough — as they did last time — to make a packet selling stuff to both sides? Would they come in right at the death-knock and then tell the world they'd won it? You could buy a fight at the pub any time on that, particularly toward closing time.

'What do you think's going to happen?' Mary asked me. 'What do you think he'll do now?'

We were walking together as we trudged out of the circle of yellow light at the end of the promenade. The others were further down the beach, running along the lacy edges of the waves as they curled up the wet sand.

It wasn't really cold. The wind off the land was loaded with the sweet dry-grass-and-gumtrees smell of the dunes, and every few seconds 'Winking Willie' over on Rottnest swung around to let us know he was still on the job. The sand was like mother-of-pearl in the moonlight, soft and luminous between the black skeins and hummocks of kelp washed up by the blow. During the previous winter I'd found a dead sea-horse among the weed: I'd never seen one before, excepting in illustrations. It was so strange and beautiful and in a way, secret. It knew things and had seen things I couldn't even begin to imagine, and as I looked down at it, the faint, salty smell of its decay drifting up to me, I felt as if I were holding all the secrets of all the oceans between my own fingertips.

You didn't have to ask who Mary meant when she said *he*. It seemed no time at all since he'd been just a big joke, and 'impressionists' were taking him off all over the country. You'd always get a laugh if you brushed a lock of hair down onto your forehead and stuck the last inch of a black comb under your nose, then flung your right hand out in the Nazi salute and gabbled a bit of mock-German: *Gebunkenspeil und glockspecken mit fuckenpot! Heil Hitler!* He was no longer a joke, though. He'd done everything he'd ever said he'd do, and it looked as if the well-known lights of Europe that Kaiser Bill had doused the year before I was born were for the chop again. Like the tiny jewels of phosphorescence that eddied about our feet as we walked to Triggs that night, glittering in the wet sand, and then washed away, after every wave.

Next morning, when the others had scoffed their weeties and milk and raced through the sandhills to the bus, Mary and Bonny and I set to to clean out the flat. Even when there was no wind at all the sand seeped in — through the cracks in the walls, up through the floorboards, down from the roof. After the blow during the week we got a truckload. Then while Mary and Bonny made their bed, I went over to the corner store for the 'West'. I sat with my back to the warm sandstone wall of the prom, out of the wind, and read all about it. There was no let-up. *HITLER MAKES WAR!* and *POLAND INVADED!* and maps of Danzig and the Corridor, and always photographs of that mad, marble-eyed stare and the out-flung hand. As I was sitting there one of the blokes from the surf club went by with his board under his arm.

'What're you going into?' he yelled at me.

'The monastery up at New Norcia!' I yelled back. I hadn't really thought much about it, although it would be the army for sure. I knew I'd never learn to fly a plane, and I got seasick on a merry-go-round.

It's curious how safe and normal things seemed when I climbed the wooden steps to the front door of the flat. The old place had been built God-only-knows-when, a couple of hundred yards off the end of the promenade, in the sandhills. Not another house around, which suited us fine. More lately, though, it had been divided into three flats at thirty shillings a time, and very nice money for whoever owned it. The dividing walls were only single sheets of asbestos, and we used to reckon you could hear the lady next door putting on her cold-cream. It didn't worry us, generally, but one summer a couple of years earlier it did worry the lady next door. She was from Kalgoorlie, and a real Tartar. She wrote to one of the papers saying how disgusting it was that the girls stayed in our flat with us over the weekends, and what was the younger generation coming to, and did our mothers know, and much else beside. Actually the girls all slept in the inner room, while we were ranged around the verandah wherever we could fit in: but you'd have had a hard time making that stick with the lady from Kal. Dirt is like beauty — most times it's in the eye of the beholder.

About mid-morning Mary and I went for a ride. There was a pretty rough sort of 'riding academy' in the sandhills a couple of miles in from the beach, with a flock of very savvy horses that knew much more about being ridden than most of the customers knew about riding. Apart from the few which we always reserved, they were barely-broken brumbies from further up the coast which had been caught and belted into submission. When they could be got to move at all it was at a slow, dogged walk — until you turned them toward home: then Darby Munro himself couldn't have held them in for a thousand quid. It cost us five-bob a throw, but it was worth it. Outside the ball season it was usually our only big outlay for the week.

There was a lovely stretch of country behind the dunes between Scarborough and North Beach, and we used to take off into it — gum forests and deep gullies, and sand-hills so high you could sit your horse on top of one and see Fremantle in one direction and almost up to Whitford's in the other. There wasn't much in the way of buildings in either direction to stop the view, in any case.

We usually rode for about an hour-and-a-half out and the same back. On the way home we were walking the horses along a sandy bush track, almost stoned on the scent of gumtrees and wild-flowers — perhaps partly just with being together and alive on that unexpectedly glorious spring day.

'Are you going, Hungie?' Mary said, without looking at me.

Again, as when she said *he*, there was no need to ask *going where?* I reckon the same question was being asked in a thousand homes, and parks, and in cars and ferries and tea-rooms all around Perth that day. *Are you going?* And it didn't mean to the pictures, or down the pub.

'I suppose so', I said. The Poms had said all along that if Germany didn't pull back they'd go to Poland's help, and if they bought into it, that meant the rest of us, too. The British Empire and our association with Britain were something to be proud of. People still stood up when *God Save the King* was played in theatres, and my mother still said we should stand up for it when the wireless closed down for the night, in our own livingroom.

'England'll be in it, and I suppose we'll be in it too, like the last time,' I said, 'so I guess we'll all be in it.'

I said it but I couldn't believe it, even though we'd talked it over among the blokes in our crowd until we were blue in the face. A couple of the students up at the studio the night before had said they'd be at the recruiting office before the bloke put down his bugle. They'd been out of work for the best part of a year and they reckoned they couldn't wait to get their hands onto some dough again. I could understand how they felt, discussing it with them, but on that bush track ten thousand miles away from where it was happening I just couldn't make it seem real. Not with the lovely bump-hump-bump of the horses beneath you, and the magpies sounding like bells in the trees all about you and the surf sounding like bells on the other side of the sandhills. Not on my Saturday off. *It'll blow over again*, I told myself. *Like it always has.* But suddenly I saw again what I'd seen in the paper that morning, that terrible block of Hitler they always used, day after day, with his mouth open, roaring hatred, and his eyes popping like a dog's balls, one arm out like a ramrod and one hand over his heart promising someone he'd tear the living guts out of the whole world. I knew then all right what was going to happen.

When we got back from our ride the others were home, and Mack was sitting on the steps waiting for us.

'Well, mate!' he sang out to me. 'She's on!'

I thought maybe he was only talking about our usual Saturday night bash after the dance — live it up Saturday and broke Monday was the pattern.

'What's on?' I said.

He held up the midday edition of the *Daily News*. He'd brought it out from town with him — not so much for the war news, I was certain, but for the horses. It was folded in half, but I could see the word WAR in what must have been the biggest and boldest type-face the *News* had. I didn't take it to look at it. I didn't want to.

'You mean — *we've* started?'

'Of course not!' Bonny managed to snap at me, even around a mouthful of clips. She was sitting on one of the beds just inside the door, putting up her hair for the dance that night. 'And shut *up* about the bloody war!' I guess she was like me — like a lot of people, for a long time. Don't talk about it and it won't happen.

That evening we all went up to the pub for an hour or so before tea, and to buy the booze for the party at our place after the dance. The girls were with us so we went into the lounge rather than in to the Saloon Bar, where we always drank. The talk was all about the war, of course, and one of the blokes really took it to heart. He'd spent the whole afternoon weaving between the pub and the SP shop on the other side of the road, I was told later, and just before we left he clambered onto one of the tables and held his arms up for silence. When he'd got a bit of it he yelled: 'Don't worry about the bloody war! If the Scarbie boys can fight as well as they can fuck they'll knock Hitler off by themselves!' Luckily for him there was still a lot of noise going on, and only the few around him heard him. His mates pulled him off the table and hustled him outside very smartly.

It was all right for Bonny to say *shut up about the bloody war*, but there it was. It was in every breath you took, and in every look anyone gave you; and in everything you did, thinking: *Will this be the last time I'll do this?* Later on, down at the dance, I was loafing around the floor to a nice slow modern waltz — *Sleepy Lagoon*, it was — and the girl I was dancing with said: *I wonder if it's the last time we'll do this: I wonder if there'll be many more dances at Scarbie?* She wasn't one of the girls in our crowd, but I knew her well, and I knew what she was thinking. She was engaged to a bloke who was already in the navy, and already at sea somewhere, on peacetime manoeuvres. If the balloon went up before he got back they wouldn't even have time for a fond farewell.

The next day, Sunday, the day it all ended, I woke early. I lay there on my back staring at the cobwebs in the ceiling. My own spider, a big, coal-black cannibal with longer and shinier legs than any other, it seemed, was crouching at the entrance to his tunnel waiting for any early business that might turn up. I made a mental note to swipe a few flies later on and to tack them to his web.

The surf was booming in, and I pictured it to myself, the long, smooth, glass-green of it sloping down under the spindrift rainbows curled back from the crests by the land-breeze. I began to count the waves. Every fifteenth beat of my heart that hollow thud, that minute trembling of the world as one of them slammed down onto the reef in front of the surf club building. It was like a metronome, and listening to it, and watching the spider, I got that feeling that often came over me while we were at the beach shack — a numbing sort of isolation, of being somewhere outside the envelope of the world listening to the waves, and the rattle of the loose sheets on the roof, and the soft-shoe-shuffle of the sand shifting around under the house. Early in the morning, or late at night when everyone else was asleep, of me alone on that thin, glittering strip of white sand at Scarborough, between the thousand blue miles of ocean and the thousand red miles of the continent.

I began to wonder whether the *Sunday Times* would be in over at the store, and whether it would have anything new in it. I would have turned on the wireless, but I didn't want to wake everyone up so early. It was funny — weekdays at home I'd stay in bed until the last second, with my mother roaring from the kitchen about my breakfast getting cold and I'd miss the boat: but I had it timed. I leap out, shower and shave, into my clothes, wolf a piece of toast and a cup of tea, gallop down to the jetty wolfing another piece of toast, and jump onto the ferry just as the boy was uncoiling the rope from around the bollard. Sundays, when I could have hugged the mattress all day if I'd wanted to, I couldn't make myself stay there. Particularly when we were out at the beach shack. Time there was too precious to be wasted in bed; and now more precious than it had ever been, I told myself, thinking of the *Sunday Times* lying on Ambrose's counter with its message for the rest of our lives.

At half-past-seven I could stand it no longer. I eased myself out of my bed, doing my best to soften the squeaking, and tiptoed around to the kitchen to light the fire for breakfast. As I passed Mack's bed he turned over and peered up at me over the edge of his blankets.

'Jesus!' he complained, as he always did. 'Can't you bloody sleep?' If he hadn't said it, every Sunday morning we were out at the beach, I'd have thought he was sickening for something. 'Clumping around in the middle of the bloody night!' He had a point, though. It'd been well after two when we'd all finally got to bed.

When I'd got the fire going I ducked over to the shop for the *Sunday Times*. One look was enough. POISON GAS RAINED ON POLISH CITIES and PARTS OF WARSAW ALREADY IN FLAMES: in about the biggest type I'd ever seen in a paper.

'Looks like it for us, eh?' Ambrose said as he handed me my change, and as I pocketed the coins it seemed to me that in some strange way I was seeing him, maybe seeing all Australians, for the first time. After I'd known him and dealt in his shop for a couple of years. He would have been about twenty-four, not very big, wiry, dark curly hair and vivid blue eyes. He was married, and they had one kid, a little girl, and he'd be right in the hole when they came looking for volunteers. Yet he stood there on the other side of the counter, ten thousand miles away from Warsaw, and quite calmly accepted the fact — the probability, anyway — that just because it was in flames we'd be in the war. No drama, no resentment, no excitement, just the acceptance of it as a natural, unavoidable step in a sequence of events. He even grinned at me as he said it. A real grin, too — no old Anzac up-boys-and-at-'em bullshit.

As I walked back to the flat I opened up the paper. Every page you turned hit you with something about the war, all the commentators and experts and retired majors having a field day about what had happened, what was happening, and what would happen. But it wasn't all pie-in-the-sky. *When the British Parliament meets at 6 o'clock tonight it is likely that Mr Chamberlain will announce that Britain and Germany are at war.* That put the lid on the kettle, all right. Ten more hours of what we'd always known — without really knowing we'd had it, I suppose — and then . . . into the bush.

The funny thing is that what really caught my eye in the middle of it all was a block of a very fancy bedroom suite for twenty-four guineas. It was a hell of a lot of money for a suite, but it looked good. Bonny and Ben were getting married in a few weeks' time. They were doing it on a shoe-string, and we were always talking about furniture and ways-and-means. One night at the studio, when we were having a blow between lessons, someone said something about a nice kitchen dresser in one of the Perth shops.

'Get the flaming bed first,' Ben said, 'the rest can follow!'

'Hold on', Bonny said. 'What about a table and some chairs?'

Ben winked around at us. 'You can eat in bed. You can't . . .'

'That'll be enough, Ben!' Bonny said.

As I was walking through the sandhills back to the shack I met one of the Greeks coming up from the beach. A mob of them lived in another shack further back in the sandhills, and you could smell the cooking from our place. He looked at my paper.

'War is on, no?'

'War is on, yes, George', I said. 'I think so, anyway.'

I was more interested in four or five squid he had, hanging from a butcher's hook like a bunch of purple grapes with eyes. 'What're you going to do with those? Going fishing?' Nobody I knew ever used them for anything but fish-bait, and for that they were the best.

'For eat!' he said. He looked surprised that I shouldn't know.

'Cook in wine. Ah-ha!' I almost gagged, thinking of all those little suckers. He pointed to my paper again. 'You go?'

'I suppose so', I said. 'If it's on. You?'

He stood there in his dirty khaki shorts, barefooted in the sand with his bunch of squid, and stared down the slope of the beach to the surf. It was such a beautiful day, all blue and white and green and gold. Somewhere, at the limits of what you could see up and down the coast, everything merged with a haze the colour of milk opals. Already you could feel it was going to be really warm, far warmer than early spring should be. I thought, as I looked at George Spikelides looking at the day: *Turning on a good one for the last!* He shrugged, and said: 'Ah, Jesus Christ. I leave Greece to get away from it. When I am a boy you could see it come. Now, it follows me to Australia. Yes — I go.'

When I got back to the shack Bonny was still the only one up. She was standing on the steps, waiting for me. When I was close enough she raised her eyebrows at the paper I was carrying. I shrugged and nodded, and without even thinking I said to her exactly what Ambrose had said to me . . . but I couldn't raise a grin.

'Looks like it for us.'

I climbed the half-dozen steps and stood with her, looking down at the beach, the old shack creaking and rustling behind us. One of the surf club members had tried to talk us into shifting out of it — he'd taken on an agency to flog off land at Scarborough, and one Saturday afternoon up at the pub he offered us a block for fifteen pounds. Up on the hill, it was, behind the prom overlooking the lot.

'You're out of your minds to go on paying thirty-bob a week for that dump,' he reckoned, 'buy this block and run up a shack for yourselves, and you'll be sitting pretty.'

'Fifteen *quid!*' Wally said. 'We haven't got fifteen bloody *bob!*'

'Rake up the five for the deposit and you can pay it off at five-bob a week', the bloke offered. He was really keen.

'Any five quid this lot rakes up'll go for a keg!' Mary said. I think she felt the same as the rest of us. Who wanted a bit of land right out at Scarborough, nothing but the promenade and not a house for miles?

Bonny took the paper from me and skimmed through it. If she saw the block of the bedroom suite she didn't say anything about it. She didn't say anything about the war, either. She just folded the paper and handed it back to me.

'Let's wake the others and get out early', she said, as she walked around the verandah toward the kitchen. 'After breakfast you can help me cut some sandwiches, and we'll go up to Triggs for the day.' I think she was feeling the same way as I was. If it's going to be our last day, let's make the best of it. The weather's gone all out, so let's do the same.

We spent a lot of time up at Triggs every summer. It was a mile or so north of Scarborough, with nothing but bush either side of it or behind it. Hardly anyone but us ever went up there, apart from the occasional rod-fisherman trying out the Blue Hole, and now and then knowledgeable folk after mutton-fish — spend half-an-hour wading around with a tyre-lever on the reef on the north side of the island, and if the surf wasn't running too high you'd fill a chaff-bag without getting your knees wet.

There was a convent retreat house in a deep fold of the dunes just behind the island, a long, low, unpainted weatherboard barn of a place with a faded red iron roof and heavy lattice work all around the verandah — just like Josie's Bungalow down in Roe Street, only Josie did at least keep her joint painted. You never saw much of the nuns. Only once, one weekday when I was on holiday, I'd gone for a walk up to Triggs by myself and surprised a flock of them having a swim. They probably thought nobody would be about, midweek. You never saw such a sight — I'd say the only article of their clothing they'd taken off to go in was that great heavy leather belt they wear to hang their crucifixes and their wooden rosaries on. They were flapping around like penguins at the very edge of the Blue Hole, and as I watched them from the sandhills I wondered if they had any idea of just how dangerous it was. Maybe they just put their faith in God — but then, so had a lot of people: it seemed that every few weeks in summer the papers carried stories about someone in trouble at the Blue Hole, either dragged out of it or drowned in it.

Triggs wasn't properly an island excepting, very rarely, when big surf or king tides washed over the neck of sand joining it to the beach. It was really an enormous sandstone rock pitted with caves and holes paved with deep yellow sand. On hot days — and that Sunday was one, almost summer-hot — with the sun beating down into the holes where the wind couldn't get at you, it was like being in an open-top oven. You could feel yourself turning brown, almost sizzling. There was a fair-sized pool in the reef on the North Beach side, and when you got up a good sweat you dived into it to cool off.

During the summer we prowled around the reef, under-water, for hours, picking up shells and bits of coral, watching the fish — but not that Sunday. Although the day was so hot the water was freezing — I can only describe it as like swimming in champagne. We didn't loiter, though. When we began to turn blue we

211

clambered out and burrowed into the hot sand again. Mack, who really didn't care about much apart from the pub and the SP shop, said that if ever he got to Heaven and didn't see something like Triggs just inside the Pearly Gates, he'd turn around and come straight back.

About the middle of the afternoon I climbed out of my oven and began to rake over the lunch-time fire to put the billy on for a brew. Mary came to help me, and she picked up one of the sheets of newspaper we'd brought to start the fire. It was that morning's *Sunday Times*.

'Hey, listen to this, Hungie!' she said, after a while. 'Your stars. They're right on the ball! *Touch and go in your affairs just now. Almost anything might happen. Certainly the unexpected will happen. You might be justified in taking financial hazards.* Golly!' She laughed at me. 'You might buy me that silver-fox we saw in Bon Marche. Only twelve guineas!'

Bonny had got up and was reading over her shoulder, the wind wrestling with the paper and the smell of salt on the wind wrestling with the smoke from my fire.

'Listen to this', she said, looking around at all of us. '*My* stars. November. *A somewhat pessimistic atmosphere* . . . my God, you ain't kiddin'!'

'What's mine, Bon?' Richard called out. He was still lying in the sand. 'September.'

Bonny looked at the page for a moment. 'You won't believe it. It says there's plenty for you to think about next week. And *travel seems probable!*'

We all laughed, but there was something more than amusement, or even disbelief, behind it. There was behind mine, anyway. I walked over and stood behind Bonny and Mary, and looked at the paper. 'That's what it reckons, all right', I said. 'Travel seems probable. Warsaw, here I come.'

'Not for you, Hungie', Mary said. 'You're May. Only the September babies get to travel.'

'Bullshit', Mack said. 'They've changed the rules. Didn't you know? Everyone's birthday's in September, now.'

When we got back to the shack I went over to the shop to get some milk. There wasn't a car on the promenade and only a few people on the footpaths. The lightd shop-fronts seemed far lonelier than if they'd been blacked out. The wind was whipping up over the prom wall, curling the sand back the way it did the spin-drift off the waves.

'Menzies's going to give a talk at seven', Ambrose said, as he handed me the bottles. 'Did you know?'

'No. We've been up at Triggs all day.'

'He's going to give us the good oil. We'll be in.'

'Or out', I said, but of course I didn't believe that myself.

'If it's on we're in,' Ambrose said, 'and it's on. London to a brick.' He almost seemed happy about it.

Most nights after tea we played cards or word games or Monopoly, and when we'd cleared away the things Richard reached up to the shelf above his head and dragged down the box with the Monopoly board in it. It had come over very cold after sundown, and we kept a big fire in the kitchen stove. The shutters rattled and the loose sheets on the roof clacked, and the surf sounded as if it was crawling up to the sandhills to get at us, personally. It was cosy in the old shack, just the same. Richard took out the board and the paper-money. I looked at my watch. It was ten to seven.

'Wait a while', I said. 'Ambrose told me Menzies's going to make an announcement at seven.'

Bonny was still cleaning down the bench, and the others were around the table — Ben peeling an apple, Mack sitting next to him looking at some racing form or other, Mary sitting next to him putting up her hair, Richard sitting next to her handing her the bobby-pins out of the tin. For one of those seconds that might have been a year, they all stopped what they were doing and stared at me. It was hours since anyone had said anything about the war, and I guess they didn't want to be reminded about it. The only sound was the wind and the surf, and the creaking and whispering of the old shack settling down for the night.

'No prize for guessing what *that'll* be about!' Mary said, flatly, slamming home her last pin. Ben put his apple down on the table and went and stood beside Bonny.

'Bloody old Pig-iron', Mack said. He was third generation Labour. He would have voted the ticket if they'd put up a ten-day corpse. 'He's going to tell us we'll be sending scrap to the Germans now, as well as the flaming Japs.'

I turned the wireless on and got the national station. Richard began to count the Monopoly money out into six heaps. We all watched him as if we'd never seen it done before, instead of four out of five of the nights we spent at the beach. In a moment the announcer introduced Menzies, and immediately that beautiful, mellifluous voice began to give us the chop. *Fellow Australians* . . .

I could have listened to him reading the market reports and still have been entranced. Richard kept on dealing out the play-money, but nobody else moved. As soon as the Prime Minister finished Mary jumped up, scattering her pins, and switched the wireless off.

'Nobody can tell us anything worse than that', she said, and sat down again. 'Come on. Let's have a game.'

'Jesus,' Ben said, 'you slobbered a bibful. Go directly to jail, don't pass GO, don't collect two hundred quid. Jesus.'

'Bugger the war', Mary said, and then, again: 'Come on. Let's have a game.'

'Who told that pompous old fart he could tell us we're also at war?' Mack demanded. 'Don't we get a say in it? It's our arses are going to get shot off!'

'Melancholy duty, my bum!' Richard said. 'And no harder task, he reckons. He enjoyed putting us in, the fat old bastard. He won't be carrying a gun!'

Ben and Bonny walked over to the table and sat down, and Bonny picked up the eggcup with the dice in it. I sat down opposite them and looked around at the others. They were all somewhere else — 'passing through Kalamunda', as we used to say. I wondered if even unconsciously they might be listening for the sound of aeroplanes and guns. I was, with at least half my mind. We'd been brainwashed about instant destruction if war was declared. Richard slid along the bench and put an arm about my shoulders.

'Coming in the RAAF with me, Hungie?'

He would be burned to death in an aircrash in Tripoli. Mack would go through it all, Middle East and then New Guinea. Ben would go down in the Perth.

'I'm after Park Lane and Mayfair tonight,' Bonny said, 'I'm tired of mucking around on Old Kent Road. I'm going to put a teashop on Park Lane and a nice, high-class knocking-shop on Mayfair.'

'Better move quick', Mack said. 'Mightn't be there much longer!'

'Might be gone already', Ben laughed. 'Poor bloody Poms!'

'Oh, for God's sake!' Mary said. 'Forget it, can't you?'

She grabbed the eggcup off Bonny and rattled it savagely, and I thought: That'll stir someone up! The lady next door said in her letter to the paper she'd been kept awake all night by the rattle of dice, and she reckoned it was the girls in our place tossing to see who they'd sleep with.